THE COMPLETE CANADIAN
HOME INSPECTION GUIDE

5/93

Books by Douglas A. Gray

▼

- Start and Run a Profitable Consulting Business

- The Entrepreneur's Complete Self-Assessment Guide

- Marketing Your Product (with Donald Cyr)

- The Complete Canadian Small Business Guide (with Diana Gray)

- Home Inc.: The Canadian Home-Based Business Guide (with Diana Gray)

- Raising Money: The Canadian Guide to Successful Business Financing
  (with Brian Nattrass)

- Buying, Owing and Selling a Condominium: A Guide for Canadians

- Making Money in Real Estate: The Canadian Residential Investment
  Guide

- Mortgages Made Easy: The Canadian Guide to Home Financing

- The Complete Canadian Home Inspection Guide

THE COMPLETE CANADIAN
HOME INSPECTION GUIDE

ED R. R. WITZKE
DOUGLAS A. GRAY

McGraw-Hill Ryerson Limited

Toronto   Montreal

First published in 1993 by
McGraw-Hill Ryerson Limited
300 Water Street
Whitby, Ontario
L1N 3B4

Canadian Cataloguing and Publication Data

Witzke, Edward R.R. (Edward Richard Rollie)
      The complete Canadian home inspection guide

Includes bibliographical references.
ISBN 0-07-551245-9

1. Dwellings — Inspection. 2. Dwellings — Canada —
Inspection. 2. House buying. I. Gray, Douglas A.
II. Title.

TH4817.5.W58 1992 643'.12 C92-094476-0

This publication is designed to provide accurate and authoritative information on the subject
matter covered. However, building codes, laws, techniques and materials are constantly
changing, and the examples given are intended to be general guidelines only.
      This book is sold with the understanding that neither the authors nor the publisher is
engaged in rendering professional advice. If such advice or assistance is required, the
personal services of a competent professional should be sought.

Cover Design: Dave Hader, Studio Conceptions
Text design: JAQ

This book was produced for McGraw-Hill Ryerson by Shaftesbury Books, a member of the
Warwick Publishing Group, Toronto, Canada.

Dedication

▼

Affectionately dedicated to my mother, Pauline Witzke,
and to the memory of my father,
Wilhelm Waldemar Witzke.
— Ed R. R. Witzke

Diana Gray, my wife,
friend and intrepid entrepreneur.
— Douglas A. Gray

Acknowledgements

It is hardly possible to mention all our associates and others who have made valuable contributions, but we are pleased to acknowledge our indebtedness to Ingrid Wood for hours of first-draft editing, help, guidance, suggestions and patience on the word processor. And to Diana Gray for her talented and constructive condensing and final editing of this book.

A special thanks goes to the staff at McGraw-Hill Ryerson, whose continuing encouragement and support has made it all possible.

Contents

▼

About the Authors

▼

ED R. R. WITZKE, B.Arch., is a graduate in history and architecture from the University of British Columbia. Since 1965 he has professionally inspected thousands of homes and commercial buildings throughout North America. He is a former architect, energy consultant, consumer information specialist and former building contractor. He has first-hand experience in carpentry, masonry, roofing, plumbing and electrical work. He is head of his own independent building inspection firm, Witco Building Inspection Services Ltd., based in Vancouver, British Columbia. He is a member of numerous building trade and professional associations, including the Royal Architectural Institute of Canada and the American Institute of Architects. He is also president of the National Home Inspection Institute Inc.

Ed Witzke conducts courses and seminars throughout Canada on a variety of topics related to home inspections, repairs and renovations. He is a frequent guest and host on radio and television shows, and gives presentations at trade exhibitions and home shows. In addition, he writes articles for newspapers and magazines on home inspections, house buying, home repair and improvements, remodelling and energy conservation.

Mr. Witzke lives in Vancouver, B.C.

DOUGLAS A. GRAY, LL.B., is one of Canada's foremost authorities on real estate and entrepreneurial development. In his capacity as a real estate and business lawyer, he has also represented thousands of clients who were buying, selling, financing, renovating, developing or investing in real estate. He has seen the problems that occur when a thorough and competent inspection has not been performed. Mr. Gray has personally dealt in all forms of real estate.

As a public speaker and educator, Mr. Gray has conducted seminars and presentations to over 250,000 people across Canada and internationally. Many of these presentations were on real estate topics. He is frequently interviewed by the media as an authority on entrepreneurship and real estate. Mr. Gray has given over 1,000 media interviews and has been profiled on the three national television networks (CTV, CBC, Global). He is the President of the National Real Estate Institute.

He is the author or co-author of numerous best-selling books including: *Start and Run a Profitable Consulting Business; The Entrepreneur's Complete Self-Assessment Guide; Marketing Your Product; The Complete Canadian Small Business*

Guide; Home Inc.: The Canadian Home-Based Business Guide; Raising Money: The Canadian Guide to Successful Business Financing; Buying, Owning and Selling a Condominium; Making Money in Real Estate: The Canadian Residential Investment Guide; Mortgages Made Easy; The Complete Canadian Home Inspection Guide; and the forthcoming books (1993) *Home Buying Made Easy* and *The Complete Canadian Real Estate Guide.*

Mr. Gray lives in Vancouver, B.C.

Introduction

▼

Why you should buy this book:

- To familiarize yourself with a house you are purchasing, so that you don't get caught with a "lemon."
- To help you assess your investment and realize the potential of the house and its renovation possibilities and limitations.
- To help you renegotiate a better purchase price after you have found out what is wrong with the house, or to change other terms of the agreement.
- To protect your investment, so that you understand the full extent of your profit (or loss), and to avoid unexpected surprises later.
- To make you aware of what is involved in a house inspection, so that you won't take 40 minutes to examine a house, but at least eight hours. A house is not a car, which you can take for a test drive.
- To assist you as a homeowner, in your decision to renovate or sell your house. If you decide to renovate, it will help you to avoid costly problems. If you decide to sell, it will help you get the maximum compensation.

A house is one of the most expensive purchases you will make in a lifetime. Yet many houses are bought based upon first impressions or a sales pitch from a real estate agent. Buyers become caught up in what real estate dealers call the "cosmetic" or "curb-appeal" aspects of a house, such as its exterior appearance, the neighbourhood, scenic view, fireplace or skylights. Most people spend more time deliberating over the purchase of a car than a house. As little as 17 minutes, on average, is spent viewing a house before deciding to buy it. Remarkably few people undertake a thorough or even cursory pre-purchase inspection. Few even think to test out the most basic systems, such as turning on the heat or flushing the toilet. They ignore the basic features, such as good insulation, an efficient heating system and a solid structure.

One reason for this is that prospective buyers or renovators often don't know what to look for. Most people don't have enough building or home renovating experience to locate defects until it's too late. We all have heard horror stories where a family's dream home was bought, only for them to discover later that the wood was filled with dry rot or that an underlying creek bed had weakened the entire structure. Let's for a moment compare a house to the human body. By knowing some basic facts about maintaining a healthy lifestyle and diet, for example, a person can learn to enjoy good health and a longer life. In the same way, facts need to be known about proper care and maintenance of a house in order to recognize a healthy one and to extend its natural lifespan. Thus the reason for *The Complete Canadian Home Inspection Guide*!

This book is intended for the prospective first-time homeowner as well as seasoned homeowners and handymen. For those experienced in minor household maintenance, this book is a complete do-it-yourself inspection guide; for the person new to household ownership and maintenance, it will provide an overall perspective of the components of a house and property. Numerous sketches have been included to help build your understanding and knowledge. A glossary of terms and list of tools referred to throughout the book (Appendix 3) are provided at the back of the book. A conversion factor table (Appendix 8) will assist you if you do not own a metric conversion calculator.

This book will help you decide whether or not to buy a particular home because you will learn where and how to look for the symptoms that indicate existing or future problems. You need to know what major repair or replacement costs will be incurred within the next five years. Appendix 2 provides a checklist giving the average life expectancy of household materials or components. Premature wear or deterioration may indicate that substandard materials or methods were used.

Chapters 1 to 3 deal mainly with the neighbourhood, the exterior of the house and the condition of any buildings and landscaping on the property. The most critical aspect of a house, of course, is the stability of the structure itself. Chapter 4 covers pointers about the structure that are visible from the outside as well as the inside. The interior rooms of the house are covered in Chapters 5 through 13. The remaining three chapters provide tips on household security, energy conservation, proper care and maintenance of a house.

Once you have finished reading the book, you should be able to conduct your own house inspection. This will enable you to eliminate some houses from your shortlist of possibilities — the so-called "dream homes" turned nightmares. A one-hour inspection checklist has been provided in Appendix 5 to draw your attention to the critical aspects you should inspect for. If the house passes this preliminary review to your satisfaction, then chances are you will contemplate purchasing the house, and this requires a more careful and thorough review. A detailed "Master Checklist of Questions to Ask an Owner" (Appendix 4)is intended to be used during a more thorough inspection process — one that should take up to eight hours to complete. For this in-depth inspection, the summary checklists provided at the end of each chapter will be useful as you go from room to room through the house. Some individuals may prefer to hire a professional building inspector to conduct a final review of some critical or suspicious items. For these people, the hints provided in Appendix 6 will be helpful.

To conduct a proper inspection, you must put on your Sherlock Holmes hat and pack your "black bag" of implements to assist you. You will need an inquisitive mind and an interest in learning everything you can about the property. Some background knowledge of household construction or repairs will be helpful but is not necessary. Or you may wish to be accompanied by a friend or relative who has more experience in this area. Be certain to demonstrate utmost care when inspecting so that damage is not caused to the property or vegetation. You will have to accept responsibility for any damage you may incur. Of foremost importance, though, is your safety and the safety of any other persons in or around the house.

A pleasant disposition and courtesy should gain you the approval and cooperation of the owner. After all, only serious potential purchasers would be inclined to spend the time necessary in conducting an inspection. Ask questions — of the owner, the salesperson, the neighbours and city hall employees. Ask for brand names of materials used and copies of product warranties. Check that the manufacturer is still in business and whether the products are still available. Make notes of your discoveries and questions to ask or investigate further. Draw sketches of each area that you inspect. Record measurements and the types of construction and finishing materials used. Double-check information that is unclear or suspicious. The more you know, the better able you will be to make a confident purchase decision.

Your inspection will enlighten you as to the overall condition of the house's health. It will reveal the history of the house and its strengths and weaknesses. Careful inspection and technical evaluation of the house should play a more important role than its emotional impact. At first you may only see what you want to see, but a second and third look will reveal what you missed earlier. A thorough inspection should leave no window unopened and no corner undiscovered.

Throughout this and the subsequent chapters, you will find housing and construction facts interspersed with variables in house design and construction. Keep in mind that items of concern to one person may be of little interest to another because of different needs, lifestyles and priorities. You will have to weigh up the pros and cons — the seriousness of any repairs and how they will affect you. If there are any areas that cause you major concern, you may wish to get a second opinion by hiring a tradesperson to re-check the area.

You may rest assured that defects will be discovered. No house is perfect, as a car or other consumer products might be. What is important is to find out if you can live comfortably in the house. Examine the quality of materials and how well they have been used, and see if problems can be remedied within your skills and budget. Keep in mind that any problem can be fixed, but at what cost? Itemize the repairs and renovations into three categories: under $100, up to $1,000 and over $1,000. Then mark the status of each of the repairs as desired, necessary or urgent in order to assess the purchase price more accurately. You should then have enough information to decide whether you should buy the house and renovate it or look for another one. It may also put you in a strong position to negotiate a better price in light of the urgency of any repairs.

In conclusion, it is hoped that this book will help you to find the best house for your budget. If, after reviewing your list of needs and carefully inspecting the property, you decide not to purchase it, then your inspection has been a worthwhile undertaking. If your inspection reconfirms your interest in the property, but alerts you to some immediate repairs required thus enabling you to negotiate the purchase price downward, then your inspection has been profitable. It will also help to eliminate the fear of the unknown, and this will let you sleep more soundly on those stormy winter nights.

Best wishes in your quest for the ideal home!

Ed R.R. Witzke
Douglas A. Gray
September 1992
Vancouver, B.C.

▼

CHAPTER 1

Neighbourhood, House Style and Grounds

WHEN YOU START your search for a new home, you should prepare a written list of the approximate size, design, location and local amenities and services you prefer. This list will help you to stay focused on the key features to look for in a house, and will be a starting point to evaluate and inspect it. Your decision of what to include on your list will be based upon your family's needs, such as a yard for young children to play in, few stairs for aging parents to climb, a garden area or workshop in order to pursue a pastime or hobby. Keep in mind that if such a feature is not present, you will have to decide whether you are willing and able to invest the time and money to undertake the necessary renovations.

Character

Your search for a house in which you will be able to live comfortably will no doubt lead you to think first about its location. Neighbourhoods will differ widely and will impact upon the resale value of your home. For instance, a modest house in an expensive neighbourhood will have greater resale value than an elaborate house in a rundown area. Usually, yards and homes are better cared for in a neighbourhood with a large percentage of owner-occupants. When looking at the neighbourhood in terms of its growth and expansion, consider whether it is improving and reaching its prime or whether the opposite is evident. Realtors will be able to provide you with comparative data on the selling prices of nearby homes. Actually, the best source of historical data on the area is the neighbours. They may be willing to share information on the population mix, incidence of crime and vandalism, water drainage and pest or parking problems.

Typical neighbourhood amenities preferred may include public transportation, shopping centre, schools, churches, parks, playgrounds, hospital

DIAGRAM 1: The Subdivision
Take a walk around the subdivision.
What do you see?

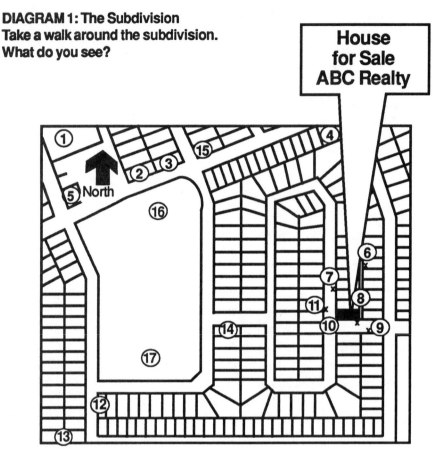

1. Shopping Mall
2. Police Station
3. Fire Department
4. Church
5. Post Office
6. Community Centre
7. Low Grade Elevation
8. Bus Stop
9. Paved Back Lane
10. Fire Hydrant
11. High Ground Elevation
12. Street Light
13. Gasoline Service Station
14. Peanut Factory
15. Corner Store
16. School
17. Park

Note: House for Sale — Lot is on a good north–south Axis and has a good exposed south side.

and community centre. If the house is located on a busy thoroughfare, you may wish to investigate matters such as traffic noise levels, air pollution and traffic congestion at different times of the day. Also, nearby factories or commercial buildings may create pollution, smells and machine and traffic noise that is undesirable. In particular, heavy industrial sites or train yards may produce machine vibrations strong enough to cause books to fall from shelves.

Zoning, Restrictions and Services

A visit to city hall to investigate the area's approved zoning, property tax assessments, property restrictions and service levels may be enlightening. Find out if there are any planned neighbourhood zoning changes such as residential to commercial. Mixed-use zoning may permit undesirable development of adjacent land, thereby devaluing the property. Residential property restrictions that may apply include removal of certain species of trees, designated heritage homes, street parking, pets, home-based businesses, multiple-family dwellings and future renovations or additions to the home. Garbage burning, fence height restrictions and noise levels are other areas usually governed by local by-laws.

The level of services that the community receives will also affect your enjoyment and the quality of the area. Three kinds of service that you would want to find efficiently administered are maintenance, protection and communication. Maintenance services include the general upkeep of the neighbourhood, such as paving, repair, cleaning and lighting of streets, regular garbage removal and sanding and snow-clearing of streets in wintertime. Check into the level of fire and police protection in the area, and look for fire hydrants, good street lighting and neighbourhood watch teams. Depending upon your lifestyle and the distance from urban centres, you may wish to ensure the efficient delivery of communication services such as cable television, telephone, mail, newspaper, department and food store deliveries and services for the disabled.

Building Style

From 1700 onwards, various house plans and architectural styles have been adopted in regions throughout North America. The characteristics of an architectural style usually have sound practical origins. These may be associated with climate, construction materials available locally, methods and labour available, cost factors, topography, soil type, water table and plain old traditions and customs.

Today few houses represent a "pure" style, as designers are continually trying different combinations of traditional details. You will likely find Colonial houses with Victorian additions, and Victorian houses with Colonial revival features, for example. By consulting illustrated history books of various styles on this subject, your eye will begin to discern what is original to a house and what has been added, or removed, in keeping with the latest fashion. Remember that fads and fancies do not persist very long, and the resale value of your home will depend upon the lasting qualities of good workmanship and simple proportions. Apart from structural soundness and practicality, the merits of appearance are a matter of taste — and opinions vary widely.

Types of Residential Construction

Like style, house types vary from bungalow, two-storey, split level, to two-storey or four-level split. And each of these has variations. For example, the split-level configuration can be arranged back-to-front, front-to-back or side-to-side. Your preference will be determined by balancing the advantages and disadvantages for your lifestyle and for the house's resale potential.

Single-storey (Bungalow)
The single-storey home has the advantage that all principal accommodations (living room, dining room, kitchen, bedrooms and bathroom) are on one floor, with or without a basement. Because there are no stairs in the main living area, getting around is less fatiguing and fewer accidents occur. Exterior maintenance is easy, and if additions are to be made to the home, it is often easier and cheaper to add to a bungalow. The single level offers scope for open planning, which can give an impression of spaciousness. On the other hand, excessive heating costs may result if the plan is too spread out. Since a bungalow needs twice as much roof and foundation for proper insulation as does a two-storey house of the same floor area, a one-and-a-half-or two-storey house is often more economical to build and maintain.

Two-storey House
In a two-storey house the main accommodation is on two floors, one above the other, with or without a basement. Such houses are compact, easily heated and can be built on narrow lots that have insufficient width to accommodate a wide-frontage bungalow with a similar floor area. However, small two-storey houses may look "boxy" because they are about as wide as they are high.

One-and-a-half-storey House
The one-and-a-half-storey house is similar to the two-storey house except that the upper level has a smaller plan than the lower floor, as a result of a sloping roof. Therefore partly sloped ceilings may exist in some rooms. This type of house probably provides the greatest amount of floor area for the least capital outlay.

Split-level House
The split-level house is similar to the single-storey house but the main floor is stepped up or down to a noticeable extent. A common example is one in which

the lower level is built slightly above grade over a low crawl space and contains the entrance hall, living room, dining room and kitchen. The adjoining upper level, built above the basement, contains the bedrooms and is reached by six or seven stairs from the main hall. An advantage of this design is that it provides for

> ### What a lovely, large lot!
> A buyer purchased a particular house because of the large lot it was situated on — ideal for a swimming pool. As the excavator was about to start work on installing the pool, he was told by a neighbour that the trees on the lot were protected by the City.

easy communication between the levels, as in a bungalow, and yet maintains the separation of the sleeping and living quarters similar to that of a two-storey. Though it can be used on a level site, the split-level is useful in solving the design problems imposed by a sloping lot.

The Lot

Sketch

Begin with a survey of the property. Draw a plan of the lot and note where the house is situated in relation to the other houses in the neighbourhood. How does the size, shape and grade of the lot compare to the neighbours' lots? Do the other homes look smaller, bigger, older, newer or better maintained than the one you are considering? Check where the water, sewage, gas, electricity, telephone and other lines or cables are coming from. How and where do they enter the lot?

Carefully check the survey plan and markers to verify the property line. Is it an odd- or pie-shaped lot? A sloped lot can be more expensive to maintain than a flat one and will affect the water drainage. Note the high and low spots, as well as the trees, shrubs, paths and outbuildings. Use your compass to orient yourself towards north and try to determine from what direction the winter and summer winds blow over the lot. The sides of the house and property receiving the greatest exposure will show greatest signs of weather damage.

Soil conditions can vary from one house to the next in the same area. Certain types of soil, such as clay, have a tendency to expand considerably when they become wet. Soil types can vary from silt, clay, sand and shale to gravel and organic matter. Ideally the sub-soil is stable and capable of bearing the weight of the house. Check to see if the soil has settled around the perimeter of the house.

Notice the water runoff patterns around the house, and ensure that the soil slopes away from the house and that there are no areas where surface water has collected. You should be most concerned about any soil erosion since it can cause serious foundation and stability problems. Wet basements, inoperative septic fields, backed-up sewage lines, standing water and drowned-out lawns make it all too clear that a drainage problem exists. A house built on a lot lower than the established grade presents the greatest problems.

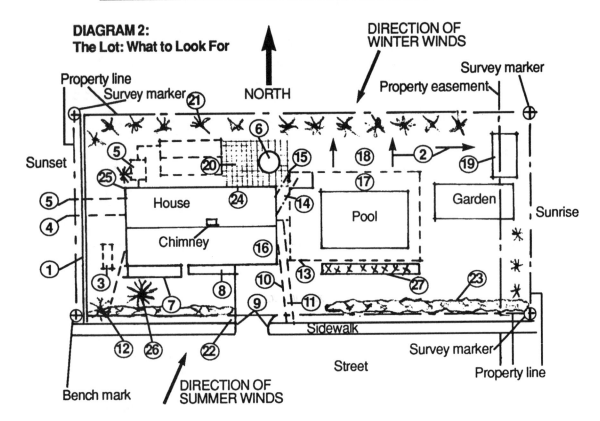

DIAGRAM 2:
The Lot: What to Look For

1. Retaining wall.
2. Arrows indicate direction of lot slope.
3. Old buried oil tank. Ask owner if fuel has been emptied and the tank filled in to prevent collapse.
4. Storm drain.
5. Sewage drain.
6. Hot tub.
7. Solarium.
8. Main entry.
9. Driveway.
10. Power line including TV cable, telephone.
11. Natural gas line, meter against wall of house.
12. Main water line with shut-off and water meter at property line.
13. Pool fence.
14. Natural gas line and powerline for pool and hot tub.
15. Shed for pool and hot tub, pump, motor heater and filter.
16. Attached garage.
17. Deck.
18. Lawn.
19. Outbuilding (storage).
20. Patio.
21. Trees along this side serve as a winter windbreak.

Trees that you should watch for:
22. Weeping willows, poplar, alder and birch lap up moisture and can crack foundation walls or pools.
23. Crimson King maple leaves a stain that can even damage car paint.
24. Ivy retains moisture and speeds wood rot.
25. Wisteria creepers can burrow under tiles and pry them loose.
26. Hazelnut or filbert — nuts attract squirrels, raccoons — the tree requires time pruning, clearing leaves, twigs and nuts from gutters, stairs, porch or roof.
27. Espalier — these trees can be trained to grow flat.

Lawn, Trees, Shrubs and Grounds

Landscaping that has been well-designed and cared for can increase the value of your property immeasurably and provide an array of colours throughout the seasons. Some owners have planted their landscapes in such a way as to reduce the use of water. The process involves choosing plants that require less water, improving the soil's capacity to hold water, using mulch and installing a drip irrigation system. On the other hand, poorly planned trees and shrubbery may cause severe drainage and structural problems to the house. If the property has a considerable amount of high-maintenance landscaping, be aware of the time and cost required for its upkeep.

Lawns

A consistent green colour with even growth and no bare, uneven or eroded spots suggests that a good-lawn maintenance program has been in place. Scan the lawn's surface, looking for dramatic slopes, surface rock, exposed tree roots and heads of buried automatic sprinkler systems. These are potential hazards when mowing the lawn. Weeds and moss flourish in shallow, poorly drained soil, making it difficult to hand-weed and hoe. Ensure that all buried cables and pipes are well beneath the lawn surface so that they will not be tripped over or caught by a mower blade.

Trees

Identify the types of trees on the property and their approximate height and location in relation to the house. Determine their growth peculiarities and root size. Tree roots are enormously strong and can cause cracking or heaving of wall foundations, sidewalks, driveways and swimming pools, and may eventually grow into the perimeter drainage system of the house. Some trees, like willows, elms, cedars and poplars, require large amounts of water, and their presence may indicate a high water table or cause settling problems in walls by withdrawing moisture from soil below the foundations. Chestnut, silver maple and tree-of-heaven types seed profusely, and seedlings have to be destroyed continually. Because of their red leaves, which stain concrete and metal surfaces, crimson king maples should be kept away from the driveway, balcony or sidewalk.

Besides adding to the aesthetic appreciation of the house, trees offer privacy, and protection from noise and wind, and may aid in the heating and cooling of the house during the year. Evergreens can enhance the property's visual appearance year-round, while deciduous trees on

---

Do You Know Your New Neighbours?

A prospective purchaser, while examining the interior of a house, heard a rumbling noise followed by vibrations of the house and a loud bang. The vibrations from the trainyard nearby were so strong that it caused books and chinaware to fall from the shelves.

Do You Know Your New Neighbours?

Soon after a homeowner moved into his new house, he discovered that the house next door was owned by a consortium of motorcycle gang members who were using it as their regional head-quarters and detox centre.

the south can provide summer shade to prevent the house from overheating. Remember, though, that in the fall they will drop their foliage onto roofs, gutters, sidewalks, lawns, driveways or neighbours' properties. Shading may be so extensive that removal of moss and fungal growth from the roof and walls and replanting the lawn will be regular maintenance tasks. Tall trees may require topping because a strong gale could sway their limbs onto the house, or they may interfere with suspended utility wires. Branches swaying back and forth can damage the exterior windows, siding and roof as well as promote visits from raccoons and other pests. Espalier trees, trained to grow flat against a building, can be a nuisance when painting. They also retain moisture, which can promote wood rot.

Inspect each tree, separating some of the branches with your hands. Shake a branch. Is the tree firm? Are there branches that require removal? If you see holes and uneven colours on the leaves, there may be a disease spreading within. Check the trunk for insect damage, rot, bark separation or fungal growth. Old tree stumps on the property should be checked for carpenter ants, termites or other pest infestation.

Shrubs and Ground Cover

Do a shrub inspection, similar to the tree inspection. Grown that is neatly trimmed and shaped and properly cared for, with no lifeless, discoloured limbs, is what you are looking for. Some shrubs require a lot of water for good growth, and most require a great deal of time for proper care. Plants that cling to exterior wall surfaces can cause enough damage, even after the plant has died, that costly-wall surface restorations are necessary. In addition, clinging vines often attract pests and insects, which find their way into the house through open windows, holes and cracks.

Gardens

A beautiful garden is a delight to have, but remember, it can take hours away from something else you would rather be doing. You will find that some flowers grow better than others in your garden and will be affected by the soil quality. There will always be the matter of pest control, watering, weeding, composting, plant compatibility and cultivating. A garden requires tools. If you take your gardening seriously, I recommend that a professional soil test be made for its chemical makeup, pH ratio (Alkalinity– Acidity), texture and moisture- holding capacity, humus content and other nutrients. If the garden has a shallow, reflecting pool, check with the owner on how the pool is cleaned and drained. Does it have a pump for a fountain? How is it winterized?

Planter Boxes

Masonry planter boxes must rest on a concrete or block foundation extended below the frost line to avoid damage caused by excess moisture penetration during the freeze/thaw cycle. For added protection, there should be an impervious lining between the dirt and the masonry wall to prevent moisture from being absorbed into the wall. With your awl, check the mortar joints along the planter. If they are soft, deterioration has set in. Weep holes along the bottom of the planter will allow natural drainage and preserve the soil.

Fences and Retaining Walls

Fences and retaining walls can provide security, a windbreak, privacy, definition of property, a microclimate or simply ornamentation. They may also provide camouflage for a neighbour's unsightly yard. How well does the fence shed water to prevent rot or rust from developing? Bevelled, rounded, sloped or capped wooden post tops drain off water and prevent rotting. Wooden posts rot quickly if not properly preserved, treated or installed. Check the construction and firmness of the fence and examine the footings of all fence posts. If there is a gate, open and close it, and check its hardware. Fasteners, such as nails, screws, bolts, hinges and hooks used in assembly, should be zinc coated or made of rust-resistant materials.

Offering similar benefits as fences, retaining walls serve the added purpose of retaining soil from eroding slopes. Construction may be of stone, brick, solid concrete or masonry blocks. To check that the wall is straight and leaning inwards towards the slope, stand at one end and look down its length. The wall foundation should extend below the ground surface to prevent it from toppling. Check the wall for signs of deterioration such as wide cracks and soft spots on top of the wall. You should find weep holes along the bottom face of the wall that allow water to pass through. Often, though, these are plugged with debris, and this causes the lawn to be saturated with backed-up water.

Driveways, Sidewalks and Patios

Driveways and sidewalks may be made out of dirt, gravel, concrete, asphalt, paving bricks or stones. Because of its malleability, asphalt surfaces are easily damaged. For example, tire depressions can result from a heavy vehicle being parked on a driveway on a hot summer day, and engine cleaner or anti-freeze dripping from automobiles can cause the asphalt to deteriorate. Asphalt surfaces will require a sealant to prevent water seepage

---

Disintegrating asphalt!

One homeowner used solvents to clean the engine of his automobile while it was parked on his driveway. Little did he know that once the job was finished, he had no asphalt driveway left. The driveway became a sea of tar!

and to facilitate cleaning. The acrylic type can be cleaned up with water before it dries.

The surfaces should be slip resistant with no irregularities, large cracks, sudden slopes or evidence of soil erosion. Check the surface for these signs of wear:

- *cracking*: caused by freeze/thaw cycles, moisture or base failures
- *ravelling*: rough surface and loose stones, which result when the stone binder loses its resiliency
- *oxidation*: discolouration and drying out due to weathering and the effects of sunlight
- *soft spots*: caused by gasoline, oil and other petroleum products that dissolve the asphalt's binding power.

Where concrete sidewalks and driveways are attached to the house, any separation gaps or expansion joints must be filled with caulking to prevent water from penetrating into the foundation. The driveway should be sloped away from the foundation and the edges thickened to prevent cracking or soil erosion and to guide the water in a specific direction to a storm system.

You may wish to drive your car into the driveway to test it for ease of access, traffic visibility and sufficient clearance so that the bottom and doors do not scrape the surface. If there is a culvert where the driveway meets the public street, check the inside for any non-draining water or collected debris.

Most patios are located at the back or side of the house and help to unify the house and garden. They are constructed of similar surfaces as sidewalks, but paving bricks and stones are most common. The better brick patios are held together with mortar. Bricks laid in sand, however, are easier to repair or replace. The brick should be laid on 3 inches of sand, with gravel underneath if drainage is a problem. Check to see how well the bricks are in place and if the edges have started to slip away. Sagging and uneven surfaces suggest improper preparation of the subsurface. Ask the owner if the bricks have been protected with a silicone sealer to prevent staining and water damage.

Swimming Pool, Spa and Hot Tub

Since a pool can add little to the value of the property, you should ensure that what you are buying is in good condition. Because of the technical aspects of inspecting an in-ground pool, you may wish to engage the services of a pool technician to undertake a thorough inspection of the pool's construction, heating, pumping and drainage systems to ensure they are functioning properly. Some considerations for a pool inspection include:

- pool location relative to wind direction and evaporative heat loss
- age and condition of the liner and when it is due for replacement
- water leakage and cracks or bulging of the floor and walls

- drainage system and relief valves, which prevent the pool from rising out of the ground when emptying it for cleaning purposes
- perimeter drainage around the pool
- heating system checked for corrosion
- sealing of deck areas
- state of repair of pool equipment (lights, electrical receptacles, underground wiring, filtration system, diving board, skimmer, automatic cleaning systems, pool cover, etc.)

An indoor pool area will have to be inspected for proper insulation, air-tightness and isolation from the rest of the house. There have been cases where severe moisture problems have destroyed major structural components of the house. Moisture always evaporates from a pool surface. The amount of evaporation depends upon the difference between the air temperature and the water temperature. The greater the temperature difference, the greater the evaporation. The best control of evaporation and humidity is a well-fitted floating blanket.

If you decide to purchase the property, you will need to become familiar with proper care and maintenance of the pool as well as safety guidelines for use. Pool maintenance requires regular care and can be time consuming. The water needs to be treated for alkalinity, tested for pH, disinfected and treated with chlorine and the filters cleaned.

Inspecting a spa or hot tub is similar to inspecting a swimming pool. Typically, spas are made of fibreglass or moulded plastic, while hot tubs are constructed of solid wood, and both rest directly on the ground or are sunk into the ground. Redwood and cedar swell when wet to provide a good seal. Cedar has a tendency to splinter; redwood can turn the water slightly tea-coloured initially. The wooden staves on the hot tub must be precisely shaped and should be at least 1 inch thick — the thicker, the better. The rilled steel compression hoops holding the staves together should be coated or tar-dipped to prevent rust and corrosion.

The pump's electrical consumption is a major portion of the operating costs. The hot tub can be equipped with a two-speed pump that circulates water through the filter and heater at low speed and operates the hydrojets at high speed. A timer on the circulating pump can reduce operating costs. The combination of high temperature and small volume of water in a hot tub means that the chemical balance must be watched more carefully than in a swimming pool. A rigid foam insulation cover should be in place when the tub is not in use.

A careful inspection of the grounds, trees and surroundings of the house will give you clues as to what you may expect to find when you start your examination of the exterior and interior of the house. For your convenience, a checklist of the major items to include in your inspection is included below.

CHECKPOINTS
✔✔✔✔✔✔✔✔✔✔✔

The Lot
____ house orientation
____ lot location
____ property line
____ lot size
____ drainage
____ restrictions, e.g., parking
____ sloped or level lot
____ flooding
____ trees
____ buried lawn sprinkler
____ electro-mechanical
       controllers
____ compost pit
____ barbecues and firepits
____ garden pool
____ fence
____ yard light
____ sidewalks
____ curbs
____ easements or right-of-ways
____ fire hydrant
____ sanitary sewers
____ storm sewers
____ shrubs
____ lawn, sod or seed
____ garden
____ security
____ survey markers
____ clothesline post
____ wind direction
____ slip-resistant surfaces
____ radiant-heated driveway
____ driveway curbs
____ driveway width
____ catch basins
____ culvert
____ natural light
____ privacy
____ noise seclusion
____ survey plan
____ earthquake zone

____ property zoning
____ air pollution
____ soil condition
____ soil contamination
____ placement of house

Architectural House Style
____ age of house
____ single storey
____ 1 1/2 storey
____ two storey
____ split level
____ historical designation
____ rectangular house shape
____ square house shape
____ T house shape
____ L house shape
____ H house shape
____ other

Patios
____ lighting
____ wood rot
____ type of finishing
____ slip-resistant surfaces
____ type of construction
____ missing components
____ drainage of surfaces
____ other

Swimming Pool
____ indoor
____ outdoor
____ shape
____ size
____ depth
____ fence
____ privacy
____ accessories
____ diving board
____ filters
____ heater

_____ special insurance
_____ vapour control in indoor pool
_____ water tested
_____ water discolouration
_____ perimeter drainage
_____ type of lining
_____ age of liner
_____ drains/hydrostatic relief valve
_____ ground fault circuit interrupters
_____ water temperature & pH level
_____ pool cover
_____ pump
_____ subsurface/surface drainage
_____ maintenance manual
_____ total operating costs

Hot Tub/Spa
_____ location
_____ heater
_____ pump
_____ filter type
_____ hydrojets
_____ accessories
_____ water temperature
_____ cover
_____ size
_____ insulation
_____ above ground
_____ below ground
_____ heated
_____ wood stave construction
_____ fibreglass construction
_____ other construction
_____ drain for tub
_____ how maintained
_____ disinfectant used
_____ ground fault circuit interrupter
_____ total operating costs

CONSUMER TIPS

Many people prefer to buy a resale house when purchasing for personal use or as an investment. Here are some of the advantages and disadvantages involved in buying a resale house rather than a new house. Like any guidelines, they are general in nature and do not necessarily apply in each case.

Advantages
- Generally cheaper than a new house.
- Has character or lived-in feeling.
- Utilizes architectural styles that are unique and no longer in common use.
- Problems in house design or construction are discernible by a competent professional building inspector, due to the aging of the house (e.g., settling, cracks in the walls, etc.).

- Landscaping is established.
- Neighbourhood is established and has developed its own character.
- Community services are established.
- Available in and proximate to the centre of the city.
- May include extras not normally included in a new home purchase, such as customized features that previous owners have built or installed.
- No GST.

Disadvantages

- May not have been built according to existing building standards, therefore could be deficient on matters dealing with electrical ventilation and energy efficiency codes (e.g., aluminum rather than copper wiring, lead-based solder rather than leadless solder for copper pipes, inefficient insulation or UFFI [urea formaldehyde foam insulation], etc.).
- Defects in the house construction may not be visible or identified unless a thorough inspection is done in advance by a professional building inspection. Buyers of new homes may not be protected by a New Home Warranty Program.
- If a resale house is in a metropolitan area, could be higher priced due to the higher value of land, whereas a new house in a suburban area could be less expensive due to lower cost of land.
- An older home may have been renovated by the owner or a handyman without a local building permit and inspection, therefore the safety or functional aspects of the house could be deficient.
- Some older homes do not have an attractive or functional design (e.g., rooms too small or poor layout), have low basement that makes that area less functional for comfortable use or rental suite, have a poor location of the building on the property (e.g., set back too close or too far from front of property line), have small or old-fashioned bathrooms and kitchens, etc. Costs to substantially renovate an older house could be expensive and time-consuming.
- The equipment (e.g., heating system) may be outdated and need repair, and appliances could be old-fashioned and lack modern features.
- Older houses could have water seepage problems.
- Not energy efficient (e.g., thin single-pane window glazing and inefficient insulation and heating source).

▼

CHAPTER 2

Garages
and Outbuildings

THE LIST OF preferred features that you prepared before starting your inspection may have included a garage attached to the house so that you are protected from unpleasant weather conditions. Perhaps the list also contained a workshop or work area for your hobbies and storage of your home repair tools. So before you can start your inspection, check to see what is not there. If you find a house with no garage, consider if there is sufficient space on the property to construct one. Be certain to check the zoning regulations and by-laws regarding building permits, set-backs and property lines. If a garage does exist, is it large enough to meet your needs? It should be long and wide enough to take any model of car and still leave space to walk around the car. An ideal width so that doors on either side of the vehicle can be opened freely is 11 feet for a one-car garage and 18 feet for a two-car garage. In addition to parking the car, check to see that there is sufficient room for garden tools, bicycles, window screens, work benches and other items, and that it is secure enough to meet your needs.

Garages may be attached to a house or to another outbuilding or they may be free-standing (detached). They may be enclosed by a solid wall or held up by vertical posts, as in a carport. Built-in garages, with living accommodation over the garage area, are sometimes used in two-storey houses. This chapter will deal with inspecting detached garages, attached garages and outbuildings.

Detached Garages

Roof
The first step is to examine the roof. Ask the owner the age of the roof and the number of layers of roofing material under the present roof. A good roof should have a lifespan of 10 to 15 years. Check the pitch of the roof to ensure

there is sufficient slope for rainwater and melting snow to run down its surface. Walk around the garage at a distance to get a good view of all sides. Use binoculars to scan all surfaces. Any depressed areas could suggest structural weakening or inferior construction. Take this opportunity to check how the roof is supported. You may find that the weight of the roof is spread evenly on the garage's exterior walls, or there may be a load-bearing structural support inside the garage. Roof framing may vary from 2" x 4" to 2" x 8" construction, spaced 16 or 24 inches apart. Be wary of irregular spacing of framing members and supports.

If the roof is not too high, you may wish to climb a ladder to examine more carefully the edge of the roofing material, flashing, ventilation vents, structural members and gutters. These are areas where dry rot or deterioration can most often be found. If the gutters are not sloped, there may be an accumulation of debris. Often this debris is saturated with water, causing water to back up to the fascia boards and rafter tail-ends. Take your awl and probe the suspect areas.

If the garage has wood, metal or vinyl gutters, check the joints for possible corrosion, leaks or deterioration. Look closely at the downspouts. Note their size and how they are secured to the wall. The ends may not be long enough, causing wall discolouration and deterioration. You may wish to use a garden hose to let water run down the gutter and listen for it to pass through the downspouts. Ideally the water should flow onto a splash pad and run away from the foundation wall of the garage or into a protected opening in the ground that leads to a perimeter drainage system. If the water runs towards the garage, an underground catch basin should be present. The basin should be covered with a rustproof metal grate and be clean of debris. Lift the grate to see how deep the basin is and where it runs to.

Walls

Walk around the outside of all four corners of the garage to check for plumbness, bulging, bowing, leaning or sagging of walls or corners. If this is noticeable, it may be due to settlement, frost heave, structural weakness or general deterioration. The exterior siding should not be in contact with the soil. The foundation wall should be at least 6 inches thick and should extend at least 6 inches above grade and below the frost level in the ground. As you are digging you will see if the soil appears to be saturated with water, indicating improper drainage. A well-compacted granular material below the concrete supports would prevent this. Problems with walls, doors and windows on the outside should be systematically inspected on the inside of the garage.

Finished inside walls limit your inspection to visible clues. Occasionally you will find openings where a flashlight can reveal the framing, vapour barrier, insulation or any deterioration. If unfinished, you can check the condition of every stud. Notice how each stud is supported at the top, the bottom and the corners. Most dry rot is found at the bottom of studs. Often foundation sills have no vapour barrier and are in direct contact with concrete or the soil. Look for inconsistent colouring in the wood. Darkened, stained areas will indicate that water seepage has occurred. Gently push the wall to see if it gives to pressure. Additional cross-bracing may be needed.

In the same way, check the sturdiness of any vertical columns that hold up the roof. Hold a level along the side of each column to ensure that they are not leaning. There should be an appropriate number of columns to prevent the deflection of the beam to which they are attached at the ceiling and to resist wind uplift. There should be a vapour barrier between the structural support and the concrete floor. Check the base of each column for dry rot or soft wood. Check the footings with a shovel to ensure they are deep enough below the grade to prevent frost heaving.

Ceilings

Examine the ceiling in the same way as the walls. With finished ceilings it is more difficult to see water seepage through the roof. Examine the ceiling for irregularities, sags and water stains. With an awl and the palm of your hand gently touch the stained areas. If the surfaces feel damp and the tip of the awl offers no resistance, water seepage is evident. Often you will find lumber, tools or sports equipment hung or tied from the rafters. These stored items can weigh enough to cause sagging of the roof and ceiling joists.

Flooring

Garage floors are usually made from dirt, gravel, wood or concrete. Check the surface for levelness and cracks or other signs of deterioration. If the floor is a concrete slab, check for a minimum of a 4-inch thickness, a gentle slope and a drain. If the concrete floor has expansion or control joints, check for any unusual movement or spalling along these joints. A sloped floor can be hosed out easily, allowing clumps of melting snow dripping from the car to run off. How are the exterior walls anchored to the flooring?

Garage Doors

Doors can be of one solid piece or sectional, with lockable hardware and protective weatherstripping attached to the threshold and the frame, and can be made out of wood or aluminum. As garage doors are constantly used, they need to be in good condition. Doors open and close on hinges, or on tracks and rollers. They can be of the overhead or swing out type. Test the doors by moving them slowly back and forth. Listen for unusual sounds. Are the hinges or tracks and rollers loose? The track should be anchored to some structural supports. Does the door close easily and smoothly? Is it light enough for all members of the family to handle? Usually counter-balance springs are mounted on the door, one on each side, to make operation easier.

The door may have a motorized opening mechanism. When testing it there should be no unusual noises or changes in the rate the door opens and closes. Most units have a feature that triggers the light switch as you open the garage door, the light staying on until you enter the house. An important child-safety feature on some garage door openers is a mechanism that causes the door to reverse if it touches anything on its way down. Should the power fail, it should be possible to operate the door manually. Door openers differ in design, from wire cables and bicycle-type chain drives to worm-screw devices. If the opener is mounted under a bedroom, the quietness of the worm-screw is preferred.

Check the door and door jambs for damage. Often you will find door jambs directly in contact with concrete or dirt floors; this can result in water damage and attract insects. Look for warpage and wide gaps between the door and the frame. Gaps or damaged weatherstripping allow heat loss. Place a mirror under the door to see if any irregularities can be noted. Check the surface of the door for veneer separation, broken glass or cracked panels.

Lighting and Heating

Since many detached garages rely on natural lighting through windows, check to see that the windows provide enough light and are not blocked. If the garage has electrical lighting, ensure the switches work. In an unfinished garage it is easier to examine the type, condition and connections of the electrical wiring. Check to see if there are electrical outlets for power tools. Are the outlets equipped with certified ground fault interrupters for safety? If the garage has its own electrical box and breaker switch, check for rust around the metal surfaces. (See comments on electrical wiring in Chapter 9.)

Unattached garages may have their own heating source, such as wood, electric baseboard, natural gas, oil or propane. Check that the heating system works and consider the annual maintenance required. Combustible appliances require their own fresh-air supply and you should check with city hall for requirements. While in the garage, be on constant lookout for evidence of mildew, water stains, seepage, efflorescence on walls and corrosion of any metal structural support brackets. Evaporation of rainwater and melting snow from a parked car are known to warp and crack wooden garage doors. Taking a deep breath through your nostrils may give you further clues of peculiar odours.

Attached Garages

All inspection principles discussed under "Detached Garages" also apply to an attached garage. However, as an attached garage is an integral part of the house, it requires a greater emphasis on safety. Toxic automobile combustion gases must not be allowed to enter the house. The entrance door from the garage to the house should be tight fitting, self-closing and fire resistant. The door threshold should be above the level of the garage floor. Some fire codes require that it open into the garage. Hardware on the door should consist of a dead-bolt to prevent unlawful entry into the house.

Foundations, framing and exterior finish of the side walls and roof should be approached in the same way as for the house. They are discussed fully in Chapter 3 (the exterior) and Chapter 4

Garages and Outbuildings

A homeowner did not check out the structural components of the garage prior to moving in. One night after a heavy snowfall and strong winds, the garage collapsed onto his new car.

(the structure). Carefully examine the wall and ceiling of the garage that adjoins the house. Municipal building codes in parts of North America require a fire-resistant material like stucco, plaster or wallboard of 5/8-inch thickness. Sometimes water will seep in between the house and garage if proper flashing between the roof and the wall of the house is not provided. If it is an enclosed garage, the walls and ceilings should be insulated to keep heat loss to a minimum, and the attic spaces above the ceiling must be properly ventilated. These garages are warmer during cold weather. When equipped with a connecting door to the house, enclosed garages keep the upper floors in the house warmer in the winter.

Houses that do not have a full basement or crawl space may have the boiler or furnace in the garage, along with the hot-water heater. These appliances should be properly partitioned, with adequate ventilation to carry off toxic fumes and allow for fresh-air circulation. The water heater pipes should be insulated to prevent heat loss and freezing. More details on heating and hot-water tanks are provided in Chapters 6 and 8.

Outbuildings

If there are outbuildings on the property, try to determine their original use. Inspect the exterior and interior in the same way you inspected the garage. Determine whether there are doors, windows or louvres for ventilation, and whether the structure can be used during the winter. Is there electricity, heating and a water source? Check for evidence of rodents, insects or bird life that could be a health hazard. There have been instances where chicken dust from outbuildings has found its way into homes, causing asthmatic and respiratory problems. Moulds of fungal spores are capable of prolonged survival in dust, and can be linked to pulmonary illness.

Remember that in the purchase of a property, a percentage of the selling price is for the garage and outbuildings. However, if these buildings are in a state of disrepair, they may in fact be a liability. If this is the case, you may be able to negotiate the purchase price downwards to offset the approximate cost of repair, renovation or demolition of the garage and outbuildings.

CHECKPOINTS
✔✔✔✔✔✔✔✔✔✔✔

DETACHED GARAGES
Roof
____ age
____ type
____ pitch
____ leakage
____ surface-worn areas
____ uneven surfaces
____ number of layers
____ missing shingles
____ straight roof ridge

Gutters
____ wood
____ aluminum
____ plastic
____ other
____ condition
____ cleaned
____ how attached

Downspouts
____ type
____ joint leaks
____ catch basin
____ how secured to wall
____ splash pad
____ leading to perimeter drainage

Fascia Boards
____ wood
____ aluminum
____ any deterioration
____ other

Soffits
____ sagging areas
____ surface stains
____ number of vent openings

Flashing
____ galvanized
____ aluminum
____ other
____ rust
____ loose flashing
____ how secured
____ caulking of connections

Roof Rafters
____ size
____ bracing
____ evenly spaced
____ condition of rafter tail ends
____ roof overhang

Paint
____ peeling
____ chalking
____ blistering
____ number of paint layers

Exterior Walls
____ load-bearing types
____ bracing used
____ insulation
____ vapour barrier
____ type of framing
____ finishing materials
____ foundation depth
____ settling, sagging or bulges
____ wood contacting ground/
     concrete

Foundation
____ concrete
____ masonry
____ wood
____ other
____ depth
____ soil condition

Ceilings
____ height
____ surface stains
____ insulation
____ finishing materials
____ uneven surfaces
____ vapour barrier

Flooring
____ concrete
____ wood
____ dirt
____ slope
____ thickness
____ length and width
____ uneven areas
____ settling, heaving, cracks
____ floor drain opening w/strainer
____ catch basin with perforated lid

Doors
____ wood
____ metal
____ size
____ location
____ security
____ warpage
____ jambs
____ thickness
____ height and width
____ hardware
____ railings and rollers
____ hinges
____ ease of operation
____ weatherstripping
____ contact with dirt/concrete
____ thresholds
____ motorized opener
____ transmitter
____ child-safety features
____ automatic door closures

Windows
____ wood
____ aluminum
____ double/single glazed
____ type and thickness
____ frame
____ hardware
____ security
____ type of glass
____ weatherstripping
____ operable hardware

Electrical
____ copper wiring
____ aluminum wiring
____ knob and tube wiring
____ screw fuse breakers
____ cartridge breakers
____ toggle switch breakers
____ push-button breakers
____ volts
____ amps
____ main source panel location
____ corrosion inside panel
____ number of breakers
____ location/number of light switches
____ location of lights
____ light fixtures
____ location/number of outlets
____ protected by ground fault
  interrupters
____ ground connection
____ last updated
____ certified testing agency approved

Plumbing
____ copper
____ galvanized
____ plastic
____ pipe sizes
____ leaks
____ location of water supply
____ condition of water tap
____ main shut-off valve
____ pipe insulation

Heating
____ oil
____ wood
____ natural gas, forced air
____ propane
____ electric
____ hot water
____ location of heating ducts or
  pipes
____ thermostat location
____ fresh-air ventilation
____ combustible gases ventilation
____ chimney condition
____ make
____ model number
____ serial number

Hot-water Tank
____ natural gas
____ oil

_____ electric
_____ location
_____ capacity of tank
_____ vacuum relief valve
_____ temperature/pressure relief valve
_____ floor drain
_____ age
_____ corrosion
_____ last replaced
_____ make
_____ model number
_____ serial number

Miscellaneous
_____ fire hazards
_____ insects or rodents

ATTACHED GARAGES
Additional to above points

Size
_____ width
_____ length
_____ ceiling height

Fireproofing
_____ doors
_____ walls
_____ ceilings
_____ joints sealed

Vertical Load-bearing Columns
_____ size
_____ concrete settling
_____ distances apart
_____ deterioration
_____ sagging of beams
_____ solid timber
_____ laminated wood
_____ depth of foundation under posts
_____ vapour barrier between wood/concrete

Floor
_____ slope of floor
_____ ease of keeping clean
_____ floor drain or catch basin

Doors
_____ type
_____ weatherstripped
_____ carbon monoxide leakage
_____ door swing
_____ automatic door closures

Drainage
_____ perimeter
_____ surface

Pet Doors
_____ size
_____ condition

Miscellaneous
_____ carbon monoxide detector
_____ storage of combustible materials
_____ pest infiltration

OUTBUILDINGS
Additional to above points:

Hazards
_____ health
_____ safety
_____ liability
_____ moulds and fungal spores
_____ lightning protected
_____ fire
_____ security
_____ insurance

Dry Rot and Water Infiltration
_____ roof seepage
_____ ceiling seepage
_____ door seepage
_____ wall seepage
_____ floor seepage
_____ window seepage

Miscellaneous
_____ foundation supports
_____ purpose of use

CONSUMER TIPS

You may wish to purchase a new house for your principal residence or investment needs. Here are some of the advantages and disadvantages of buying a new house over an older resale house.

Advantages
- Tend to be better designed in terms of room layout (e.g., larger kitchen, bathrooms, ensuites), functional purpose (higher ceilings in basement, patios, family room), and brighter atmosphere (skylights).
- Frequently a builder has several house models to choose from in the area you desire. In addition, you generally have the ability to select certain features to customize your needs, if you contact the builder before the house is fully completed. Optional or standard features you may be able to select include such items as carpet colour and fabric, kitchen appliance colours, kitchen and bathroom floor coverings, paint colours, etc.
- Has been constructed in compliance with current building code standards (e.g., structural plumbing, electrical, heating, ventilation, fire, security, etc.).
- Looks clean, modern, fresh, and smells new.
- First occupant in the house, which to some people is a psychological plus because you can personalize the house to meet personal or family needs rather than undoing the previous owner's personality or taste.
- Market evaluation of the house is easier because of similar comparables built in the same area.
- Price of house could be lower or house could be larger, compared to a similar resale house, if new house built in a suburb with lower land costs.
- Many new homes are built by builders who are registered with the New Home Warranty Program in their province. Therefore, if problems occur after the sale is completed, the builder or the New Home Warranty Program will correct them if the specific problems are covered by the program. You can check with your provincial New Home Warranty Program to verify if the builder is covered by the program.
- More energy efficient, e.g., improved insulation techniques, doors, windows, appliances, heating and cooling systems.
- Builders have taken up to date construction courses on building technology.

Disadvantages

- Pay GST.
- The builder may not be registered with the New Home Warranty Program, thereby creating a potentially high risk to the purchaser if problems occur.
- Due to land availability and cost savings, many builders construct new houses a considerable distance from the city core, thereby causing a potential increase in commuting time plus a loss of the services you may find in more metropolitan areas.
- It is not uncommon to have construction delays (e.g., paving of driveways, landscaping, finishing touches) and defects, both of which cause frustration and possible expense.
- Purchase documents prepared by the builder tend to be more complex and detailed compared to resale house contracts.
- Builder may be an amateur, with no experience in new house construction and may not be financially stable.
- Construction materials used may be new on the market and may have no proven record for quality or durability, e.g., roof, windows, concrete additives, specialized wood used in framing.
- The deposit funds you pay to the company could be lost if the builder ceases to operate. In some provinces there is consumer protection legislation that protects these funds. Unless you put the funds in a lawyer's or realtor's trust account, though, you could lose your deposit. It is particularly important that you check on the builder's reputation thoroughly beforehand through your Provincial New Home Warranty Program, local Home Builders' Association, and Better Business Bureau.
- Unstable and/or unpredictable geological, climatic or topographical conditions, resulting in mud slides, structural settlement.
- Some landscaping may be difficult to start, e.g., some tree or shrub varieties may not grow because of unusual soil, wind or sun conditions.

CHAPTER 3

▼

The Exterior

MOST PEOPLE'S FIRST impressions are made quickly by viewing the exterior finishes of a house, its placement on the lot and the enhancement of well-planned landscaping. However, the old adage "Don't judge a book by its cover" holds true when inspecting a house for potential future purchase. Some houses have attractive finishing and landscaping that is nothing more than a veneer for a damaged roof or rotting wood. Other houses of sturdy construction may not immediately appeal to you because of their plain appearance. The important factor to keep in mind is the relatively low cost of adding decorative features as opposed to reconstructing walls or roofs. Therefore your task is to look beyond the veneer of the exterior features, and to verify that the products chosen and the construction methods used offer a trouble-free lifespan.

This chapter will take an in-depth look at roofs, exterior walls, doors, windows, stairs and balconies. General comments will be given on each topic followed by specific care and inspection tips for a variety of building materials.

Roof

A roof can make the strongest visual impact on a house. The shape of the roof, and how it is proportioned, does more to establish the character of a house than any other single feature. To look at the roof critically, notice whether it is flat or pitched. If the roof is too steep, roof repairs may be difficult. If it is too flat, will water and snow collect on the roof? This is especially important in climates where heavy snowfalls can be expected, as serious roof damage can result from excessive moisture or the accumulation of snow that cannot run off easily. A roof overhang should prevent runoff from striking exterior walls, doors, windows or another roof below. The slope, pitch or angle of the roof can be obtained using your carpenter's level in a perfectly horizontal position against the rafter, fascia board or wall. Place the middle point of your protractor on the point where the roofline slants down to meet the level. Then read the angle in degrees on the protractor. A steel framing square is another tool that can be used to calculate the slope of the roof.

View the roof from a distance, using binoculars if necessary, and inspect the roof for a sagging or lowered ridge, sagging edges or roof surfaces, or lifting soffits and edges. These are all indications of structural problems due to settlement or problems that have arisen during renovations. Check the roof for moss growth, which will damage roof surfaces. Moss functions like a wick, using its root system to provide a direct path for water to penetrate further. Surfaces that receive little sunlight, such as north sides and areas hidden by tall trees, are particularly prone to moss growth.

The roof edge has the highest rate of decay, and therefore requires careful design and maintenance attention to keep repair costs down. You may need to climb a ladder to check the prime areas where moisture collects: the edges of roofing material, rafter tail-ends and sheathing, moulding at the roof edge, the fascia boards and joints between the fascia boards. Quality shingle applications will have metal drip edges installed to protect the edges of the roof. Edges can also be finished by extending the shingle 1 inch over the eave. Be careful when walking on a roof when inspecting it. Often it is not worth the risk of being held responsible for a leaking or damaged roof.

Types of Roofing Material

The purpose of roofing material is to protect the house and its contents from wind, rain, hail, sun and snow loads. The material used should be durable and offer some fire resistance to protect against falling sparks from a nearby chimney. A black or dark-coloured roofing material will absorb more heat during the summer season, creating a hot attic.

By checking along the edge of the roof and carefully lifting the roofing material, you may be able to decipher the types and the number of layers of roofing material. A roof may be covered as many as three times. However, if a fourth roof is needed, it is recommended that all the old roofing be removed and a completely new one installed. If only the original roof is present, there should be an underlayer of roofing paper or other form of moisture protective membrane. Ensure that the nails holding down the sheathing are not lifting or rusting.

There is a variety of roofing materials on the market, and some are mere imitations of old materials. Ask the owner for copies of warranty or other documentation provided by the roofing contractor to verify the quality of the materials used and the length of the warranty. While all may claim "greater lifespan" and "most fire-resistant," look for materials that have a proven history and are still being manufactured. If a house is ablaze, by the time the fire gets to the roof, there may be no structure left to hold up the claimed fire-resistant roof! Likewise, there is no point in having a roof with the best insulating

DIAGRAM 3: Features of a Roof

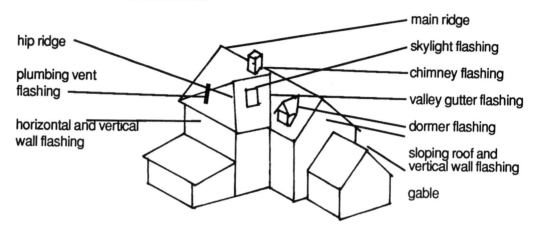

hip ridge

plumbing vent flashing

horizontal and vertical wall flashing

main ridge

skylight flashing

chimney flashing

valley gutter flashing

dormer flashing

sloping roof and vertical wall flashing

gable

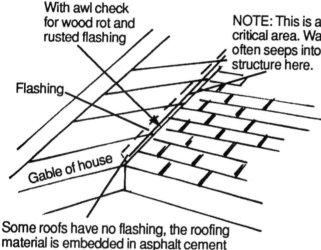

With awl check for wood rot and rusted flashing

Flashing

Gable of house

NOTE: This is a critical area. Water often seeps into the structure here.

Some roofs have no flashing, the roofing material is embedded in asphalt cement

Sloping roof and vertical wall flashing. Horizontal and vertical wall flashing similar.

NOTE: Three types of valley finishes you will find on roofs.

1. OPEN VALLEY

flashing

check flashing for: width, holes, breaks and tightness of joints

2. CLOSED CUT VALLEY

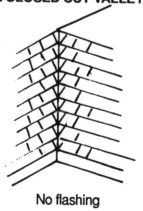

No flashing

Carefully check under all valleys in the attic for moisture and water seepage.

3. WOVEN VALLEY

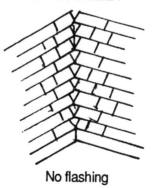

No flashing

Freezer in the Garage?

One house inspection found that the freezer in the garage was actually being used to store garbage because of bear problems in the area.

value when the attic is well ventilated and the cold air travels under the roof's sheathing. Consider the weight of the material and the bearing it will have on the structure. Too much weight may cause broken rafters and bracing supports and cracked interior ceilings. Beyond these obvious factors, some materials may be better suited to certain climatic conditions such as high wind velocity, heavy snowfalls, etc. Interlocking shingles, for instance, offer better protection against strong winds than the tab variety, which are prone to lifting. Advantages, disadvantages and maintenance considerations for a variety of common roofing materials are detailed below.

Asphalt Shingles

Asphalt shingles come in two basic types: fibreglass and organic. The fibreglass shingles are composed of an asphalt-saturated fibreglass mat; they look the same, but last five to 10 years longer than the 15- to 20-year-lifespan of organic shingles. Excessive mineral granules inside rain troughs or at the base of splash pads from downpipes are signs of an aging, weathered roof. Bare spots will show in areas of the roof where granular surfaces have worn off. The mineral granules also may clog the perimeter drainage system. Look for fine fissures over the surfaces that have widened through weathering, and for missing and broken shingles. It is common for older shingles to curl, claw and buckle, making them highly susceptible to wind, hail and ice damage as well as water penetration and decay under the subroof. You should find a galvanized zinc piece of flashing under the asphalt ridge finish to control moss growth.

Asphalt Roll

Asphalt roll roofing is usually made from felt material, saturated in asphalt and coated with mineral granules, and is applied by exposed or concealed galvanized nails. In both cases, all joints should overlap and be bonded together with roofing cement. The concealed nail method will give the roof a longer lifespan of approximately 20 years, depending upon the type of roll used. While this material is not the most attractive, it is the easiest to install, and is ideal for areas with heavy winds. It is commonly found over shallow-sloped carports or yard shed roofs. Inspect the roof surface for ridging, air bubbles and separations of the lap. Joints applied directly to the edges of the roof deck should have a metal drip edge.

Cedar Shakes and Shingles

Shingles are taper sawn, smooth on both sides, front and back and therefore have uniform lines and gentle appearance. Shakes, on the other hand, are handsplit and resawn, taper split, straight split or taper sawn, each with a slightly different appearance. The textured surface of the natural woodgrain is visible, which gives the roof a more dominating appearance. For quality and durability, the product should be free from knots. Shakes or shingles of good-quality rating are number 1 grade,

100% edge-grain, 100% heartwood, 100% all clear, or premium gold label grade. The shakes or shingles should be pressure-treated to prevent decay and fire-proofed to prevent combustibility. Stainless steel nails should be used with pressure-treated shakes and shingles. Both materials boast a 40- to 60-year lifespan when properly installed on a steep sloped roof. Lower-pitched roofs will have more collection of debris, and slower water runoff, and are therefore slower drying. When shakes and shingles are properly laid on narrow, widely spaced strips of wood, without paper sheathing, both outward and inward drying is permitted after a heavy rainfall. A non-breathable type of underlay will restrict uniform drying and cause decay.

Shakes and shingles will warp and show stains when nails rust. If copper flashing has been used, spacers are a must; otherwise, copper will oxidize, leaking a green stain into the cedar, and the cedar's acids in turn will corrode the copper. If the house is in a shaded area and a humid climate, leaves and moss will gather on the roof and build up between shingle or shake joints. They can cause enough lifting to allow wind to break the shingles or carry water deeper into the roof, causing decay. Wood shakes and shingles may increase the cost of house insurance.

Concrete and Clay Tile
Concrete and clay tiles come in various shapes and sizes ranging from flat to barrel-shaped. A high-quality vitreous clay can be as durable as concrete. Concrete tiles don't absorb moisture as easily and are less susceptible to frost damage, chipping and cracking than clay. Clay tile is unsuitable in wet climates as it can absorb as much as 18 per cent of its weight in moisture, and moisture and freezing cause it to crumble. Since both concrete and clay tiles are heavy, the house structure should be checked by a structural engineer to verify adequate support and bracing before these materials are used. Both products look best on a simply designed roof, and have a 50-year lifespan when properly installed. The tiles break easily, so the roof is not meant to be walked on. Check for chipped, cracked or damaged tiles. Tile flashing around the ridge, dormers, porches and valleys are potential rain leakage areas at the joints. This type of roof is best inspected from inside the attic, where you

should not see the underside of the tile. Instead, the tile should be attached to wooden battens under which is a continuous metal foil, wood-fibre material or felt-covered half-inch plywood sheathing. Check for cracked roof rafters or supports and water seepage between the joints.

Slate

Slate resists deterioration and requires little maintenance; therefore it adds significantly to the value of a house. If unaffected by high winds, a slate roof can last over 100 years. Within 40 years, though, the metal fasteners holding the slate in place may require replacement. Like concrete and clay tiles, slate is heavy and requires extra structural reinforcement. Synthetic slate shingles are available, and weigh and cost less, but they do not have the same durability. Since there are few slate roofs in Canada, finding replacements for broken pieces is expensive.

Steel Tiles

Steel tiles are best used in regions of heavy snowfalls because the snow slides off the roof. Some galvanized steel tile has a factory-baked finish that is manufacturer warrantied for 25 years against cracking, blistering or peeling. With lower-quality steel tiles, the colour can fade within five to 15 years. Since steel tiles are installed using wooden strapping, they can be removed and replaced with ease. Houses located close to salt water should ensure the fasteners have been treated against galvanic corrosion. Also, sudden temperature changes from hot to cold can cause fasteners to pull loose from the nailing base. Leaks can develop at loosened seams where steel tiles have been damaged by screws or nails. Steel tiles can be noisy in heavy rain or hail, although the sound can be reduced by acoustic insulation in the attic. This type of roofing is easily dented by falling tree branches or by walking on it to repair a TV aerial or clean the chimney.

Built-up Roofing

Tar or asphalt-and-gravel types of built-up roofing are commonly found on flat or low-sloped roofs and consist of built-up layers of felt, tar or asphalt and gravel. Their durability depends on the number of layers but can range between 20 and 30 years. Such roofs are difficult to inspect because you can't lift anything to look underneath, and walking over the surface can puncture the membrane or an air bubble and cause a water leak. Look over the surface for any repair patches and separations or cracks at the joints. Is there any moss buildup? Check the seals around projecting pipes and drains and ensure the flashing is well secured around vents, skylight and chimney. The main problem with this type of roof is getting water to drain from its surfaces. After a heavy rainfall, water may be seen ponding over areas away from drain openings or over plugged drains. This may cause the roof to sag. Check to see that there is a gravel stop or cant strip used in conjunction with the flashing, running around the perimeter of the roof to prevent the gravel from washing off the roof. Repairs on this type of roof can be expensive as special equipment is required. A rival to the tar-and-gravel roof is torch-down rolled roofing material.

Corrugated Sheet Metal / Fibreglass Panels

This is a relatively thin and lightweight type of roofing commonly found over porches and extended patios. The edges of each panel should overlap and be nailed down, and there should be rubber-type washers between the nail heads and the roofing. Examine how the panels fit against the house, as this is where most leaks occur. A sheetmetal roof should be treated with a rust inhibitor. Fibreglass roofs, if directly exposed to ultraviolet rays, get brittle and crack; otherwise they will last over 10 years. During heavy winds and rains both of these roofs can be noisy. If a strong enough wind blows underneath it, the roof may be blown off entirely. Any solid or translucent roof attached to two or more walls of a house needs ventilating provisions. Heat and light will radiate through the roof, and if the air does not have a chance to circulate, there may be an uncomfortable heat buildup. More than one patio cover has been rebuilt because it cooked rather than cooled those who sat beneath it!

Flashing

Building codes permit several different metals to be used for flashing, including hot-dip galvanized steel, lead, copper, zinc and aluminum. One material is basically as good as another for the purpose, but dissimilar metals should not be used together as they can "attack" one another, causing electrolytic corrosion and failure. Of course, galvanized flashing must be rust-proofed. Flashing is used to prevent water from entering joints such as at the junction of walls and roofs, chimneys, vents, over door and window openings, in roof valleys or between different building materials. Check the flashing for signs of rust and nail pulling. Where flashings are applied around the roof, nails or screws can become exposed, opening gaps at the connections, thereby causing water seepage and wood decay behind the flashing and cant. Laps and joints in flashing materials must be caulked.

Eave Projections

All houses should have some sort of eave overhang that protects the walls and windows around the house from rain, and sheds the snow further from the foundation walls. A properly designed overhang can allow the low winter sun to warm the house, and provide a summer shade over the exterior walls and windows, thus having a cooling effect. The area under the eave projection should be finished with a soffit. Check any areas of the eaves that have stain marks. This may indicate water seepage from the roof.

Gutters and Downspouts

Stand back and look at how water is to find its way from roof surfaces. In regions that do not experience heavy winter snow conditions, you should see a gutter system around the pitched portions of the roof, along with downspouts. Some houses have a gutter system that is recessed

and hidden behind fascia boards. Roofs that have low slopes or are flat may have no gutters, only downspouts. Both gutters and downspouts can be made from a variety of materials including wood, vinyl, aluminum or galvanized metal.

When properly maintained, the life of wood gutters is usually equal to that of the main structure. Vinyl gutters have unsealed seams that permit the material to expand and contract with changes in temperature. The diameter of the gutter depends on the size of the downspouts, which in turn depends on the roof area to be drained. Downspouts may be round, square or a corrugated shape. You will find that water travels more smoothly (and quietly) down a round downspout, than down a square one. Those built-in corrugated shapes tend to freeze less rapidly than other models.

Gutters can be attached to the fascia boards or rafter tail-ends, using strap hangers or spike-and-ferrule. Spikes are easier to install but can cause the gutter to sag more readily under heavy loads of snow and ice. Often you will find a leaf strainer over the opening where the downspout is attached, as well as a leaf guard laid over the gutters to prevent leaves from falling in and clogging the downspouts.

Gutters can become a problem if not properly sized, sloped or maintained. Rusting, clogged gutters and missing downspouts can lead to overflow of water and serious wood decay. Gutters that are pulling away from the side of the roof, are an indication that there is rotting wood. Recessed gutters must be carefully inspected for adequate slope and to see if any leakage has occurred causing damage to the soffit and fascia areas. Check the ends, elbows and connections of the gutters and downspouts as most leaks occur here. Soldered joints and seams should be inspected for breaks. You can look inside the gutters by using a small mirror from atop a ladder.

The water should run freely through the downspouts onto a splash pad, turned away from the foundation wall, or through a pipe to empty into the perimeter drainage system. Examine carefully the ground level area where the downspouts connect with the perimeter drainage system. Often the connection is loose or damaged and soil has crept in, blocking the opening. Where the downspout penetrates the soil, see if you can move the downspout aside and with your flashlight look down into the opening. Water should not be pooled inside. Can you decipher whether the drains run to a separate storm drain, sump or dry well, or into the sewer drain? Some municipalities call for a two-pipe storm system for all buildings, consisting of a tight joint piping system to pick up all roof downspouts and a second perforated piping system to pick up subsoil drainage.

Trim

Trim around the exterior of the house is referred to as soffits, fascia, gable ornamentation and finishes around doors and windows. The trim should be securely fastened and joints tightly mitred. Better-quality wooden trim will have a rain drip kerfed under the edge to prevent water running back into the wall of the house. If wood trim is covered by metal flashing, check underneath for soft areas indicating rot. Rust stains at the nail heads are a sure sign. Too much trim on a house allows for weathering and water to enter the joints, and requires extra painting and maintenance.

Exterior Walls

A wide variety of exterior wall claddings are in use today. The most common types will be described along with features to look for when examining them. When making your observations, try to determine the condition of the material and how much time and money you would be prepared to spend each year to keep it in good shape. It is not unusual to come across a house with up to four different exterior materials. For example, the bottom quarter may be finished with brick, the area around the main entrance with stone, the rest of the house with stucco, and the gable finished with wood siding. Note that there should be at least 8 inches between the bottom of most wall finishes and the ground cover to prevent decay of the structural sill plates of the house.

Brick

A brick exterior, when properly installed with a suitable footing and protected from water damage, has an indefinite lifespan. All bricks are graded for their durability when exposed to weather conditions. Non-weathering, salvaged or recycled bricks should be kept dry and only used for decorating interior walls. Masonry brick can expand and contract, due to temperature, moisture, shrinkage and creep. Look for expansion and control joints, which can prevent cracking caused by masonry movement. Clean weep hole openings should be evident around the base of the brick wall. These holes serve to drain water and act as a venting device for the air space in the wall.

Check for surface spalling and broken, missing and cracked bricks or mortar joints. Cracks will allow water to seep into the wall and cause decay, or freeze and cause further damage. Vertical cracks usually indicate inadequate footings. If the wall moves slightly when light pressure is applied by hand, perhaps the metal ties behind the brick have deteriorated or have not been installed. Examine all openings on a brick house, including windows and doors. Spanning each opening is pre-cast concrete, reinforced concrete or steel angles or "lintels." Steel angle lintels often cause problems if they have not been correctly sized or anchored to the wall. Under too much load they will deflect and can crack the stiff masonry above the opening, resting on the window or door frame and transferring load to it. This can distort or deform the frame, prevent sliding doors from opening and even break the glass.

Stone

A stone wall will provide the greatest variety of natural texture and beauty. Examples include granite, marble, limestone, quartz, slate, bluestone and sandstone. It may be ashlar, which is composed of sawn and squared stone, or rubble, which consists of stones gathered from quarry pits or in fields, either split or in their natural state. For exterior applications, the stone, like brick, should be low in porosity, permeability and absorption. Stone masonry is expensive and may be difficult to match for future repair or renovations. Building with stone is a craft that requires creative ability as well as knowledge of masonry. If there is missing mortar at the joints, moisture may cause the stone to spall or crack with freezing temperatures.

Stucco

A stucco wall may have many different types of texture or design. Stucco contains water, sand and gypsum and may be applied over a wire mesh that is attached to the house, or directly over a masonry wall. In the prairies, where the winters are harsh and the climate is dry, stucco is more durable than wood and can easily last 50 years. Any problems with stucco are primarily related to water damage and cracking due to movement and settling of walls. Check for cracks around doors, windows and wall surfaces. Using a rubber mallet or your fist, gently tap the stucco surface around cracked areas. If you hear hollow sounds, this could suggest that a harder tap might cause a chunk of the stucco to fall off the wall.

Asbestos Shingles

Asbestos shingles are vermin-proof, will not burn or rot, need no protective coating and are inexpensive. While they are hard to scratch or mark, they are very brittle and break easily. Since they are porous, the house may feel damp or lose heat during humid or rainy weather. Often you will find that damaged asbestos shingles have been replaced with wooden shingles and painted to match the existing finish. Examine the corners for wood rot underneath the shingle. If you find building paper, this will provide some protection against moisture penetration.

Asphalt Siding

Asphalt siding comes in either shingle or roll and is installed in a similar way to the conventional roof. The surface may be embossed to resemble stone or brick. Check the surface areas for signs of deterioration or nails that have pulled away from overlapping joints.

Wood Shingles

Wooden shakes and shingles used for roofs may also be used for walls. When properly applied, most are naturally decay resistant, especially if they have been treated with a water-repellent preservative. Red cedar shingles, native to the Pacific Northwest, are more resistant to insect attack and decay than white cedar found in Eastern Canada. However red cedar wood can cause asthmatic reactions in people who are predisposed to allergies. Check the shakes and shingles for surface rot by gently touching and lifting the bottom edges.

Wood Siding

Wood siding may be smooth surfaced or textured in a variety of patterns and may be installed either horizontally or vertically. Tongued and grooved patterns usually have greater resistance to rain penetration than shiplap patterns. Where there is no roof overhang, the exposed edges of wood sidings should be treated with a water-repellent preservative. Nails should be placed evenly along the siding and be rust-free. Gently tap the wall surfaces to check for insulation throughout the wall cavities. A variety of sounds will indicate whether insulation is present.

Properly maintained and protected, wood sidings will last well over 100 years. However, the siding's only protection is the wood preservative, paint finish or stain. Try to determine from the owner what the finish consists of, as you will need to match a new layer of paint or stain with the one underneath to ensure that it will bond adequately. Failure of the finish will result in rapid deterioration. With your knife, make a small scratch in an inconspicuous area. Count the layers of paint or stain that have been applied.

During your inspection you may see signs of deterioration (decay, splitting or missing knots) on the south and west sides due to the sun's rays. The north exposures may show signs of moss growth and moisture penetration. Black or grey discolourations of exterior paint at the joints and nail areas of the siding are usually due to fungi growing through the paint from wet wood. Pronounced vertical streaking on cedar siding can indicate that condensation has occurred on the back of the wood, with water seeping down and out at the horizontal joints. Fungal stains, mould and water stains on unpainted wood indicates that interior wetting has taken place.

Aluminum and Vinyl Siding

Vinyl siding is more durable than aluminum, although early types were subject to breaking easily. Vinyl can become torn, punctured and brittle, and can crack in cold weather. In the early 1960s aluminum siding was subject to extensive chalking, fading and unattractive oxidation and pitting. Aluminum siding products now have a baked-on finished enamel that protects from the natural elements. As the siding will conduct heat and cold (especially darker colours), you will hear cracking sounds from expansion and contraction during temperature changes. It may corrode in salt air.

Due to expansion and contraction of both materials on hot and cold days, some of the panels may bulge, bow or twist. Aluminum siding should be grounded as a precaution against faulty wiring or lightning strikes. Its surface may be easily damaged by dents, scratches, climbing vines and bird droppings. Both types of siding can outlive the house, and the only maintenance required is an annual hosing.

When it is properly installed, it should be possible to slide any piece of siding back and forth along the wall. By pressing your hand over the siding, you may be able to detect a backing board that has no insulation value but makes the siding more rigid. Notice the trims and finishes around doors, windows and corners and inspect for proper sealing and caulking. Condensation should be able to drip down and out of pre-punched weep holes along the butt edge of each panel. Poorly finished connections will allow moisture and insects to enter and cause rot. You should be particularly cautious if the aluminum or vinyl siding has been placed over an old wall surface. Both forms of siding offer good hiding areas for a variety of destructive insects.

Log Homes

Log houses are common in rural areas. They can survive a fire easier than conventional homes. Logs used for homes must be carefully selected and cured. They should be felled during winter months, when the sap isn't running, to avoid later fungus growth and insect attack. If the grooving, notching and shaping of all connecting logs is accurate, the load will be transferred efficiently with no distress to the building or heat loss. Logs should not protrude beyond the roof line, and you should check that the logs have been protected from sun exposure and moisture penetration. The most common pests that invade untreated logs are termites, powder-post beetles and carpenter ants.

Doors and Frames

Exterior doors should provide good security and insulation as well as style and serviceability. Doors will vary, depending upon their positioning and function. For instance, doors in the path of prevailing winds should have a windbreak near the door opening. Be certain to check pet door openings, as there is usually a lot of cold air blowing through the edges of these small doors. Weatherstripping should evenly contact the door all around, without any bent, crimped or missing pieces. If the door has any glazing, it should be tempered or safety glazed and securely fitted so as not to rattle when the door is slammed shut. A door that opens into the house is called "normal swing," and one that opens out is called "reverse swing." This terminology will be important when purchasing a screen door, as you don't want the screen door and the main door swinging in the same direction. (Comments about security and locks are found in Chapter 15.)

Open and close each door slowly to ensure that it swings easily and does not rub anywhere. All six sides of the door should be sealed. Take your mirror and look under and over the door. Does it look as if someone has cut a strip off or added a piece? Look for delaminated corners and edges. Check to see that the door properly fits its frame, and that no daylight shows through when it is closed firmly.

Door frames are usually made of wood, although some are made from heavy-gauge steel, vinyl, fibreglass or aluminum. Some are finger-jointed or glued-up from many small pieces of wood. How a frame has been pieced together is difficult to see after paint has been applied. There should be a thermal break, and the two sides are kept apart by a plastic or rubber spacer. Examine the door threshold for wear. Test the bottom of the frame and threshold with your awl for signs of soft or decayed wood. The frame should not move when you grasp it in your hand and shake it. There should not be any cracks along the hinges of the frame. Hinges should be securely fastened, and the leaves of the hinges should be an even depth in the frame and in the door. There should be at least three heavy-gauge metal hinges that have a security tab (a pin that secures the door even after the hinge pin has been removed). All of the hinge screw heads should be consistent.

Wood Doors
Wood is a natural insulator, but it is no match for the synthetic foam insulation inside steel doors. Wooden doors can be made of almost any kind of wood, such as cedar, pine, fir, oak, and so on. The quality within each species will vary greatly. A fine grain on a solid door is an indication of a better-quality wood. Exterior doors should be solid core and a minimum of 1-3/4 inches thick. All wooden doors require maintenance and, depending upon the quality, some swell more than others when the humidity is high. Excessive weathering and swelling may cause the door to warp, preventing easy closure of the door. This in turn may cause misalignment of the door frame and increased heat loss. Find out what type of paint, stain, varnish or lacquer has been applied to the wood surface. This will be helpful when applying additional coats or stripping off the present finish. Examine the bottom of the door for kick marks and pet scratches. If these are too deep, they may be difficult to repair.

Steel Doors
Steel doors don't crack, warp, split, shrink or swell. They consist of a metal panel or skin made of 22- to 24-gauge sheet metal (about 1/32 inch thick). The

skin covers a reinforced frame-work, consisting of either wood or steel channels, which gives the door its strength and stiffness on both sides. Between the metal skins the door cavity is filled with plastic foam insulation. A strip of plastic or other non-conductive material separates the metal parts of the door to create a thermal break so that heat won't travel from one side to the other. Steel doors are almost maintenance free, except for oiling the lock cylinder and hinges. The door skins should be galvanized and painted for corrosion protection. Steel doors cannot be planed or sanded at the edges. By rubbing your hand over the surface of older steel doors, you may notice cold spots indicating the insulation has settled.

> **All fixed up for the sale!**
>
> One prospective purchaser neglected to inspect all sides of the house. After he bought it, he discovered the front of the house had been redone using top quality products. However the old, deteriorated wood finishing on the back and sides of the house had only been repainted to give the appearance of being new.

Fibreglass Doors

Fibreglass doors are made like steel doors but with skins of moulded fibreglass. They can be stained or painted like wood and the edges can be trimmed with a saw. The lifespan of these doors is well over 25 years.

Storm Doors

Storm doors are constructed out of wood, aluminum, aluminum-clad wood or steel. A storm door can protect the main door from the elements, reduce the drafts in the winter and provide summertime ventilation through screening. Screen and glass panels are usually interchangeable. Most storm doors are not in good condition due to wind and weather abuse. Check the storm door's closing device, which may consist of a hydraulic, pneumatic or spring closer. The door hardware should be lockable.

Dutch Doors

Also called a cottage door, this is a hinged door divided into two horizontal sections, which can be opened and closed independently or together as a single unit. Often they are used as exterior doors to better control ventilation on older houses. For example, in the summer the bottom half of the door may be kept shut to keep out pets, while the upper half is left open to allow in fresh air. If these doors are made of wood, it can be difficult to control air leakage around the edges.

French Doors

French doors have a maximum of glazing with individual panes separated by strips called muntin bars. Fake muntin bars snap into place over large glass panels and can be removed easily for window cleaning. French doors usually come in pairs, hinged at the sides or to each other, or with one door operable and the other fixed. There may be hardware in place to allow the door to be propped open in a fixed position for ventilation. The doors can swing out or in. If the doors swing out, make sure that all six sides are coated with paint, stain or a wood preservative. Run your mirror around the edges to check for proper seals. Check the quality of hinges and door hardware. Tap the window panes with your finger to ensure the window does not rattle because it is loose.

Patio Doors

Most patio doors are made out of wood or aluminum, although steel, vinyl and fibreglass are also used. Some glide in tracks while others swing open. Wooden sliding doors are subject to swelling and warpage and will feel heavy and harder to move. Open the door to test how easily it glides along the tracks. Do the wheels sound worn? When the door is closed, you should not feel a breeze at the edge of the door. Check the corners of the wooden frame to ensure it is not coming apart. The door should be equipped with a locking mechanism so that it cannot be lifted out of its tracks from the outside. If the sliding door opens onto an uncovered deck, there should be a raised threshold to prevent snow from piling up along the bottom of the door. Check the condition of the weatherstripping and frame. Decayed wood around the floor areas may be a sign of cold moist air passing over worn weatherstripping. Check the condition of the insect screen and how easily it glides in the tracks.

The door glass may be bevelled, leaded, etched, tinted or plain. Double, thermally broken panes will provide greater insulation than single panes. If the glass has had condensation problems, you will notice a stain (and possibly rot) over the wood surfaces near the bottom. Examine the rubber gasket holding the window in place for signs of deterioration.

Windows and Skylights

Windows contribute to an appealing and harmonious exterior appearance, so uniformity in placement and selection of materials is an important design feature of the house. Study the design, shape and size of each of the windows and skylights. Notice if one window has a different style or if it looks out of proportion to the others. Count the number of windows and skylights; note their locations and whether they have aluminum or wood frames. Some windows, depending on the size and design of the frame, incorporate a removable storm pane on the same sash as the permanent pane. If these windows are properly fitted and weatherstripped or caulked, they can be just as efficient for reducing heat loss as a sealed unit. They are also less expensive and easier to replace in the event of breakage. You will find storm windows either inside or outside the prime window. The panes may consist of either glass or acrylic. If these windows have been removed for the summer, ask the owner where they are stored.

Storm windows
screens ?

Windows and skylights are the weakest link in the entire building envelope. They have little insulating value and cause air leakage and condensation problems. Evaluate each window and skylight based on the following criteria:

- *Energy efficiency* Windows must control air flow, heat flow, condensation and water vapour flow. Are windows single, double or triple paned? Are they tinted, heat absorbing or do they have reflective coatings or films? What is the condition of the glazing compound, gasket, window seals or weatherstripping? The fewer or smaller the windows, the lower the heat loss. Will solar and other radiation cause problems?
- *Acoustics* Will you hear outside noises from traffic or trains, or from nearby playing fields?
- *Ventilation* Can you open the windows? Do they slide or swing open? Do they offer adequate cross-ventilation within the house? Operable windows placed away from exterior corners achieve the best air movement through internal rooms.
- *Rain protection* The tops of framed openings should be flashed. Are the frames and sills protected from weathering? Can wind, rain and snow blow around hinged-type windows?
- *Security* Walk around the house and see how easy it is to obtain entry without breaking the glass. Is there any stiffness or strength to the window sash and frames? Is there a possibility that small children could fall out of an upper-floor window?
- *Hardware* An assessment of the ease of operation of the hinges, latches, locks and knobs is easier to make when inspecting the interior living spaces. Make a note of missing hardware, or windows that you can pull open from the outside.
- *Cleaning* How will you wash windows on the outside? Do you need a tall ladder? Are the window frames designed to pivot, lift or tilt out? Are insect screens and storm windows easy to attach and remove? Note that certain light- and heat- reflecting glass must be cleaned in a special manner to prevent scratching of the surfaces.
- *Light, view and privacy* Will neighbours be able to see you move through the house? Ensure bathroom windows are of a mottled-type glass for added privacy. Check the glass panes for visual distortions.
- *Warranty* Quality windows have a 20-year guarantee. Check the wording to ensure the warranty is transferable, and note the terms and conditions.
- Further discussion of windows is provided in Chapter 11, which deals with interior aspects of the house.

Large, sloped windows facing south or west can lead to overheating in the summertime unless there are large trees or awnings to provide shade. They will also cause premature fading of interior finishings. If a window is sloped or tilted more than 15 degrees, safety glass such as tempered, wired, laminated, heat-treated or acrylic must be used. Check for an approved safety sticker attached to the corner of the window pane or in between the panes. Sloped windows, if not properly installed, do not seal well around the edges, and allow for leaks. Notice any broken windows, and possible reasons for them, such as malfunctioning hardware or major structural settlement and stress problems within the building. Windows on a wall with no roof overhang protection are likely areas for wood rot in the window frames.

There are at least five different types of window frames: wood, aluminum, vinyl, fibreglass and steel, as well as combinations of these materials. Wood is the most desirable because of its low thermal conductivity. However, wood requires treatment to prevent rot and always poses a maintenance problem. If a low grade of wood is used, it will swell and warp over time. Gently press the bottom surface of the frame next to the sill with the point of your awl to test for rot. If the point disappears quite easily then the answer is clear.

Aluminum, reinforced vinyl and fibreglass are strong and corrosion resistant. Steel frames are heavy, will rust and conduct heat, and are subject to condensation. When storm windows are used, the space between the window frames acts as a thermal break. Due to their lower thermal conductivities, wood, vinyl and fibreglass frames do not require thermal breaks. The multiple dead air spaces found within some extruded vinyl frames can result in a frame that is thermally equal or better than a wood frame. Some windows will have a thermal break built into the frame. They consist of a high thermal resistance material that insulates and separates the interior from the exterior side of the frame. Heat loss and condensation can be a problem with those frames that do not have a thermal break. Condensation can occur on the frame even if the window is double-glazed.

Check the top of basement windows and door frames for drip caps. These are thin, almost invisible strips of sheet metal perched above the frames to prevent rain and melting snow from leaking into walls, where it could soak insulation and rot structural members. Check how water drains away from the window and foundation wall. If the window has a light well, ensure it is not filled with moss and debris. This is an invitation for decay and pests. If the light well has walls made out of concrete, they should be free from gaps and cracks so moisture does not seep into the window framework.

The window sill is supposed to slope downward to prevent rainwater from running back into the house or down the wall. Usually you will find a kerf along the underside of the sill, forming a drip trap to allow the water to drain away properly from the sill. Where windows have a weep channel along the sill, check to see that it is free from debris and allows water to drain out the holes.

Some houses have metal or fabric awnings built over the windows to provide shading and weather protection. The awning material should allow air to pass through to avoid buildup of hot-air pockets. If the awning is retractable, pull it up with the rope to test that it retracts easily, and that the mechanism is fully functioning.

Stairs, Verandahs and Balconies

Most often the porch, along with the stairs and handrails, is the first part of the house to suffer structural damage. This is because they are heavily used, exposed to freeze/thaw weather conditions and may not be as well built as the rest of the house. Step treads, porch and balcony flooring, exposed beams, handrailing and some window sills have broad flat surfaces that wet easily if they are not sloped properly and exposed to direct weathering conditions.

Since wood is most often used on porches and stairs, it is worth noting some basic facts about this material. Water is drawn into wood by capillary movement, gravity flow and wind-carrying rain. It penetrates the end grain of a piece of wood more easily than the side of a board. This is why decay is frequently found at joints. Flat-sawn lumber tends to swell and shrink more than vertical grain. This is particularly true in the use of wide boards. Flat-sawn step treads, handrailing and porch and balcony flooring will cup and hold water. Siding and trim of the same material will twist, warp and split with severe weather exposure. Wood flooring above a wet basement or crawl space will frequently buckle, cup, bow or twist because the lower sides of the boards become wet and swollen with moisture.

Stairs should be level except for a slight downward slope to allow water to run off the stairs. For safety reasons, the height and width of each step should be the same, and the nosings rounded. Stairs protected by a roof overhang will show fewer signs of weathering than those out in the open. Exterior stairs leading up to the main floor or down into the basement of a house are often made of concrete. Check for settlement cracks and large gaps where the concrete has pulled away from the house. Tap each stair for a consistent sound. One prospective purchaser investigated further after hearing uneven sounds. Numerous hairline cracks were discovered, indicating that the entire coat of concrete, applied over an old staircase, was ready to fall off.

Anti-slip vitrified tiles are designed for exterior use as they absorb no more than 3 per cent water and can withstand freeze/thaw conditions. Otherwise, glazed tiles are hazardous and should never be used on exterior steps. Normal freeze/thaw conditions will destroy the structure of the tile.

Metal, vinyl and wood materials are commonly used for handrailing. Wrought iron railings must be treated with a rust-inhibitor paint. Check the sturdiness of the handrailing by grasping and shaking it. The base of wooden handrail and latticework should be inspected for rot. Check the strength of the anchorage and any infill material like balustrades used under the handrail. Run your hand over the surface of the railing to check for smoothness.

Porches serve to protect the entrance from rain and snow and, if large enough, may offer sufficient space for a seating area. Ideally, for weather protection, the porch should have a roof overhang. If a large marble, placed in the centre of the floor, rolls off the balcony or to a recessed floor drain, then water will do likewise. Sometimes a deck will be fitted with removable duckboards to allow water to run in between the openings. The boards can be easily lifted to clean out debris that has fallen between the slats.

Patios and balconies with no living areas below may be finished with an indoor/outdoor carpet material. Decks over living areas require a thicker, waterproof material and should overlap at the seams. Quality finished floor surfaces will be slip/skid and ultraviolet resistant, and have good abrasion and impact qualities. In situations where the porch floor has settled, you may *N.B.* find that the roof has pulled away from the exterior wall. This creates a gap under the flashing and allows water to find its way into interior wall surfaces. If this is the case, check interior walls for cracks. Where balconies are cantilevered from the house, the floor joists should be held in place with joist hangers. Walking on the balcony should not cause floors inside the house to vibrate.

Check the bottom of the porch, wood posts, foundation, steps, floors and roof for wood rot. The edges and underneath the porch should be finished with flashing. Areas under enclosed wooden porches, balconies and stairs should be treated as part of the crawl space in terms of foundation damp-proofing, waterproofing, ventilation, footing drains and soil cover. Footings either rest on or are sunk into the ground, and support the porch deck or balcony posts. The footings may be concrete blocks, poured concrete pads, precast piers or prefabricated tubes. Good footings are key to the structure's stability. As a rule, a footing should be about twice the size of the post it supports. In most cases, they are required to extend below the frost line and should extend above the ground to keep wood posts away from ground moisture. With a flashlight and awl, probe the footings and framing for decay, rot and excessive water stains.

At this point in your inspection you have already started to look at the foundation of the house. Notes that you have made concerning cracks in the concrete, excessive wood rot and poor perimeter drainage will provide clues to further damage that you will discover as you inspect the foundations and interior of the house. The following chapter will provide you with in-depth considerations on the basic structure and foundations of the house, the basement and framing and pests you might find there.

CHECKPOINTS
✔✔✔✔✔✔✔✔✔✔✔

Roof

- ____ shape
- ____ pitch
- ____ colour
- ____ age
- ____ roof type
- ____ asphalt shingles
- ____ cedar shakes
- ____ cedar shingles
- ____ concrete tile
- ____ slate
- ____ corrugated sheet metal
- ____ fibreglass panels
- ____ steel tiles
- ____ torch-down roof
- ____ other
- ____ built-up roofing
- ____ roof edge condition
- ____ drip edges
- ____ surface deterioration
- ____ roof overhang
- ____ existing layers of roofing
- ____ galvanized zinc strip
- ____ accumulation of moss
- ____ roof underlay
- ____ last cleaned
- ____ manufacturer's warranty
- ____ certified testing agency approved

Trim

- ____ gable ornamentation
- ____ fascia boards
- ____ painted
- ____ stained
- ____ condition
- ____ how finished
- ____ areas of decay

Eave Projections

- ____ projection over doors
- ____ projection over windows
- ____ gable and projections
- ____ length of projection
- ____ soffit finished
- ____ gable end condition

Flashing

- ____ galvanized metal
- ____ aluminum
- ____ felt
- ____ other
- ____ rust
- ____ nail pulling
- ____ caulking over gaps
- ____ condition around chimney
- ____ condition around plumbing
- ____ vents
- ____ doors
- ____ windows
- ____ roof valleys

Gutters and Downspouts

- ____ wood
- ____ vinyl
- ____ aluminum
- ____ galvanized metal
- ____ built-in gutter
- ____ other
- ____ gutter size
- ____ gutter slope
- ____ downspout shape/size
- ____ downspout location
- ____ last cleaned
- ____ age
- ____ how attached
- ____ condition
- ____ drainage ease
- ____ perimeter drainage condition
- ____ leaf strainer/guard
- ____ splash pad
- ____ elbows
- ____ drainage leads to sewage drain
- ____ drainage leads to storm drain
- ____ drainage leads to dry well
- ____ other

Exterior Walls

- ____ brick
- ____ stone
- ____ stucco
- ____ asbestos shingles

_____ asphalt siding
_____ wood shingles
_____ aluminum siding
_____ vinyl siding
_____ wood siding
_____ other
_____ condition
_____ age
_____ deflected lintels
_____ manufacturer's warranty

Doors

_____ aluminum-clad with wood
_____ insulated aluminum
_____ wood
_____ insulated wood
_____ insulated steel
_____ insulated fibreglass
_____ insulated vinyl
_____ French doors
_____ sliding doors
_____ other
_____ aluminum storm door
_____ aluminum-clad wood storm door
_____ insulated aluminum storm door
_____ insulated steel storm door
_____ wood storm door
_____ steel storm door
_____ closing device
_____ age
_____ style
_____ direction of swing
_____ door condition
_____ hardware condition
_____ number of hinges
_____ brand name hardware
_____ door size, width, height
_____ thermally broken
_____ window
_____ loose window panes
_____ how surface finished
_____ door thickness
_____ deadbolts
_____ knobs
_____ handsets
_____ combination lock
_____ decorative trims
_____ manufacturer's warranty

Door Frames

_____ steel
_____ vinyl
_____ aluminum
_____ aluminum-clad wood
_____ vinyl-clad wood
_____ fibreglass
_____ other
_____ adjustable threshold
_____ threshold condition
_____ thermally broken
_____ insulation in frame
_____ how finished
_____ drip caps
_____ manufacturer's warranty

Windows

_____ size
_____ square
_____ rectangular
_____ how opened
_____ skylights
_____ sloped windows
_____ joint conditions
_____ opened for ventilation
_____ view and privacy
_____ glare
_____ acoustic features
_____ fire escape
_____ child safety features
_____ shutters
_____ awnings
_____ cracked glazing compound
_____ remote or electronic controls
_____ removable or tiltable
_____ window size, height, width
_____ tinted
_____ broken windows
_____ safety glass
_____ broken seals
_____ obscure glass (washrooms)
_____ energy efficiency
_____ cleaning ease
_____ rain protection
_____ brand name hardware
_____ replacement flexibility
_____ last cleaned
_____ security
_____ insect screens

_____ drip caps
_____ weep holes
_____ special features
_____ manufacturer's warranty

Window Frames
_____ wood
_____ steel
_____ aluminum
_____ vinyl
_____ vinyl-clad wood
_____ aluminum-clad wood
_____ fibreglass
_____ other
_____ thermally broken
_____ strength and stiffness
_____ joint conditions
_____ manufacturer's warranty

Stairs
_____ steel
_____ pressure-treated wood
_____ concrete
_____ other
_____ condition
_____ wood decay
_____ age
_____ treads on step
_____ tredel and riser dimensions
_____ step nosings
_____ finished
_____ width
_____ number of stringers
_____ open or closed stringers
_____ other

Balcony and Patio
_____ wood
_____ fibreglass
_____ vinyl
_____ other

_____ age
_____ condition
_____ wood pressure treated
_____ handrailing continuous
_____ ventilation
_____ surface drainage
_____ raised door threshold

Handrailing
_____ wood
_____ pressure-treated wood
_____ metal
_____ vinyl
_____ condition
_____ balustrades
_____ handrailing loose
_____ age
_____ height
_____ how secured
_____ how graspable

Porch/Verandah Condition
_____ roof
_____ flashing
_____ gutter
_____ downspout
_____ ceiling condition
_____ lighting
_____ floor
_____ handrailing
_____ steps
_____ load-bearing posts
_____ load-bearing beams
_____ foundation walls
_____ footing

Porch/Verandah Type
_____ enclosed
_____ open
_____ ventilation

CONSUMER TIPS

You may at some point consider buying a condominium, for example, an apartment or townhouse condominium. There are many different variations of the condominium format. Although you would obtain a title to the property as with a house, there are considerable differences from a house environment. In a situation of shared ownership and community living there are of course advantages and disadvantages. Here are some of the common ones:

Advantages
- Ready availability of financing in the same fashion as a single-family home.
- Range of prices, locations, types of structures, sizes, and architectural features available.
- Availability of amenities such as swimming pool, tennis courts, health clubs, community centre, saunas, hot tubs, exercise rooms, sun decks, etc.
- Benefits of home ownership in terms of participation in the real estate market and potential growth in equity.
- Individual ownership of living units.
- Pride in home ownership.
- Enables people of moderate and middle income to own their own home.
- Freedom to decorate interior of unit to suit personal tastes.
- Enhancement of security by permanence of neighbours and, in many cases, controlled entrances.
- Elimination of many of the problems of upkeep and maintenance often associated with home ownership, since maintenance is usually the responsibility of a professional management company or manager.
- Often cheaper than buying a single-family home because of more efficient use of land and economy of scale.
- Good transitional type of home between rental apartments and single-family houses for growing families or singles or couples; conversely, good transition for "empty nesters" who wish to give up their larger family house.
- Reduction of costs due to responsibilities for repair and maintenance being shared.
- If a home inspector sees structural or other problems in a resale condo, many of these could be corrected by the condominium corporation for any problems affecting "common property" that is any problem areas outside the internal walls of your unit. You are responsible for repairing any problem internally within your unit. If you are buying a new condo,

make sure you have New Home Warranty Program coverage, as well as ideally, warranty protection by a reputable and experienced builder.

- Enhancement of social activities and sense of neighbourhood community by relative permanence of residents.
- Participation of owners in the operation of the development, which involves playing a role in budget-setting and approval, decision-making, determination of rules, regulations, and by-laws, and other matters affecting the democratic operation of the condominium community.
- Different forms of construction, e.g., wood, concrete.
- Improved security, fire safety and noise-proof, especially in newer complexes.

Disadvantages

- Real estate appreciation is generally not as high as for a single-family house, due to the total ownership of land when owning a house. (It is land that goes up in value, of course, as mentioned earlier.)
- May be difficult to accurately assess the quality of construction of the project. It is easier to do so with a house.
- Unacceptable loss of freedom may be experienced through restrictions contained in the rules and by-laws (e.g. restriction on the right to rent, restriction on pets, restriction on operating a business, etc.).
- People live closer together, thereby potentially creating problems from time to time; frequent problem areas include the "Five P's": pets, parking, personality, parties, and people.
- One could be paying for maintenance and operation of amenities that one has no desire or intention to use.
- Management of the condominium council is by volunteers, who may or may not have the appropriate abilities and skills.
- Possible apathy of owners, so that the same people continually serve on council.
- Some elected councils behave in an autocratic fashion.
- Some units could be rented out and tenants may not get along with owners of the complex.
- Pests, e.g., complex could be infested with cockroaches.
- Expensive to repair should major structure or plumbing problems develop, e.g., leaking plumbing pipes in a concrete highrise.
- Poor management and administration of the complex occupants, personality and political conflicts for those that sit on strata boards.
- Unit may not be fire safe or sound proof.

CHAPTER 4

The Structure

THE STRUCTURE OF a house is made up of the foundation, wall and floor framing, and roof trusses — basically, all the construction underneath the finishing materials, which you inspected on the house's exterior. The structure should be considered a waterproof envelope designed to keep the building up and prevent it from settling. Underground footings increase the supporting capacity of the foundation wall by spreading the load of the house over a larger area. When a foundation fails to support the house, signs such as wall and ceiling cracks, sloped floors and doors that refuse to close properly will be evident throughout the entire structure. Once this happens, moisture, fungi and pests will be able to find their way inside and cause considerable structural harm. Deficiencies with the structure of the house should be seen as most critical because the cost to repair usually means rebuilding the inside and outside finishings as well. If the problems are serious, the time and money required to renovate and extend the life of the house may be extensive. The majority of your inspection of the house's structure will be done inside, but some aspects will be visible from the exterior.

Foundations

Good construction begins with a well-prepared subgrade. The strength of the soil, its load-carrying capacity and resistance to movement is important to the performance of the structure on the ground. Soil strength is greatly affected by the degree of compaction of the soil and its moisture content.

The main reasons why houses fail structurally at their foundations, has to do with the composition of the underlying soil and climatic conditions. In different parts of the country where floods, hurricanes, earthquake tremors and slides are not uncommon, unavoidable weakening of the foundations can result. Houses built on steep slopes where soil (such as silt and loess) has marginal bearing capacity are particularly vulnerable. Other weak soil compositions include landfill sites, expansive soils such as clay and non-expansive soils such as sand or gravel that contain peat, silt and clay. Severe frost can cause cracks and heaving if the underlying soil was not properly compacted or had too much moisture at the time the foundation was poured. Excess ground water caused by a high water table, leaking water pipes, unsettled soil and shallow tree roots can all lead to decay or cracks in the foundation.

Drain tile or perforated pipe surrounded in crushed gravel is intended to collect subsoil water at the base of foundation walls to ensure that no water collects beneath the house. In some situations high groundwater levels may make foundation drains for collecting subsoil water impossible, and you will see water from downspouts running over the surface of the soil — hopefully away from the house.

The foundation should be designed to support the load it is meant to carry. The foundation wall should extend below the frost line. Most foundation walls and footings are made of concrete because of its durability, although masonry, slab on grade and treated wood are also used.

Concrete Foundations

Concrete comes in a variety of strengths with different water/cement ratios and variable coarseness of aggregate, and can contain any number of added mixtures to meet specific building code requirements. Current building codes have air entrainment requirements for cement used for footings, driveway slabs, walls and other exposed surfaces. Air entrainment improves durability and resistance to freeze/thaw cycles, as tiny pockets of air are embedded in the concrete to allow room for moisture to expand. Temperature conditions at the time the concrete was poured, proper curing and trowelling all affect the strength of the concrete. At a proper strength, it should be very difficult to hammer a nail into concrete. If the nail goes full-depth into the wall, the soft concrete has weakened due to excessive water in the original concrete mix. Use a magnetic stud-finder or strong magnet to test whether the foundation wall is reinforced with steel. Concrete will crack due to inadequate site conditions, materials or construction methods used. Backfilling against uncured concrete can cause major cracking in foundation walls. Inspect the foundation walls and floors for any horizontal, vertical or diagonal settlement cracks larger than 1/4 inch. These indicate serious structural problems exist. Hairline cracks are not uncommon but should be repaired and sealed from the exterior if the house has a basement.

Slab-on-grade Foundations

A footing and slab that is poured as one complete unit is safer from termite attacks and decay of wooden sills than a foundation with the footing and slab poured separately. In addition, if the soil was not prepared properly, an independent slab is more likely to settle, resulting in a sloped floor. Newer construction will probably have reinforced rods or mesh in the concrete, rigid insulation and a vapour barrier under the slab and against the foundation walls.

In finished rooms where floor coverings are glued to the slab around the perimeter of the floor, it is difficult to inspect for cracks and deteriorated concrete. On thinner floor coverings you can run your foot over the surfaces to check for irregularities. An uneven hollow sound when tapping the floor areas with a rubber mallet can reveal a crack underneath.

Wood Foundations

Preserved wood foundations should be designed and approved by a certified engineer with relevant experience to ensure that proper construction practices have been followed to guarantee the best structural performance. Extreme care is needed in selecting and fabricating the materials. As many owners will know little about preserved wood foundations, you should check with the building authority in your area for any special requirements for ventilation, drainage and construction techniques. Superior wood-preservative treatments such as creosote, oil-based chemicals or water-borne inorganic compounds should be used. Keep in mind that all wood preservatives are considered pesticides and are poisonous and dangerous around young children.

Round poles generally have an advantage over squared ones because they have more sapwood, which lends itself to easier treatment than heartwood. It is also less susceptible to decay. Nails and fasteners should be of a corrosion-resistant material. Check the footings and drainage around these poles to ensure they are stable. Often independent footings have settled over time, leaving sagging roof and floor surfaces in the house. The floor in a pressure-treated wood foundation can be either treated wood or a concrete slab.

Pile Foundations

Where there is soil instability, pile foundations made of concrete, steel or timber are used. There are generally two types of piles: friction and point bearing. Friction piles depend on friction between the pile and the soil to support the load. Point bearing piles, on the other hand, transmit loads through unstable soil to firm areas below. Examples of both types of piles include houses built on a steep slope, on a rock surface or at the edge of a river delta where the soil is primarily silt and sand.

Foundation Columns and Footings

Some house designs will include a section of the structure that projects beyond the lower level and is held up with a column. Where a column meets the ground there is often a slab of concrete that also serves as a sidewalk or patio. The size of the footing should be determined by the weight to be supported, the soil-bearing capacity and local building codes. Be cautious when inspecting this type of structure, because there is no way to determine properly the depth or type of footing used below the concrete slab. Check to see how the column is anchored to the footing and at the ceiling. If a wooden column is used, has the bottom been protected from dampness? If the posts and beams are of a steel construction, they should be free from rust. Do the columns appear to be straight?

Locate the load-bearing beams. Ensure they are not sagging and that the supporting columns are resting on adequate footings, which should extend below the ground frost level. There should be a moisture-barrier membrane between the wooden supports and the footing. The load-bearing partition walls can be made of 2"x 4"s, 2"x 6"s or columns made of solid timber, laminated wood or steel. Check for cracks, splitting and bulges along the columns. Carefully inspect all interior foundation walls for horizontal and vertical cracks. There should be a vapour barrier between the sill plates and the top of the concrete on which they rest. The sill plates should be anchored down with bolts or metal strapping to the foundation wall. If insulation found in a crawl space is damp, wood rot will result. Always remember to check how the house is anchored to the conrete load bearing foundation walls. Are anchor bolts or metal brackets used?

Crawl Spaces

A crawl space with a soil grade at or above the outside grade line is the easiest to keep dry, regardless of moisture conditions. All that is needed is a soil cover, insulation and ventilation. In all cases the outside grade should slope away from the foundation. Downspouts should have splash pads or drains to keep surface water away from the foundation. Keeping a crawl space dry is difficult when the crawl space grade is below the water table.

Access to a crawl space may be through an outside door, an inside door sometimes at the back of a closet, or through a floor hatch. Care should be taken during inspections as head clearances are often very low and the ground will not always be smooth. You will need a flashlight, measuring tape, awl, compass, mirror and notepad. Some crawl-space floors will consist of exposed soil, a layer of sand or a rough pour of concrete. If asphalt roll roofing or polyethylene sheeting has been used, the joints should be overlapped 3 inches. Ground-cover vapour retarders are needed to stop moisture migrating up from the soil. Check the floor for moisture and efflorescence. If there is a subfloor, check underneath for signs of rotted and bug-infested boards. You should notice cross-bracing between the floor joists. There should be a floor drain in concrete floors to allow water to escape into the perimeter drainage system.

In an unheated crawl space there should be at least two unobstructed vents opposite each other. The screened vents should be found in the foundation wall, near corners where dead air space is greatest. The basic minimum vent opening size is 1 square foot for each 500 square feet of crawl space area. Where there is no free movement of air or ventilation, crawl spaces will often leave the upper portions of the house with a damp, musty smell. Check if the vent openings can be closed, as

---

What's under that floor?

One prospective purchaser lifted up the polythylene floor covering of a crawl space, only to find a family of frogs contentedly living there!

---

in the winter the pipes can freeze and heating ducts will have difficulty maintaining heat inside them. Inspect inside the vent openings for signs of wood rot. Condensation is most likely to occur in unheated crawl spaces with wet soil, and will cause rotting of wood framing, joists, plates and sills.

Basements

Examination of a basement is similar to that of a crawl space. You must inspect the concrete or block walls and floors for cracks and moisture. When you spot a diagonal, horizontal or vertical crack in the basement, go outside and see if the same crack is visible there. Insert your awl point into the opening and see if you can detect any loose mortar at joints or sand running out of cracks. Water is more likely to pass through concrete blocks than through poured concrete. Being careful not to damage plants and shrubs, dig into the ground along the foundation wall to see if there are footings. You should see evidence of damp-proofing or waterproofing — a black membrane tar-like application over the cement that deflects moisture. With a flashlight and mirror, look up under the exterior finishing material of the house for signs of wood rot. This is likely to be found where dirt has been pushed against the siding. Exterior basement doors, windows and their frames should be treated with a water-repellent preservative. Where support posts, partition walls and floor joists are embedded in concrete, check the wood surfaces for signs of rot. Be alert for wood-burrowing pests that may have found their way into the basement along with sawdust or shavings used as fuel for heating. They can cause considerable damage to wooden framing.

When exploring a completely finished basement, it is difficult to know what is behind the ceilings, walls and floors. The only way to see what is behind the ceiling is to look at openings found in the furnace room (if it is a forced-air furnace). Sometimes, with care, wall panelling or corner finish moulding can be gently pried loose to check for moisture, vapour barrier and insulation behind the wall. If the main electrical service panel is in the basement, check around its opening for corroded metal, dampness and rot. Does the air around this opening smell musty?

If no floor drain can be detected in a finished basement, ask the owner if there is one. Perhaps it has been accidentally covered up. Where concrete floors are exposed, take your rubber mallet and tap various floor surfaces and

Check around fuse box

Loc. of basement floor drain?

listen for irregular sounds. This could mean a cavity under the concrete floor or a thin floor slab. An unusually cold concrete floor may indicate that a high water table is causing heat loss. Set your marbles on the floor surface to test if the floor is level. The marbles should roll in the direction of the floor drain. If they roll to one side or a corner, this may indicate that some settling has taken place. (Further comments on flooring are included in Chapter 11.) Measure the floor-to-ceiling height in various areas of the basement. A variance of more than 4 inches indicates considerable settling has occurred.

Wooden Structural Framework

An inspection of the framework of a house has a lot to do with identifying different grades of lumber and their designed use. So you may wish to visit your local lumberyard or sawmill to familiarize yourself with the terms, how to read the grade stamps on wood and performance rating labels on panels, the characteristics of the different species of wood and where you should expect to find them in a house. Lumber will be graded at the sawmill for its appearance, strength, wood species and moisture content, as well as other identification data. This grade stamp will indicate how the lumber should be used. Of course, the drier the wood, the more stable it will be. Wood with a moisture content of over 19, for example, is likely to warp, twist and shrink as it dries out. As you conduct your inspection, make a note of the grade stamps. These should be consistent, especially around the load-bearing structure of the house. Be wary of a wide range of grade stamps.

Just as lumber is grade stamped, structural panels used as sheathing for roofs, floors, walls and exterior siding are labelled with a performance rating. The label provides information on the panel's thickness, how well it can withstand weather conditions and the span rating (the maximum distance between floor joists, rafters and wall studs that hold up the panel). The 4'x 8' panels may be plywood, particleboard, hardboard, waferboard, oriented strand board or other similar types. Again, each type and grade is designed for different purposes.

Floor Framing

In a wood-frame house the floor framing consists of joists, beams, columns and sills. To support centre bearing partitions and floor joists, stud walls are commonly used instead of beams and columns. Wood columns and beams (girders) are of three types: built-up, solid timber and glue-laminated. In newer construction engineered wood I-beams are used for roof rafters and floor joists as they offer the greatest strength with the least weight. I-beams are made by gluing two strips of lumber, called chords, to the top and bottom edges of a thin middle section, known as the web. Instead of wood, steel I-beams are sometimes used to avoid shrinkage.

In an unfinished basement or crawl space, check how the floor joists are held in place at the beam. The joists can be lapped, notched or resting on a ledger. Joists may also be supported by metal joist hangers or brackets attached to the beam. Where beams and columns come in contact with concrete, they should be treated with a preservative or have a piece of asphalt roll roof or polyethylene film to prevent decay. Depending on the load and strength of the beam that supports the floor joists, columns are generally spaced 8 to 10 feet on centre. Wood columns should be the same width as the beam that is being supported. The floor joists extend between the walls and support the entire floor. There should be double joists directly beneath areas where there is a bearing partition on the floor above. Cross-bridging, where diagonal pieces of wood or metal are nailed in an "X" pattern at right angles to the joists, is a means of stiffening floors and distributing the load. Continuous wood strapping nailed to the underside of each joist is another means of accomplishing this, and it also keeps the joists from twisting. If there is a forced-air heating system, you can measure the thickness of the subfloor and identify the material used by lifting out the heat register. When you pry your awl between the metal duct and the floor opening, you may detect a layer of felt building paper sandwiched between the finish floor and the subfloor. This is to prevent moisture from rising from below.

> **What's holding up that ceiling?**
>
> While inspecting a crawl space, a prospective purchaser used the corner of a column to satisfy the itch on her back. As she was rubbing back and forth, the entire column fell out of its vertical position!

Foundation Wall/Floor Joist Connection

The box-sill and joist-embedded are two versions of platform floor joist framing. With the box-sill method the sill plate is anchored on top of the foundation wall and floor joists fasten into the header ends. The joist-embedded method is used when the joists, headers and beams are embedded in two-thirds of the foundation wall concrete. Balloon-frame construction is no longer in use because of its reputation as a fire hazard. With this method, a wall framework of 2"x 4" studs, spaced 16 inches apart, runs the full height of the building. The studs pass through the floors and end at the top plates, which support the roof framing. Floor joists above the first floor are carried on a ledger board and nailed into the studs. Renovations to houses with balloon-framing can be difficult.

Notice if, on the exterior of the house, a bay window or wall projects beyond the foundation wall. The cantilevered portion of the floor should not extend beyond 2 feet from the foundation wall without the support of a load-bearing column. When checking around stairway openings, note that double joists are required. Notice whether the joists are held in place with headers, joist hangers or timber connections.

Wall Framing

Walls consist of interior and exterior horizontal and vertical members to which covering materials are attached, and which support the upper floors, ceiling and roof. Wall thicknesses will vary, depending on the materials used. You will find clues about the framing materials under the exterior and interior wall finishes by looking carefully at a window and door jamb, by removing an electrical face plate or by examining under the sill plate. Your notes of the various layers from outside to inside may read, for example, as follows: bevelled wood siding, building paper, sheathing, 2"x 4" studs, insulation, vapour barrier, gyproc. If you come across steel studs that serve as load-bearing walls, be certain that they have been approved by a structural engineer as the metal gauge used may not be adequate for load-bearing purposes.

Post-and-beam construction consists of plank decking, posts and beams that are spaced farther apart than conventional framing members. The posts must be strong enough to support the load and large enough to provide bearing surfaces for the ends of beams. The large loads are carried by the posts and allow for any size of wall openings between the posts without need for extra structural support. Walls become non-bearing, and are simply infill, although they may serve to provide lateral stiffness to the structure. The simplicity of framing around window and door openings is an advantage. Also, wide roof overhangs can be achieved by extending roof beams. Exposed beams and high ceilings create interesting design effects. This type of construction provides a high fire-resistance factor as the wood beams will not collapse under high temperatures as will steel beams. However, the lack of concealed spaces in outside walls and ceilings makes installation of plumbing, heating and electrical wiring more difficult. This should be a consideration when planning future renovations.

Prefabricated Homes

Panelled, precut, sectionalized, mobile homes and log homes are five basic types of prefabricated houses. They can be fully or partially assembled before leaving the manufacturing plant. Many houses are erected using conventional methods, but the components consist of various factory-built parts, such as the roof truss, walls, floor truss, windows, door units, stairs, soffit systems and built-in cabinet work. The factory-built components are made of engineered wood and high-tech adhesives, and are put together in controlled factory conditions using computer-aided design and assembly. Because of this precision, wood splits, knots, twists and warpage are eliminated entirely in engineered houses. Floor squeaks and nail pops are unheard of. Engineered wood is easier to handle, lighter and stronger than solid-sawn wood of equal dimensions.

Inspection attic (handwritten)

Roof Framing

Rafters are the most important framing members in roofs. They roughly corre-spond to the joists in the floors and provide a frame-work to support the sheathing and roofing material. Instead of rafters you might see roof trusses, which carry the roof and ceiling surfaces. They rest on the exterior walls and span the entire width of the house. Adding another storey to a house with a truss system may not be as easy as adding to one with rafters. With a rafter system, the ceiling joists can be used as floor joists if they are properly rein-forced. The steeper the roof, the easier it is for water and snow to run off, but repairs are more costly and difficult because of the special equipment needed.

The best place to examine the roof structure is in the attic. The attic hatch is usually found in the ceiling of a closet, hallway, kitchen, bathroom or stair-well. Sometimes it is found on the outside of the house under a soffit or gable end. Should the hatch be located in the kitchen or bathroom, notice how the lid is held in place and insulated, as these rooms can be areas of high humidity and condensation. When entering the attic, be careful that dust and insulation does not damage clothing and valuables stored in closets. If the lid has been painted shut, a good thump with your fist should jar it loose. You will want to ensure that the opening and space in the attic is large enough to carry in mate-rials should repairs be needed at some future time. Older houses and those with cathedral ceilings may have no attic access, making it impossible to inspect the roofing materials.

Before you proceed with your inspection, be aware of any visible ceiling cracks. You will not want to be held responsible for claims that your walking in the attic caused ceiling cracks that in fact pre-existed your visit. Walk only on ceiling joists. If you are unsure, it is best to stand on a ladder and just look around with your flashlight from the attic opening. A foot through the ceiling could make your inspection very expensive!

To keep the roof from collapsing, you should find vertical supports (struts) inserted between the rafters and the ceiling joists. Horizontal mem-bers (collar ties) which run from one rafter side to another provide bracing and stiffening, and help to hold the ridge and rafters together. Note the spac-ing, length and connections of the rafters. Are there any split or broken rafters? End rafters should be toe-nailed together. Examine the framework of all intersecting roofs. In your sketch of the attic, make a note of the location of the load-bearing walls below the ceiling joists. (It may be necessary to double-check the location of the load-bearing walls on the main floors in relation to the direction of the ceiling joists.)

The ceiling joists should be over-lapped at the beams. Remember that when renovating, non-bear-ing walls are easy to take out, whereas load-bearing walls re-quire special attention. Notice

---

Have you checked the attic?

A prospective purchaser, on inspecting the attic, found broken rafters and ceiling joists held together with hockey stick handles and bits of wire.

the type and thickness of the roof sheathing material. If it is not tongue-in-groove plywood, the panels may be held together with metal H-clips. These clips provide a strong, rigid surface and prevent differential deflection between adjacent panel edges.

After you have investigated the basic stability of the rafters and load-bearing walls, the next considerations are insulation, ventilation and moisture. Check the type and thickness of insulation, especially around skylights, stair openings and heat and ventilation ducts. Blackened insulation will indicate lack of air movement and excess moisture. Proper ventilation should be provided through vents along the ridge, gable or soffit. Inadequate amounts of ceiling insulation will result in heat loss in cold weather and heat buildup in the living areas during summer months. Check the condition of roof sheathing and flashing around vents, chimney and skylights. Inspect for water penetration in these areas. Excessive moisture caused by high humidity, condensation and water leaks will promote wood rot. Rusting nails, truss gussets and electrical box corrosion are other signs of moisture buildup. An attic inspection may also show evidence of bird or hornet nests or a previous house fire. Remember some areas in Canada may require special wind, snow loads or earthquake supports or strapping to prevent the roof structure from collapse or from blowing off the house. Check with the building inspectors at city hall to obtain more information.

House and Yard Pests

House and yard pests are unsanitary and destructive, and some cause health hazards. Most thrive in areas that are protected and offer dampness, darkness and warmth. Sometimes neighbours may mention problems in the area with local pests such as mosquitoes, bears, woodpeckers, porcupines, raccoons and skunks. Raccoons and skunks are known to hide under enclosed wooden stairs and porches. Look at the lawn and garden for mole mounds. Moles usually live in pairs and are difficult to get rid of. Check for pests in eave projections and chimney surrounds. Mosquitoes are known to breed in wet, swamp-like debris found in rain gutters. If you spot a number of patched holes on exterior wall surfaces, it is likely that the house has been treated for some type of pest. Although the patches may look old, the pests may still be present in the house. Ask the owner for details.

Brick and concrete block walls have small hollow voids that may serve as a shelter for tiny insects. Some homes have a metal strip between the sill and the foundation wall that provides an effective termite shield and prevents them from reaching the wood behind it. Many different types of animals and insects utilize wood as food, either directly or indirectly. Few can digest it unless there are wood-destroying fungi or other plant forms present. Other pests burrow through it or can make their way into the house through almost imperceptible cracks.

Next to earthquakes, wind, fire and wood rot, termites are known to cause the greatest structural damage to a house. Because termites work slowly, it can take literally years before any serious structural damage is noticed. The sub-terranean termite can be found in warm, moist areas of Canada and the United States. They build long shelter tubes of about 1/4 inch to 1/2 inch in width, consisting of excreta, wood particles and soil. These tubes can be free-standing or attached to walls or behind shrubs, and provide a passageway between the food supply and their nest. The non-subterranean termites consist of drywood and dampwood termites. They live entirely within the wood and can go undetected for long periods of time. While you are looking over all damp and decayed wood for termites, watch for carpenter ants and powder-post beetles. Unlike termites, they don't eat wood but simply chew it up. Warning signs are piles of fine sawdust on horizontal surfaces, spread on spi-der webs or around small, suspicious holes. If the holes are light in colour, they are fairly fresh.

Almost without fail, pests will be found during your exterior and interior inspection of a damp, dark and unfinished crawl space, basement, subflooring and posts. They may be spiders, mosquitoes, silverfish, carpenter ants, mice, rats, moths, sow bugs, earthworms, earwigs, slugs, snails, crickets, weevils, termites powder-post beetles. They may be crawling about or there may be frass clinging to spider webs or other evidence of their presence in the texture they leave behind in the ground or wood.

The most common pests found in the main living quarters are spiders, ants, carpet beetles, mites, ticks, moths and fleas from household pets. Areas inside electrical wall receptacles, behind cupboards and drawers and under fridges and ranges provide a safe, warm area to breed and hide. The kitchen and bathroom are preferred hideouts for cockroaches, which are especially difficult to eradicate. Look inside cupboards, drawers, heat registers and clos-ets for droppings and mousetraps. In the attic be prepared to see evidence of raccoons, bird nests, drywood and wetwood carpenter ants, termites, rats, mice, wasps, bees, bats and spiders. They find their way into the house under soffit vent openings and through loose boards where knots have dried and fallen out and other small openings that have developed as a result of poor construction. Keep in mind that although pests may be discovered on the exte-rior or interior of the house, they can be treated and stopped before further damage is done. Most cities have pest control exterminators and poison con-trol centres, which are listed in the Yellow Pages of your local telephone direc-tory. Your local library or university or the federal Department of Agriculture may be able to answer your pest-related questions.

As you are inspecting the structure of the house, keep in mind that most creatures have four primary needs: an entrance for shelter, food, water and reproduction. Without all four of these, there are no pests. The goal is to reduce or eliminate all four basic factors.

CHECKPOINTS
✓✓✓✓✓✓✓✓✓✓✓

Crawl Spaces
____ concrete
____ block
____ brick
____ stone
____ wood
____ other
____ heated
____ unheated
____ framing
____ dirt floor
____ concrete floor
____ vapour retarder on floor
____ insulation
____ ventilation locations
____ ventilation opening size
____ ventilation screened and operable
____ perimeter drainage
____ dampproofing
____ cracks
____ wall thickness
____ termite flushing
____ crawl space accessibility
____ head clearance
____ wood decay, damp or dry
____ presence of moisture
____ type of supports
____ location of supports
____ position of supports
____ footings
____ waterproofing
____ musty air
____ sump pump location
____ structural engineer approved

Basement
____ finished
____ unfinished
____ concrete
____ block
____ brick
____ stone
____ wood
____ other materials
____ wall thickness
____ depth
____ footings

____ waterproofing
____ insulation
____ termite flashing
____ soil tests
____ signs of moisture, rot
____ sump
____ concrete floor
____ dampproofing
____ settling signs
____ perimeter drainage
____ structural engineer approved

Slab on Grade
____ finished
____ unfinished
____ dampness
____ perimeter drainage
____ termite flashing
____ signs of cracks/settling
____ cold breezes
____ depth of foundation
____ frost line
____ sub-slab radon
____ ventilation system
____ location of radon exhaust fan
____ structural engineer approved

Column and Footing
____ column size
____ footing depth and size
____ pressure-treated wood
____ structural engineer approved

Wood Foundation
____ type of wood preservative
____ approved by certified engineer
____ certified testing agency approved
____ soil conditions
____ perimeter drainage
____ wood or concrete floor
____ manufacturer's warranty

Floor Framing
____ bridging
____ joist hangers
____ board subfloor

_____ plywood subfloor
_____ other subfloor
_____ damaged floor joists
_____ sill plate secured
_____ load-bearing floors
_____ location of double joists
_____ joist lengths/spans
_____ size/location of joists
_____ size/location of beams
_____ size/location of columns
_____ built-up columns/beams
_____ solid columns/beams
_____ glue-laminated columns/beams
_____ steel columns/beams
_____ truss columns/beams
_____ other columns/beams

Wall Framing
_____ balloon framing
_____ box-sill platform framing
_____ joist-embedded platform framing
_____ stair opening framing
_____ post and beam
_____ prefabricated framing
_____ load-bearing partitions
_____ steel stud load-bearing partitions

Ceiling Framing
_____ joist size
_____ distance apart
_____ joist lengths/spans
_____ steel I-beam
_____ load-bearing joists

Roof Framing
_____ truss
_____ rafters
_____ size
_____ spacing dimensions
_____ bracing
_____ pitch/slope
_____ shiplap board subroof
_____ plywood subroof
_____ other subroof
_____ end gable finish
_____ dampness
_____ load-bearing sections
_____ sheathing thickness

Note: *If entire house is factory-built or assembled:*
_____ construction plans/specifications
_____ manufacturer's warranty
_____ certified testing agency approved
_____ snow roads
_____ high winds
_____ earthquakes

Pests
_____ location of pests
_____ pest-control exterminating certificate
_____ traps/poison inside house
_____ bats
_____ bears
_____ bees
_____ birds
_____ carpenter ants
_____ carpet beetles
_____ caterpillars
_____ cockroaches
_____ crickets
_____ deer
_____ earwigs
_____ fleas
_____ flies
_____ grasshoppers
_____ mice
_____ mites
_____ moles
_____ mosquitos
_____ porcupines
_____ powder-post beetles
_____ rabbits
_____ raccoons
_____ rats
_____ silverfish
_____ slugs
_____ skunks
_____ snails
_____ sow bugs
_____ spiders
_____ wasps
_____ weevils
_____ wood-destroying fungi
_____ other

CONSUMER TIPS

- Land appreciates in value; buildings depreciate in value, therefore older houses do not necessarily mean lower taxes. Check with city hall to see if there are any major property tax increases planned in your area, and the reasons for them.

- Short-list a minimum of three home inspectors before deciding who to select. Look in the yellow pages of your telephone directory under "Building Inspectors". Ask for references, credentials, experience, memberships in trade/professional associations, and length of time in business. Essentially, you get what you pay for.

- Always get competitive quotes in writing — for inspection, renovation or repair — before making any final commitment. Always check with the Better Business Bureau. Ask additional questions as outlined in the point above. Ask where materials are purchased from to do the job. Check with credit managers.

- If you are serious about buying the home, take pictures of it inside and out, then review the pictures without time pressure. Better yet, if you happen to have a video camera, use that as well. Recall of detail can be fleeting. If you decide to buy the house, file these pictures in a three-ring binder along with other gathered information. Come selling time you will have a complete package to present to the next prospective purchaser.

- Ideally, view at least 20 houses, that could potentially meet your needs before making your final selection. The more homes seen, the more discriminating and selective you become. This will increase your confidence and quality of decision-making and reduce the risk of buying impulsively, due to pressure, or for emotional reasons.

- If buying on your own, bring a relative or friend to view your preferred home and ask for constructive and candid feedback, including what negative features they see. You want a realistic viewpoint. It is stressful making such an important decision in a vacuum.

- See a real estate lawyer before submitting an offer to purchase. Have conditions put in the offer, such as "subject to inspection by an inspector of purchaser's choice within 10 days of acceptance of the offer, such inspection to be satisfactory to the purchaser." Look in the white pages of your phone book under "Lawyer Referral Services" for names of real estate lawyers in your community. The initial consultation is normally free or with only a nominal fee. You may wish to obtain competitive quotes for home purchase and mortgage preparation fees and expenses, from a minimum of three lawyers before deciding who to deal with.

CHAPTER 5

Fireplace
and Chimney

A FIREPLACE, WHETHER IT is used or not, creates an ambience and coziness in the home by its mere presence. In fact, you will find fireplaces that serve no purpose other than as decoration. If one of the features in the dream house you are looking for is a useable fireplace, then it will be helpful to have some basic knowledge about fireplaces and chimneys. This chapter will review various construction materials used for the chimney, flue liner and fireplace; their efficiencies and durability; and, of course, potential problems that might arise from their inadequacies. Because of the high fire risks associated with fireplaces and chimneys, proper care and maintenance is essential for worry-free enjoyment.

Chimney

The purpose of a chimney is to remove smoke and unwanted products of combustion by creating a "draft" that draws the smoke from the fireplace and out through the chimney. A chimney may be constructed of brick, stone or concrete block. As the mass of a stone chimney is substantially higher than that of a brick chimney, it provides a greater heat sink for keeping flue gasses hotter. However, during the winter the joints may be subject to freeze/thaw damage. Because of its porous nature, a concrete block or masonry chimney should be waterproofed, painted or stuccoed to prevent water saturation and deterioration. A chimney with a brick exterior and a clay pipe or tile liner is the most common. Factory-built chimneys consist of two metal cylindrical casings with insulation packed between them. Problems may arise if the insulation settles between the inner and outer casings, creating voids. This can be spotted on the exterior casing by dark rings or corrosion of the metal. The inner casings can also come loose and buckle or warp. Stove pipes should not be used as they accumulate creosote and deteriorate quickly.

The size and temperature of the chimney liner and the height of the chimney are factors that affect the draft. The lining increases the chimney's strength, provides a tighter flue fitting and increases the temperatures within the stack, and this results in less condensation and a continuous smoke-tight surface. The liner can consist of lightweight poured-in concrete, clay tile or flexible or rigid stainless steel. Gas furnace chimneys may need steel liners to avoid icing and blockage in cold weather.

A chimney that is too low will not draw smoke satisfactorily; one that is too high will be difficult to clean and keep hot during operation. A general rule is that the chimney should rise at least 3 feet above the highest part of the roof, and at least 2 feet higher than any part of the roof within 10 feet. A chimney that is unusually high should have lateral bracing in place to provide support in gale-force winds. If a neighbour's chimney is too close, downdrafting from an air inversion can cause neighbouring smoke to come into your house. Tree branches within 10 feet of the chimney top are a fire hazard.

A chimney in the interior of a house will deteriorate less and have a more efficient draft. The heat absorbed by the masonry will be radiated back into the living spaces, which will result in more even room temperatures. A chimney built on an exterior wall, on the other hand, will lose heat to the outside. Therefore it should be out of the path of prevailing winds, situated on the most sheltered side of the building. The flue's exposure to cold temperatures will lead to increased creosote and condensation from hot gases rising out of the fireplace. In such situations it may be more difficult to start a fire in the fireplace, as the natural downflow of cool air within the flue must be overcome before a good draft is established. Houses built on hillsides sometimes require windproof chimney caps to avoid backdrafting from downhill breezes. A cap or hood will keep rainwater and snow from entering the chimney, will control the air flow for a good draft, and will protect the top of the brick from deterioration. The upper section of a chimney should be corbelled to help strengthen the chimney and create a lip to keep rain from running straight down masonry walls. If the roof slope is low and the chimney is very wide, often you will find a saddle in place. This helps to shed the water and prevent it from backing up along the chimney and roof intersections and seeping under the shingles. Some chimneys are equipped with a spark arrestor to keep leaves out and sparks from emerging and starting a fire on combustible roof material. When two chimney flues are side by side, one should be higher than the other, or a hood and narrow brick wall should be in place between them, to prevent smoke or fumes from backdrafting into the house.

The chimney's rate of deterioration is dependent upon the original construction techniques, outdoor ambient temperatures, flue

---

Have you used that fireplace lately?

On deciding to light a fire for the first time after purchasing a home, a home-owner opened the fireplace damper before striking the match. Out fell a squirrel nest containing two live adult squirrels. It took four hours to get the squirrels out of the house.

and gas temperatures and exhaust air/moisture contents. A poorly constructed chimney can be the weakest link in the heating system. Start the chimney inspection on the outside of the house, using binoculars to avoid the risks of climbing on top of the roof. Most deterioration occurs above the roof line, where loose or missing

> **Where did that chimney go?**
> A masonry chimney on the exterior wall of a house had no concrete footing. During a heavy wind and rain storm, the entire chimney pulled away from the house and came crashing down into the next door neighbour's yard.

mortar and bricks may be evident. Some older chimneys may lean, because of moisture and mortar expansion. An offset chimney will draw unevenly and can allow for the accumulation of soot and ashes. Examine the flashing for signs of deterioration where the chimney comes through the roof. Notice how water is taken away from the valley between the slope of the roof and the wall of the chimney.

If the chimney is located on the exterior wall, check for horizontal and vertical cracks. This could mean settling or an old chimney fire. Sometimes foundation settling that has caused the chimney to pull away from the house is disguised by large amounts of caulking along the corners. By digging into the ground next to the chimney foundation you will be able to see if this is the case. If the chimney is in the interior, look at its foundation for deterioration and water stains. Some chimneys end at a fireplace. In the basement you may see vents connected to the chimney. Check which flues are venting specific appliances. A clothes dryer or other sources of mechanical fan venting must not be attached to the chimney flue.

Take your flashlight and mirror and check the interior opening of the ashpit. Note the type and condition of the flue liner. Round flues are more effective than square or cornered ones, as smoke spirals as it rises. An insulated flue lining maintains the temperature better for a stronger draft. Obstructions, broken liners, fallen or loose bricks, bird nests, improperly installed chimney connectors and creosote accumulations can all cause serious blockages. If you notice lots of ash and soot on the inside surfaces, it is likely it has not been cleaned recently. It is difficult to inspect the liner in an uncleaned chimney. Examine the chimney interior for unused openings or breachings, which once served chimney pipes leading to wood-burning stoves. These openings, often covered by thin metal "pie-plate" caps, plaster or wall panelling, may be a fire hazard if they have not been safely sealed.

Continue your inspection by taking your flashlight into the attic to observe all sides of the chimney. Inspect the flashing for signs of water penetration. Shine your flashlight along the gap between the chimney and the structural framing at the roof and the ceiling joists. If you spot charred or black deposits on the wood, there may be leaking smoke or gases from the chimney. You should see a 3-inch clearance between the chimney and the structural framing. With your awl, check the firmness of the mortar between the bricks or blocks.

Cold and wet conditions will reveal any leakage by moisture stains or escaping flue gases on the exterior of bricks or blocks. Moisture penetration is particularly damaging to both inside and outside the chimney. Uncleaned, non-operational fireplaces will smell in cold weather. Keep in mind that all code-approved chimneys are reasonably safe during normal use, and that chimney fires are avoidable through proper operation and maintenance.

Wood-burning Stoves and Appliances

Some of the common wood-burning appliances you may encounter during your inspection are the airtight stove, catalytic stove, fireplace insert, heat-cir-culating fireplace, factory-built fireplace, free-standing fireplace and zero-clearance fireplace. Construction materials, features and prices of these appliances differ dramatically. It is best to consult the supplier or manufacturer for operating manuals, safety standards, certification and maintenance proce-dures. An airtight plate-steel woodstove means the stove is made of plate steel, fabricated with continuous airtight welds and fitted with tight-sealing cast-iron doors and positive draft controls.

Stoves are classed according to their combustion and heat transfer efficien-cies. Combustion efficiency refers to the effective burning of fuel. One-half to two-thirds of the fuel value of wood is locked-in gases and volatile liquids that are released as the wood is heated in the combustion chamber. Heat transfer efficiency is a matter of getting the maximum benefit of stored-up heat trans-ferred effectively from the stove to the room, and a minimum heat loss up the chimney. The unit should be firebrick lined to retain the heat in the firebox, which helps hold the fire for a longer period and protects the steel areas from burning out. The handles on the doors should be made of open-coil springs to assure dissipation of heat for safety. The glass should be ceramic. Tempered glass will expand and cannot withstand high temperatures. Around the bottom you should find a clean-out door and ash pit. The door over the ashpit opening should fit tightly to reduce air infiltration. If you find water running out of the clean-out door or around the bottom of the chimney, this will require urgent attention. It indicates water and moisture penetration inside the chimney.

Check the fit of the flue connector that vents the flue gases directly through the throat of the fireplace. With the handle of your awl, tap the con-nector and listen for dullness. This can be a sign of creosote build-up. If you do not notice a flue connector, the flue outlet or the insert must be directly below the throat of the fireplace. You should see flashings tightly fitted against the fascia brick and the opening in the fireplace. These flashings must be remov-able for regular creosote inspections. You may decide to pull out the insert to make a more thorough inspection of the fireplace and chimney. Check the smoke shelf for creosote and debris.

Fires have resulted when single-walled flue pipes have been used as con-nectors between a wood-burning appliance and the chimney. Items to check on these pipes include screwed joints, accessibility for cleaning, extent of penetration into a masonry chimney and clearances between a flue pipe serving a solid fuel-fired appliance and combustible material. Note any signs of corrosion. There is a restriction prohibiting the connection of a wood-burning appliance and a gas-burning appliance to the same chimney.

Wood-burning Fireplaces

A wood-burning fireplace may be constructed of brick, stone, concrete block, ceramic tiles, granite, marble or other material. A house without a basement, or in an area of frost heave, will have a fireplace resting on a thick cement slab. The area inside the fireplace is called the firebox, and the hearth is the flat surface extending from the inside of the firebox to the front. The firebox should never have right-angle corners, nor should the walls be absolutely vertical. This would prevent any heat from radiating back into the room. A Rumford fireplace differs from a conventional one in that it features a shallow firebox with obliquely flared sides and back, thereby allowing more heat to be radiated into the room. The lintel is the support across the top of the fireplace opening on which the masonry sits. It can be made from steel, iron, pre-cast concrete or stone. The throat is the open space above the lintel inside the fireplace. The formation of the throat should begin no less than 6 inches above the lintel. Its purpose is to help control the draft that draws smoke into the flue.

Newer fireplaces will have a damper, a pivoted metal door that swings open and closed. The door is usually controlled by a lever, turnscrew or chain, which should be adjustable to various opening positions. The damper's purpose is to keep warm air in the house whenever the fireplace is not in use. It is also used to control the fire and regulate the draft when the fireplace is in use. On the floor of the hearth there should be a metal door leading to the ashpit where the burned ashes collect. Fireplace doors should be equipped with a locking mechanism and the door handles should have low heat retention. Glass doors should fit well. Better-quality ones are made out of ceramic or tempered, heat-resistant glass.

The fireplace should have direct access to outside air; otherwise, rooms with an open fireplace will suffer from cold drafts and cold floors while warm indoor air is taken up the chimney. By using a glass door and a fresh-air duct, draft for the fireplace is isolated from the rest of the house, improving comfort and energy efficiency. In older homes a window may be slightly opened to give this effect. In some homes outside air is channelled to the fireplace through a duct extending into the firebox or to the front of the hearth. Examine the combustion air duct for size, location, insulation, bug screens, damper, fireproofing, register and grille. The smell of creosote or smoke leaking into the room when the fire-

---

Besides smoking, what other bad habits does your fireplace have?

The remains of an old alcohol still, attached to the chimney, was found by a prospective purchaser!

place is not in use is a sure sign of backdrafting. An air-starved fireplace can be dangerous. The draft of the fireplace can be so strong that dangerous products of combustion (or from other combustion equipment such as the furnace and hot-water heater) can be sucked down the chimney and into the house. Where a fire is only smouldering, the draft up the flue may be so weak that the start-up of the furnace or bathroom fan may cause the fireplace draft to be reversed, drawing flue gases into the house. Therefore, when a fire is lit in an airtight house, where there is an imbalance of air between air exhaust and air supply, the air pressure in the house is lowered relative to outdoor pressure.

Be on the lookout for signs of escaping smoke or gases. Black streaks under the mantel or over the stone or brick veneer probably mean that the fire inside the firebox and the draft up the chimney are not working properly, causing the fire to smoke. A large number of dark surfaces around mortar openings and wall surfaces adjacent to the fireplace and chimney could mean that combustible gases are leaking into the living areas of the house. Severe surface marks may mean that the concealed combustible framing behind the wall has been ignited by flue gases escaping up behind the facing brick.

Check each item of the fireplace to ascertain its working condition. Evaluate the fit of the glass doors to its metal frame. Doors should not rattle. A tight fit will reduce air leakage into the fireplace. Clean glass promotes cooler glass surfaces and thus reduces temperature strains. Take your awl and scratch the surface inside the firebox. Are there cracks? Loose or missing mortar and firebrick indicate it is disintegrating. Fireclay mortar joints should be 1/16 to 3/16 inch (1.6 to 4.8 mm) wide to reduce thermal movement and mortar joint deterioration. If the damper will not open wide, it could be rusted or blocked. When in the closed position, no daylight should be seen. With your flashlight and mirror, reach in behind the opened damper to check out the area known as the smoke chamber. The walls of the smoke chamber should be parged to ensure smoke movement is not impeded. Further back, under the flue, you will see a flat or concave shelf projecting from the back wall, known as the smoke shelf. Look up the flue to determine the condition and support of the flue liner. Notice any obstructions, smells and excessive wetness. Some fireplaces and their chimneys have deteriorated so badly that they are on the verge of collapse. If the house you are inspecting has a fireplace on the floor above, check to ensure that within the chimney each fireplace has a separate flue. No other type of appliance is permitted to be connected into a flue serving a fireplace.

Gas Fireplaces

A gas fireplace, built into an existing fireplace, can eliminate the overheating of a room that is commonly associated with wood burning. To be classified as a heater, the model must meet certain gas inspection requirements. A label on the unit should indicate the heat output and gas input rating. If it doesn't, perhaps it is just for decorative purposes. The more efficient units offer piezoelectric ignition, thermostatic control and multiple levels of firing. Some are located in highly radiant fireboxes that provide a cozy heat. Others have blowers incorporated into furnace-type heat exchangers. The operation manual will indicate if it has vent requirements or if it is a sealed combustion type that does not draw air from the room. Make a note of any corrosion, unusual smells and banging or hissing noises. These are all signs of something not functioning properly.

Don't be fooled when you are inspecting a house and you see a roaring fire in the fireplace. A fire will draft out any damp or unpleasant smells in the house. Also, with a fire going, it is impossible to check out the inside condition of the fireplace. Make another appointment and check the fireplace when it is not in use.

CHECKPOINTS
✔✔✔✔✔✔✔✔✔✔✔

Chimney
____ brick
____ concrete block
____ factory built
____ stone
____ other
____ location
____ age
____ condition
____ orientation to wind
____ fuel type
____ height
____ size of flue
____ flashing
____ foundation or supports
____ rigid liner
____ flexible liner
____ steel liner
____ stainless steel liner
____ galvanized liner
____ double-walled liner
____ other liner
____ saddle
____ mortar intact
____ bricks missing
____ clean-out door
____ ash pit
____ chimney hood
____ rain cap

____ last cleaned
____ creosote buildup
____ unused openings
____ liner in masonry chimney
____ clearance of combustible
materials
____ certified testing agency approved

Fireplaces
____ age
____ location
____ type
____ factory built
____ insert
____ manufacturer
____ fire permits
____ glass door
____ flue connector
____ opening dimensions
____ cast-iron damper
____ throat, smoke chamber and shelf
____ hearth extension and height
____ creosote buildup
____ combustion air supply
____ fire brick
____ clearances
____ last inspected and cleaned
____ insurance company approval
____ certified testing agency approved

CONSUMER TIPS

- Check with city hall on the zoning of the property, and any future development planned in the area that would affect the value or attractiveness of the property, such as apartment buildings, shopping centres or highway expansion.
- Ask city hall, as well as the next door neighbours, about any historical, existing or potential risks of nature that could affect the property, such as flooding, mudslides, rockslides, animals, insects, etc.
- Look for evidence of revitalization in the neighbourhood as well as assess how the surrounding houses will affect the value or desirability of the home you are considering. A geographic area will typically go through a series of stages, phases, and plateaus over time. For example, the normal stages are development (growth), stabilization (maturing, plateau), conversions (from apartment to condos), improvements of existing properties, decline of improvements (deterioration), and redevelopment (tearing down of older buildings and new construction, more efficient use of space).
- Look at the mix of people in the neighbourhood to satisfy yourself that they are compatible with your investment and/or lifestyle needs such as renters vs. owners, single adults, couples with or without children, older retired people, ethnic and language composition, etc.
- Look for recreational, social, cultural, religious, educational or health facilities in the neighbourhood. Are there shopping centres nearby, or playgrounds, parks or schools? How close is the house from where you work? How important are these aspects to you?
- Look for transportation facilities, such as bus routes, if that mode of transportation is important to you.
- Ask the local police department about what crime prevention measures you can take and the crime statistics in the neighbourhood. Determine if the crime rate is increasing or decreasing. Compare with other communities.
- Ideally, look at the property at least 3 different times, during the day time, in the evening and on a weekend. Check for noise in the neighbourhood, such as traffic noise from a busy intersection or highway. Is the property near the flight path of an airport? Are any fumes present in the air that may be coming from an industrial site? Talk to the neighbourhood residents and be alert to any concerns they have.

CHAPTER 6

Heating, Cooling and Ventilation Systems

A HEATING SYSTEM MUST be designed to replace the heat lost through the floors, walls and roof of a house and also that lost by infiltration and exfiltration of air through windows and doors. The rate of heat loss is determined by the construction materials used, the outdoor temperature and the velocity of prevailing winds. The thermostat, supply and return ducts and furnace filters, fan, motor and burn chamber are all interlinking components that work together to ensure the effectiveness of the heating mechanism. These components will be discussed first as they relate to some or all of the heating systems described. This chapter will also cover solar panels, heat recovery ventilators and controls, air conditioners and humidifiers.

Heating Device Components and Accessories

Thermostats

Depending on the type of heating system, some houses have thermostatically controlled heating zones. One zone, for example, may control the first floor while another may control the second floor. Separate thermostats allow you to heat either floor as necessary instead of heating the entire house. As thermostats are sensitive to cold walls and drafts, their locations may give misleading signals. Thermostats may, for example, be located next to a fireplace, a heat-releasing appliance, a concealed duct or pipe, an uninsulated exterior wall or a spot where sunlight strikes it at a particular time of the day. The thermostat monitors a room's actual temperature and compares it with the setting. If the two readings differ by degrees, the thermostat turns on the heating or cooling systems.

Thermostats are classified as low-voltage, line-voltage or electronic. The low-voltage unit can be recognized by its light construction and is the most accurate system of control, offering the best comfort at lower operating costs.

Heating comfort

A first-time buyer did not see the need to inspect a brand new home. So, it wasn't until after he and his family moved into the three-storey house that they discovered the single forced air furnace, located in the basement on a side wall, wasn't nearly sufficient to heat the entire house. The rooms above the furnace were uncomfortably hot while the rooms further away were cold.

It is designed to handle light electrical loads. Line-voltage thermostats are constructed heavier, which results in a slower response to temperature changes and causes noticeable differences in room temperatures. Electronic thermostats operate on solid state or electronic components that are programmable. Features may include pre-programmed time settings and temperature set-back, weekly cycles, seasonal settings and temporary overrides. The unit may have a battery backup that saves a program in case of a power failure.

You can check the accuracy of the thermostat by taping your thermometer to the wall. To examine the thermostat for dust and grease, remove the cover plate. Remember that a poor thermostat will reduce the performance of the best heating system and will wear out quickly.

Heating duct damper (cutaway view)

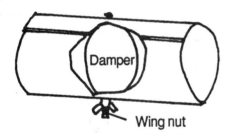

Damper

Wing nut

Check screen for blockage

Fresh air intake grill found on outside wall of house

Supply register

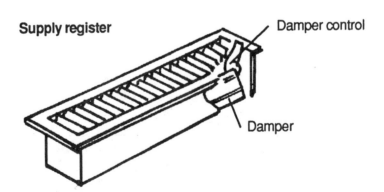

Damper control

Damper

DIAGRAM 4:
A Cross-Section View of Control Heating

Check for asbestos around the register openings, around duct connections and in the ceiling above the furnace.

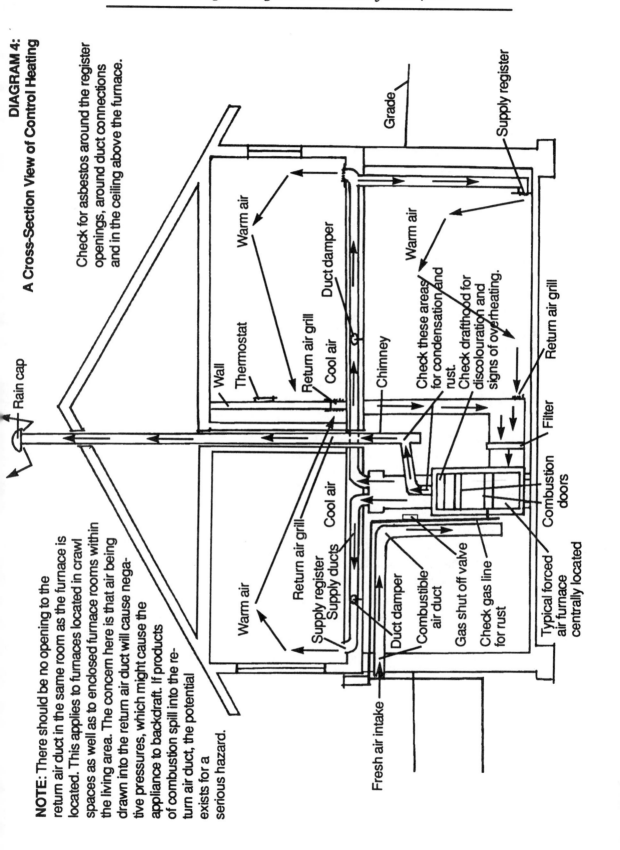

Rain cap

Wall

Thermostat

Warm air

Return air grill

Cool air

Duct damper

Chimney

Warm air

Check these areas for condensation and rust.

Check drafthood for discolouration and signs of overheating.

Return air grill

Filter

Grade

Supply register

Warm air

Return air grill

Cool air

Supply register

Supply ducts

Duct damper

Combustible air duct

Gas shut off valve

Check gas line for rust

Combustion doors

Typical forced air furnace centrally located

Fresh air intake

NOTE: There should be no opening to the return air duct in the same room as the furnace is located. This applies to furnaces located in crawl spaces as well as to enclosed furnace rooms within the living area. The concern here is that air being drawn into the return air duct will cause negative pressures, which might cause the appliance to backdraft. If products of combustion spill into the return air duct, the potential exists for a serious hazard.

Supply and Return Ducts

Supply ducts channel the warm air from the heating source to various areas in the home, and then take the stale air back to the furnace through return ducts. Plenums have a similar function but are larger. Ducts and plenums are made of galvanized sheet metal or aluminum. All ducts should be hung with straps, rather than being nailed directly to joists. Note their size, shape, location, balancing dampers, insulation, elbows, number of connections, fastenings and duct taping. Check all joints and connections for air leakage. Notice any areas that appear corroded. Noises coming from the ducts or furnace could mean anything from a worn belt, or motor bearing to air leaking through openings in ducts. Locate the supply and return ducts by turning up the temperature on the thermostat and waiting a few minutes. Then by touching the ducts you will be able to identify the supply (hot) and return (cold) ducts. From on top of your ladder, shine your flashlight along the ducts in search of hidden dampers or asbestos-wrapped pipes. Ducts passing through vented crawl spaces should be well insulated to minimize heat loss. In a slab-on-grade floor construction, ducts can be buried in the concrete.

To keep air circulating, each room of the house should be equipped with a supply and return register. They may be located on the floor, walls or ceiling. In finished basements it is common to find supply grilles mounted on the ceiling. These basements may be cold, however, if there is no fresh air return on the floor near the furnace. To prevent chimney backdrafting, the return grille should be more than 6 feet away from the furnace. Where registers are mounted on walls and ceilings, check the walls for black streak marks projecting from the register. This may be an indication of dirty ducts or that the heat exchanger inside the furnace is cracked and gases are leaking into the house rather than going up the chimney. Identify the supply and return air grilles by holding a tissue in front of the opening. Dampers should be adjustable for various opening positions. Remove the register to check for any obstructions around the openings. The return air grille must be at least as large as the return air duct or the whole system will suffer. Ask the owner if some registers give off more heat than others. Sometimes, during a slab-on-grade concrete pour, a duct may become crushed, thereby rendering it useless for transferring heat through the registers. Other factors that may cause some rooms to be warmer than others include: long, smaller-sized uninsulated duct runs; numerous bends, elbows and junctions in the ducts; air leakage at joints; closed balancing dampers; obstructions within the ducts; and location of the furnace.

Furnace Filters

Filters fit into the return ductwork of a forced-air heating, ventilating or air-conditioning system and may be disposable, washable or electronic. The disposable filters are thrown away when they become dirty. Washable filters, cut to fit the specific system, can be made from fibreglass, aluminum filler or plastic foam. The high-efficiency are usually pleated and are more effective in removing dust. An electronic filter is the most expensive and delicate. Unless you have hay fever or allergy problems, you may not need this type. It traps dust, smoke and pollen particles that pass through ordinary filters. A crackling noise will indicate that it is working, and some have an indicator light that comes on when they need servicing. To ensure optimal effectiveness, electronic air filters must be sized and installed correctly.

Fan and Motor

The fan most often seen in forced-air furnaces is known as a squirrel cage. In some furnace servicing, the cage and fan are pulled out as a unit. However, if the motor requires replacement it may be difficult to find an identical motor with a similar speed, shaft size, mounting brackets and size to fit inside the fan. For safety reasons, turn the power off before checking the area. Check the motor for areas that require oiling, and the axle ends of the fan for lubrication openings. A different style of fan may have a belt that connects the fan shaft to the motor. The speed of the fan can be changed by adjusting or replacing the pulley on the motor. Check the belt for tightness, alignment and wear.

Burn Chamber

As only furnace service personnel should touch anything in this area, just shine your flashlight around the burner assembly area. The pilot light should be a blue colour, similar to that for natural gas hot-water heaters described in Chapter 8. The burner flames are made up of many small blue cones, which should be uniform in shape and size. They should look clean, with no permanent yellow showing. (Dust particles in the air will cause temporary yellow flecking in the flame.) In a furnace designed for blue-flame operation, yellow-tipped flames indicate incomplete combustion. If a humidifier is running and the water in the area is soft, the flame could be orange.

Types of Heating Systems

There are literally hundreds of heating devices on the market today. The heating system in the house you are inspecting will depend upon the age of the house and the extent to which the home has been made energy efficient. You may find a combination of types of heating in a house, such as wood/gas, wood/electric, oil/electric, oil/wood, etc. The system may have been chosen by the original owner or contractor based on its price, efficiency, safety, ease of installation, appearance, durability and/or size. Because of their natural resource conservation features, forced-air gas furnaces are becoming the most popular type of heating. Oil, hot-water, electric and radiant heating as well as heat pumps will be discussed as they are commonly found in homes constructed over the last 50 to 60 years. A comparison chart has been provided which summarizes the advantages and disadvantages of different types of heating systems. The utility company will be able to give you an assessment of the costs involved in heating the house. However, keep in mind that the number of occupants in the house and their lifestyles will affect the heating bills.

FORCED-AIR FURNACES

Advantages

1. Installation and maintenance costs are low.
2. When a house is cool, the air is warmed quickly.
3. Duct system can be used to humidify, dehumidify, clean and cool the air.
4. No danger of components freezing up during cold weather.
5. Air can be filtered to a high level using an electronic filter.
6. Repair costs low as no plumbers required.

Disadvantages

1. Space is required around the furnace for servicing. Large ducts lower the ceiling clearance in the basement.
2. Some rooms can get an irregular flow of heat through the ducts, causing drafts and uncomfortable air movement.
3. May be noisy as sound travels along the ductwork.
4. A faulty heat exchanger can cause combustion products to enter the house.
5. The further the ducts are from the furnace, the less heat will come out of the registers.
6. Filters and ducts need to be cleaned regularly.

HOT-WATER HEATING

Advantages

1. Low maintenance, quiet and clean operation; long life expectancy.
2. Takes up less space than forced-air furnaces. Piping is concealed and easy to install.
3. Even temperature distribution; no drafts; less cyclical air movement.
4. After furnace reaches desired temperature, convectors remain warm for a considerable time as water retains heat longer than heated air.
5. Convectors can be added to a house without interfering with the heating capacity of the system.
6. Hot-water heating can be tied into any fuel-fired system.
7. Rooms can be individually temperature controlled by separate thermostats.

Disadvantages
1. More expensive installation costs than forced-air systems. Depending on house design, a large number of convectors may be required.
2. Hot-water systems respond slowly to a cool house.
3. Expensive to add air conditioning; difficult to humidify the air.
4. Baseboard convectors may become an obstacle when decorating.
5. Water pipes can corrode or leak.
6. Expansion and contraction of pipes may create noises.
7. Replacing a worn-out pump is very expensive.

ELECTRIC HEAT

Advantages
1. No chimney required, therefore no combustion products.
2. Inexpensive to install; minimal servicing required.
3. Electrical wires take up little space.
4. Quiet operation.
5. Components do not freeze up during cold temperatures.
6. Each room can have a thermostat.

Disadvantages
1. Large main electrical capacity required; electricity costs can be high.
2. Slow heat recovery when temperature drops suddenly.
3. Without any ductwork, you can't clean, cool or humidify the air.
4. Requires extra wall, window and door insulation to maintain heat.
5. Lint from carpets can block air circulation under baseboards, causing increased moisture levels in winter.
6. Inexpensive thermostats for the heaters can result in high electricity bills.

RADIANT HEATING

Advantages
1. Efficient where design heat requirements are small.
2. No noise or drafts.
3. Space saving as no mechanical room, ducts or baseboards required.
4. Furnishings, walls, windows and floors are all warmed by radiant energy.
5. Temperature differences between ceiling and floor are small.
6. Lower velocities of air currents result in less streaking and dust on walls and ceilings.
7. Individual room temperature controls.

Disadvantages
1. Repair costs can be high if panels become damaged.
2. Difficult to add more ceiling lighting due to risk of damaging panels.
3. Expensive compared to baseboard heating, especially in areas where electrical rates are high.
4. Slow response time.
5. Requires special insulation and thermostats.
6. Special floor, wall or ceiling preparations are required.
7. Difficult to affix anything to the ceiling (like hooks for hanging plants).

HEAT PUMPS

Advantages
1. Efficient in areas where the climate is mild and the cost of fuel is high.
2. One system of distribution can be used for both heating and cooling.
3. Clean operation with no danger of fumes or gases.

Disadvantages
1. Without a maintenance contract, repairs can be expensive.
2. Requires special positioning to minimize sound and vibration.
3. Relies greatly on fluctuating outdoor air temperatures, and its efficiency drops in very cold weather.

SOLAR HOT-WATER HEATING

Advantages
1. Quiet operation.
2. Environmentally safe as they do not burn fossil fuels.
3. Some systems have no moving parts that can wear out.

Disadvantages
1. Not efficient if improperly installed.
2. Water storage tank can take up valuable space.
3. In the winter some systems may require special attention.

Forced-air Gas Furnaces

Forced-air gas furnaces are available in conventional, medium-efficiency and high-efficiency models, with the latter type delivering the greatest amount of heat. Commonly found in older homes, a conventional furnace is considered inefficient due to the heat loss up the chimney. An upgraded conventional furnace has electronic ignition, two-speed fan, programmable thermostat and automatic flue dampers. The electronic ignition improves combustion efficiency by replacing the constantly burning pilot flame with a device that only ignites when the thermostat calls for heat. The automatic flue damper reduces heat loss up the chimney by closing the chimney flue when the furnace has stopped operating. Dilution and combustion air are still required when the furnace is operating. These furnaces use a draft hood, which ensures good burner combustion and compensates for pressure differences in the chimney flue due to wind or blockage. A two-speed fan offers continuous air circulation and provides a better temperature control, minimizing air stratification.

A medium-efficiency furnace combines an induced draft fan and electronic ignition for improved efficiency, or a vent damper controlled by an electric motor, which regulates the opening and closing of the damper, may be used. The fan draws a controlled amount of combustion air into the furnace and exhausts combustion gases to the outside through a small vent, which passes through an outer wall, or through the existing flue with a natural gas hot-water heater, if one is present. Since there is no draft hood, the need for dilution air is eliminated and the unit's efficiency is increased. Another type of medium-efficiency furnace has its combustion unit outside the house. The advantage is that house air is no longer required for combustion. This unit circulates a heated glycol/water solution to an outdoor blower coil, which distributes warm air throughout the house. However, maintenance costs and difficulty in finding qualified service personnel can be a disadvantage.

A high-efficiency furnace has a built-in draft fan, an electronic ignition and an extra heat exchanger that further extracts heat from the combustion gases. A chimney is not required as the combustion byproducts are vented to the outside through a small pipe. When the temperature of the gases falls below a certain level, water vapour condenses out, releasing additional heat. This acidic and corrosive condensate is piped to a floor drain. Furnace parts are usually made out of plastic or stainless steel. A "pulse combustion" furnace operates with the force of rapid combustion pulses, which induces combustion air movement into the unit and exhausts gases out of it through plastic tubes, eliminating the need for a chimney. The loss of house air when the furnace is operating is completely eliminated with combustion air being drawn directly from the outside. Disadvantages of high-efficiency furnaces include the initial high cost of installation and the fact that, it cannot be vented with a hot-water heater and the condensate is slightly corrosive and acidic. Over time there can be unknown maintenance costs as qualified service personnel may be difficult to find.

The furnace should be in a fairly central location of the house and an adequate distance on all sides from walls and appliances. Examine the vent carrying exhaust gases up the chimney and the fresh-air intake vent. An upflow duct system means that air flows up through the furnace, with the duct sys-

[handwritten margin note: get Make & model of furnace to get age.]

tem usually under the floor. Where space is limited, you may find a downflow furnace where the arrangement of the components is exactly the opposite and the fan is at the top of the furnace forcing the air down. With a horizontal furnace, the fan is at one end and the heating components are on the other. By prying off the service panel you will be able to identify the heating source (gas, oil, hot water, hydronic, electric), the furnace name, the model and service stickers. Make a note of this information so that you can later find out from the manufacturer the age and condition of the unit. All forced-air furnaces will have a filter, fan with motor, burner area, supply and return air plenums and ducting. When replacing the service panel, be certain it is closed properly. Deaths have occurred when furnace doors were not replaced, causing air to be drawn down the chimney instead of its venting its gases upwards.

Forced-air furnaces found in older homes are frequently oversized. When a system is too big, it will spend less time operating at or near peak efficiency. Instead, the furnace will deliver a large amount of heat over a short period of time, causing frequent temperature fluctuations. During cold temperatures the furnace will cycle on and off constantly. A properly sized unit will run almost continuously during the coldest weather. Noises heard travelling through the ductwork may indicate a damaged belt, misaligned pulley or expanding and contracting ductwork.

Oil Furnace

A typical oil furnace consists of the following components: an oil tank, filling and vent pipes, fuel level indicator, oil line, flue pipe and chimney furnace casing, flue damper/draft diverters, ductwork or hot-water pipes, burner combustion chamber, heat exchanger motor, fan filter and oil pump. The burner itself differs from a gas furnace in that oil has to be pumped through the system and the pressure has to be great enough to atomize the oil as it passes through a nozzle. In order to provide for rapid ignition and effective burning, oil must first be changed from a liquid to a vapour. The efficiency of the furnace is diminished if the oil does not burn properly. The burner flame should be bright yellow in colour. In cold weather, if the smoke at the top of the chimney is white, the oil furnace appears to be operating satisfactorily. If the smoke is grey or black, the burner needs retuning. All oil-fired furnaces and boilers require a masonry chimney lined with clay flue tile or a double-walled, insulated, pre-fabricated metal chimney with a stainless steel lining. While oil furnace chimneys rarely if ever need to be cleaned, the oil furnace itself requires more regular servicing than a gas furnace.

Check the location of the oil tank and the number of gallons it holds. If it is buried, it should have a lockable filling cap for safety reasons. If the tank is above ground, examine oil line connections and oil filters for leaking connections or crushed or broken tubing. The furnace should be thoroughly checked for rust, large soot marks, soot buildup, loose connections and noise.

Hot-water Heating

A typical newer residential hot-water heating system relies on a circulating pump to move hot water from the boiler through baseboard convectors to heat air in the house. All makes of boilers offer a different life expectancy and performance. The piping system may be a loop, one pipe or a two-pipe system and may consist of the following components: piping joints, convectors, pressure differential regulator, motors, circulation pumps, flow control valves, expansion tank, pressure-relief valve, pressure-reducing valve and air scrubber. Proper arrangement of piping, controls and equipment is critical to the proper operation of the system. Radiant panel heating along the floors, walls or ceilings is sometimes used in conjunction with hot-water heating systems because it can be tied into the same piping system. In the case of needed repair because of corroded or leaking pipes, a drainage system should be in place. This is usually located at the boiler and radiators or baseboard convectors. All exposed pipes should be well insulated to avoid freezing. If the insulation was installed prior to 1972, it may contain asbestos. Be careful not to disturb this material, as it will release countless small fibres into the air that can cause major health problems.

Locate the manufacturer's label on the boiler to determine its type, age and service details. Boiler problems are usually caused by lime deposits in the water which form scales inside the pipes. Examine all areas for leaking fittings, sooting and rust. Sooting occurs when combustion products adhere to surfaces of the boiler. Soot creates an insulating blanket that holds heat and has corrosive characteristics that will cause problems. Check for any damaged or missing fins on the convector piping. Servicing a hot-water heating system usually consists of maintaining the water level, occasionally adding a corrosion inhibitor, bleeding air from the system and lubricating the motor and circulation pumps with a few drops of non-detergent electric motor oil. As some plastic piping is permeable to air, the internal components may become corroded over time. In addition, air seepage in the pipes can result in corroded boiler components.

Electric Heating

Electric heating systems include radiant ceiling panels or elements, floor drop-in heaters, wall heaters, baseboard heaters and electric furnaces. Electric furnaces operate with resistance wire installed in the furnace and the number of these depends upon the amount of heat needed. An electric furnace does not require a chimney but has a duct system and a fan to force the heated air to various rooms. Each heating element within an electric furnace is protected by its own fuse and circuit breaker. Some electric heaters will discharge air by means of a fan.

Note the location and rating of the heaters, which circuits they are on, the size of the conductors and the rating of the breakers at the main service panel. If the capacity is less than 100 amps, a new service, sized for electric heating and other loads, should be installed. Electricity bills may be high in some regions because of the large electrical capacity required. Also, to maintain the desired temperature levels, the added insulating effect provided by double-paned windows, storm doors and 2"x 6" wall construction is required. Use of high-quality thermostats will also achieve better temperature control. If the unit is not properly fitted to the wall, dust particle streaks can occur above the baseboard. Heaters located on exterior walls will lose much heat to the wall behind them and may rust if rain passes through open windows above them. Window curtains close to baseboard heaters are a fire hazard. Air circulation can be blocked by accumulation of carpet lint under baseboard heaters. This can cause increased moisture levels during winter months. Also, the smell of burning dust can become nauseating. You may wish to contact the manufacturer to ensure that replacement parts are still available for these heaters.

Radiant Heating

You may come across electric or hot-water radiant systems installed in ceilings and floors to heat the surface and turn it into a radiator or emitter of infrared radiation. The system consists of a flat foil that carries the electric current. This foil is sandwiched between two sheets of plastic film, which is laid underneath the floor or above the ceiling coverings. Because of their insulative qualities, floor coverings will determine the actual floor heat output. The lower the R-value, the better suited it is for radiant floors. It is helpful to have access to the plans that show the layout of the system and the location of the branch circuits. Low voltage controls are most important when a radiant heat system is used. Radiant hot-water piping should be protected by an oxygen barrier to prevent air from mixing with the water and corroding the heat exchanger in the boiler. Hydraulic or air pressure tests may be performed to check for leaks. The use of certain oil-based paints is not recommended on ceiling surfaces.

Heat Pumps

A house may also be heated or cooled by a heat pump. The heat pump uses the same basic principles as the household refrigerator, where heat is extracted from a space at low temperature and discharged to another space at a higher temperature. The system consists of two heat exchange coils. One is the condenser, which gives off heat, and the other is the evaporator, which picks up heat from the outside. In the cooling phase a compressor reverses the roles of these two coils. A four-way valve is used to switch the heat pump from the heating to the cooling cycle. The refrigerant is a liquid with an extremely low boiling point so that it changes from liquid to vapour as it is compressed and picks up heat. It returns to liquid as it is decompressed and loses its heat. An air-to-air heat pump may be found operating independently, although you may also see an oil or gas furnace combined with an air heat pump, a solar-assisted heat pump or a ground- or water- source heat pump. They all work on the principle that it takes less energy to extract heat from one source and move it to another place than it takes to create heat. Even when it is cold outside there is a great deal of heat energy in the air.

The heat pump may be located in the attic, basement or outside. If outside, the heat pump should be at least 18 inches above the ground to avoid snow and ice buildup, and should be situated away from doors, windows and neighbours who might be aggravated by the noise. Turn up the thermostat and notice any vibrations or irritating noises. To help minimize noise, the compressor should be mounted on rubber pads. Check all electrical controls that operate the thermostat, defrost cycle, overheat protection, resistance heater, reversing valve relay, compressor motor and fan pump. Other components include the filter, dryer, crankcase heater and warning lights. The compressor may be a piston or rotary type.

There should be easy access to the control panel to reduce repair costs. If neglected, the heat pump can get plugged with dirt and other materials, which greatly reduces its life expectancy. Make a note of the warranty coverage, the type and the model and check with the manufacturer regarding the availability of parts.

Solar Panels

Some houses use solar panels as an extra source of heat for domestic water heating, space heating or swimming-pool heating. The solar panel is basically an energy trap to capture sunshine. A well-designed panel should be located in a sunny, unshaded area such as on the roof, facing due south. For at least six hours around midday it should be unshaded. The panels must be of a proven design, built from durable materials and performance rated. This information should be available from the owner or manufacturer.

Evaluation of the solar panel should include an inspection of the glazing, seals, gaskets, caulking, connectors, heat-absorber plate and enclosure. Check the glazing for watertightness and the ability to pass solar radiation. Clouding on the glass may be due to condensed water vapour. If the solar panel along with the piping is an integral part of the roof, notice how easy it will be to remove the components when the roof needs repair. Does the roof sag in the area of the panel? Check how well the components are plumbed, fastened down and protected from adverse weather conditions. Are there signs of corrosion over any metal components?

Mechanical Ventilation Systems

With the advent of the airtight, energy efficient houses of the 1980s and 1990s, building codes have insisted on the provision of a controlled ventilation system for comfort, health and safety reasons. Some ventilation standards are based on air change rates, while others are based on a minimum amount of fresh air per person or per room in the house. Houses that are not airtight do not require a mechanical ventilation system as they have enough natural, uncontrolled infiltration of fresh air through window openings and the loose-ness of the building envelope. The three types of mechanical ventilation are: exhaust, supply air and balanced systems. The first two are known as central ventilation systems. With such systems, a single exhaust fan, usually located in the attic, exhausts air only. Ducts from the main sources of pollution, the bathroom, laundry and kitchen, lead to this fan where it is vented to the out-side. Space must be found under each interior door to let intake air circulate throughout the house.

Exhaust Ventilation System

An exhaust system uses either a number of individual fans or a centrally locat-ed fan connected with ducting to rooms of the house. Make-up air (air that is required to replace the air leaving the house) is drawn into the rooms through leakage paths in the building envelope and through adjustable air inlets locat-ed in each room. If these inlet openings are not carefully sized or regulated to ensure even distribution of fresh air, you can expect to find high levels of neg-ative pressure, cold drafts and backdrafting of appliances. Also moisture and radon can be drawn in from the soil.

Supply Air Ventilation System

A supply air ventilation system operates in reverse principle to exhaust sys-tems. Fans are used to provide outdoor air while exhaust air leaves the house through deliberate openings or leakage paths in the building envelope. As this system pressurizes the house, condensation problems may occur when warm moist air is pushed into the walls and ceilings of the structure. During cold temperatures this moisture can condense out of the air and freeze the insula-tion within the perimeter walls and attic. Besides the risk of reduced insula-tion and moisture levels, windows and door locks can freeze.

Heat Recovery Ventilators (HRV)

A balanced, or heat recovery ventilation (HRV), system relies on both supply and exhaust fans to provide ventilation while interior pressures are equally maintained to those outdoors. The HRV air-to-air heat exchanger draws warm stale air from the house and transfers the heat in that air to the fresh cold air being pulled into the house. An HRV system brings fresh air from the outside, heats it in the winter and cools it in the summer, and then distributes this air to the entire house. The unit may be found in the attic, basement or utility room and should be supported by vibration-resistant material and located away from quiet areas like bedrooms.

Most HRVs consist of two fans, controls, a heat exchanger chamber and a duct system for air distribution to the various rooms. Two ducts should con-nect the ventilator to the outside, with one bringing in fresh air and the other exhausting stale air. These ducts should be short, straight and insulated, with a sealed vapour barrier taped and caulked around the insulation. The two ducts should terminate on the exterior wall of the house, well above the ground and separated from each other by a distance of at least 6 feet. These ducts should be finished on the exterior wall with rain hoods and equipped with a wire mesh bird screen.

With a window or wall-mounted HRV system, there is no ductwork and the unit is merely plugged into an electrical outlet. However, because the fresh and exhaust air outlets are so close together, the fresh air can be exhausted before it mixes adequately with room air. With a system designed to service the entire house, the ventilator should have a capacity to exchange one-half the total volume of air in the house per hour.

Inside the heat exchanger chamber there are channels that form a plastic or metal core, consisting of a plate, a drum or pipes that are arranged so that fresh and stale air passageways are in close contact with each other, without the streams of air actually mixing. The system should have a frost mechanism to melt any ice or frost that may build up inside the core of the heat exchanger during cold weather. In order to maintain the efficiency of the heat exchange, the inside core of the ventilator should be cleaned regularly. Some units have drains so that water can be used to wash them out. Similarly, the air filters in the fresh air and stale air ducts require cleaning.

An HRV system should operate continuously. Most operate at two or more speeds. When a speed setting is selected, the control switch overrides the low speed fan setting that is used for continuous operation. Typically one or more of the following control switches are used: manual high speed switch for kitchen, bathroom and laundry rooms; rheostat; timer; and dehumidistat switch. A dehumidistat switch should be in a central location where it senses average house humidity and away from ventilator supply grilles. The dehumidistat operates the ventilator fans at normal speed when the humidity is below a set point but automatically increases the fan's speed when the humidity rises. Humidity measurement is the most practical method of controlling the operation of a heat recovery ventilator. The healthiest setting is between 40 and 60 per cent.

On the outside of the house, locate the intake and exhaust ducts. Ensure that there are no sources of air contamination close to the intake duct, such as exhaust fumes from the house next door, gas meter, oil tank or garbage containers. Trace the ducts through the house in your notebook, and make a note of any whistling noises in the room registers. Ensure that range hoods, clothes dryer vents, attic spaces and combustion appliances are not connected to the ventilator ducting.

Air Conditioning

A well-designed air conditioner should control and regulate humidity, temperature and ventilation, as well as filter, clean and recirculate the air within the conditioned space. Air conditioning is accomplished by using the principles of mechanical refrigeration in an air recirculation system. Heat is absorbed from the air within the house and is transferred to the outside walls of the structure. The load the air-conditioning system has to bear will be less in the summertime if the south sides of the house are shaded by trees or awnings.

Individual room units, mounted to walls or windows, are less expensive but will not cool the entire house. The size of the unit relative to the area it is supposed to cool is important. A unit that is too small will run continuously without cooling the room sufficiently. On the other hand, too large a unit will cool the room quickly but shut off before it has removed enough moisture to lower the humidity to a comfortable level. Newer units will be more energy efficient and dissipate the heat better. From outside, notice the location of the air conditioner to ensure it will not receive direct sunlight. The sun will heat the metal parts that are trying to dissipate the room's heat. Ensure the switches and automatic timers work properly and the filters are clean. A dirty filter will run up an electrical bill by having to work harder to push the air through spaces clogged with pollen, soot and dust.

The most efficient type is central air conditioning which is designed to service the whole house. A heating/cooling furnace will provide air conditioning in the summer by shutting off the burner and allowing air to pass by the heat chamber without being heated. A heating/cooling furnace will have a larger fan motor to help circulate the heavier cool air. It will also have a foil-backed, insulated duct system so that moisture won't condense on the ducts and cause them to rust. The condensate pipe will lead from the furnace plenum, where the coil case housing is located, to a floor drain. The coil case houses the cooling evaporator. The refrigerant is pumped into the evaporator from the compressor and motor located outside the house. The cool air passes through the furnace and is blown by the fan throughout the same ducts that hot air travels during the winter. The air is then recycled through the return air ducts. Even though the heating and air conditioning operate from the same system, you may find that some installations have separate heating and cooling registers in each room.

From outside the house, examine the condenser fan, compressor and motor. They should be mounted on a level slab. Check for signs of corrosion, leaking refrigerant tubes and areas filled with debris. Ask the owner if there is an existing warranty on the compressor and how frequently the system has been serviced. Where the refrigerant pipes enter the house from the outdoor compressor, check for wood rot. If these pipes are insulated, minimal wetting and decay of wood will be present. Check for dirt on the furnace filter and evaporator coils. With the owner's consent, set the thermostat to turn on the cooling system. Listen for any vibrations and loud noises. These could indicate the unit has not been properly installed. Check each register for cool air. Allow the unit to run for about 30 minutes and check the system again. This time look for major icing on components. Icing will reduce the efficiently considerably. If the air-conditioning unit is in the attic, check the amount of insulation around the ducts. There should be a drip pan under the unit to collect water. As a rule, if you have an air-conditioning system, you won't need a dehumidifier.

Humidifiers

If the house you are inspecting is equipped with a humidifier, it will probably be installed on the warm air side of the duct system close to the furnace. This is because warm air absorbs more moisture than cold air. Most humidifiers have an electric motor, a pan at the bottom of the humidifier, a regulating float, an inlet valve with a water line and a water line shut-off valve close to the humidifier. Inside the humidifier, absorbent elements like plates, roller bristles or a sponge hold the water to be absorbed by the air passing through the system. In some systems the motor, which is wired into the furnace fan and rotates the absorbent material on a roller, is switched on by a humidistat when the ambient air is excessively dry. It will shut off when the desired moisture level is achieved. Air with a lower temperature or a higher moisture content will take less moisture from the humidifier.

One of the major problems with a humidifier is the mineral deposit buildup left behind when the water evaporates. This is particularly serious in regions where the water is very hard. Unless the unit is cleaned regularly, these deposits will settle over the float and water inlet valve, and cause malfunctions or overflow problems. When you check the pan, look for any discolouration or bacteria growing on the surface of the water. Mould growth can cause respiratory problems for occupants of the house. Mineral deposit stains also may be found on the side of the humidifier and duct system.

Improper installation of a humidifier can shorten the life of a furnace by rusting its internal components. Check the operation of the humidifier by adjusting the setting of the humidistat and the furnace thermostat. Everything should operate smoothly. If the rotating drum does not move, the motor or transformer could be burned out, an electrical connection could be loose or the humidistat could be stuck. If the humidifier is allowed to run continuously, there will be too much moisture in the air. Condensation will build up in areas of the house where the excessive moist air meets cold surfaces. The condensation will reduce the effectiveness of insulation and cause paint to peel and wood to rot. When the humidistat is not properly adjusted during cold winter months, excessive air moisture may cause heavy frosting on the windows, which could later lead to water damage to the woodwork. Similarly, if the humidistat is located in an area of abundant moisture, such as in a wet basement or next to a bathroom shower or clothes washer, the humidifier will be ineffective.

A careful review of the type of heating, ventilation and air-conditioning systems will provide valuable information for your house purchase decision. Are the systems so old or inadequate that they will require replacement in the near future? Are you financially prepared for this major cash outlay, or can an adjustment be made to the purchase price to offset this factor? How do the costs of maintaining these systems compare with your present usage and servicing bills? Perhaps you will need to add components to meet the comfort and lifestyle needs of your family. As you proceed with your inspection, be aware and make a note of the air quality and temperature in the various rooms in the house.

CHECKPOINTS
✓✓✓✓✓✓✓✓✓✓✓

Heating
_____ type
_____ manufacturer
_____ manufacturer's warranty
_____ mechanical engineer approved
_____ serial number
_____ model number
_____ age
_____ installer's name
_____ location
_____ condition
_____ corrosion
_____ operating instruction manual
_____ fire stops and separations
_____ asbestos
_____ crawl space heater
_____ main fuel shut-off valve
_____ pilot light colour
_____ burner flame colour
_____ oil tank fuel level indicator
_____ combustion air supply
_____ last serviced
_____ filter cleaned
_____ type of fuel burned
_____ fuel tank location
_____ safety relief valves
_____ distribution system
_____ balancing of dampers/ducts/ registers
_____ pipes
_____ wires
_____ duct location
_____ pipes/ducts insulated
_____ ducts cleaned
_____ exhaust breaching

_____ furnace casing condition
_____ hidden dampers inside ducts
_____ efficiency of unit
_____ cost effectiveness of unit
_____ certified testing agency approved

Thermostat
_____ location
_____ manufacturer
_____ certified testing agency approved
_____ manufacturer's warranty
_____ line voltage
_____ automatic
_____ zoned controls

Heat Pumps
_____ manufacturer
_____ serial number
_____ model number
_____ last serviced
_____ age
_____ operating manual
_____ service contract
_____ manufacturer's warranty
_____ certified testing agency approved

Air Conditioning
_____ manufacturer
_____ serial number
_____ model number
_____ location
_____ age

_____ last serviced
_____ total cooling capacity
_____ type of refrigerant used
_____ pipes insulated
_____ corrosion
_____ filter
_____ compressor
_____ operating manual
_____ control switches
_____ zone control thermostats
_____ weatherproofed electrical controls
_____ ease of access to controls
_____ speed controls compressor/
condenser fan
_____ manufacturer's warranty
_____ certified testing agency
approved

Solar Panel
_____ manufacturer
_____ location
_____ support
_____ flashings
_____ age
_____ mounting brackets
_____ access to panels
_____ roof penetration
_____ piping insulated
_____ manufacturer's warranty
_____ certified testing agency
approved
_____ system properly sized
_____ fluid fill and drain valve
_____ automatic air vent sensors

Pumps
_____ manufacturer
_____ type
_____ hot/cold water connections
_____ age
_____ last serviced
_____ oil holes
_____ electrical grounding
_____ last serviced
_____ availability of parts
_____ manufacturer's warranty
_____ certified testing agency
approved

Tank
_____ manufacturer
_____ type
_____ safety valves
_____ insulation
_____ bypass piping
_____ back-flow preventer
_____ expansion tank
_____ preheat tank gallon capacity
_____ auxiliary tank
_____ floor drain
_____ tank drain
_____ shut-off valves
_____ check valves
_____ supply valves
_____ water supply need conditioning
_____ sensors
_____ combination pressure/temp
gauge
_____ pressure relief valve
_____ certified testing agency
approved

Heat Recovery Ventilator
_____ manufacturer
_____ serial number
_____ model number
_____ location of unit
_____ last serviced
_____ core cleaned
_____ filters cleaned
_____ intake/exhaust fair opening
locations
_____ location of registers
_____ quiet operation
_____ balance ventilation exhaust/
intake
_____ remote switch controls
_____ timer switch controls
_____ dehumidistat controls
_____ condensate drainline or drain
pan
_____ ductwork sealed
_____ operation manual
_____ certified testing agency
approved
_____ manufacturer's warranty

Humidifier
_____ manufacturer
_____ serial number
_____ model number
_____ location
_____ age
_____ last cleaned

_____ humidistat location
_____ humidifier location
_____ water shut-off
_____ manufacturer's warranty
_____ certified testing agency
approved

CONSUMER TIPS

- Find out the real reason that the house is for sale. Frequent reasons include: marital separation or divorce, death of owner or co-owner, loss of job or business failure, financial problems, job relocation, ill health of the owner, retirement, downsizing or upsizing due to family needs, desire to move up to a nicer neighbourhood, crime in the area or wanting to get a good price in a seller's or hot market.
- Attempt to negotiate a reduced price on the house purchase if you find the property inspection shows that repair work or replacement drainage, roof, electrical, wiring, plumbing, furnace, chimney fireplace is required. Show the owner the inspection report and an estimate of the cost to correct the deficiencies.
- Target a specific geographic area or areas when house searching. This means restricting your choices to specific communities or areas within a community. This makes your selection much easier and gives you an opportunity to get to know specific areas thoroughly. Obtain street maps of the area as well as zoning map from city hall.
- If you are buying for personal use and eventual resale or buying as an investment, the issue of climate is important. Certain areas of your city or community may have more sun, shade, rain, snow and wind than others, depending on historical climate patterns.
- Look for factors that would have a negative influence on your interest in living in the house, on a prospective tenant or future purchaser when you re-sell. For example, unpleasant odours coming from an industrial plant, poor lighting because of too many trees, lack of street lighting that impairs safety, inadequate municipal services such as septic tanks rather than sewer facilities, roads that need repair, open drainage ditches, etc. Awareness of these negative factors will also assist you in your negotiating approach to get the best price.

CHAPTER 7
▼
Plumbing

S IMILAR TO HEATING systems that carry warm air through the house using ducts or pipes, a plumbing system delivers water through a piping system to various faucets and takes the excess water and waste out through a drainage system. The location of the house will determine whether water is supplied by the city's underground water main system or from a well. Likewise, drainage may be connected to the city's system if the house is in an urban area, while a rural area is more likely to have septic tanks. This chapter will review the components of water supply and drainage systems, indoor and outdoor plumbing, water treatment systems and features to look for during your inspection.

Water Supply Systems

City Water Main System

In most cases the city's water main connects with the house supply system near the property line just below ground level. Here there will be a water meter and valve, or stopcock. The Public Works Department uses the stopcock to turn the water service on or off. In colder climates the valve may be a few feet underground and the meter located inside the house. Water accumulation around the stopcock could indicate a high water table, poor drainage or a leaking pipe. Over time metal pipes can develop pin-hole leaks because of soil acidity and will require replacement. If the water line cannot be located, contact City Hall to view the property survey plan. At the same time, by checking the date of the water connection application you can determine the age of the house.

Well Water Supply

The quality of well water depends on the type of well and the area. Old wells were often dug by hand and then lined with bricks, wood, rocks or other sup-

---

> **Perimeter Drainage**
>
> After testing the perimeter drainage around the house with a garden hose for about three hours, one prospective homeowner decided to look into the crawlspace. He found that the water had filled up the entire crawlspace!

porting materials. The area below the water table was generally lined with loose gravel and stones through which the water seeped. Newer drilling methods are more hygienic. Usually 15 to 50 feet deep, a well collects rainwater that filters down through the soil and seeps into the well.

If the well is too deep it may be contaminated with sulphur or salt water. Heavy rainfall can also contaminate a well by its runoff. Be certain to have the water tested for bacteria. Ensure the well opening has a tight-fitting lid for safety.

Pumps are used to raise the water from the well and temporarily hold it in a storage tank before it is delivered to the house. Old-fashioned lift pumps have been replaced by more modern submersible, jet and deep-well piston pumps. The complete pump, tank, controls and piping system must be protected from severe temperature extremes and lightning strikes. If the pump is in a pumphouse, the building and pipes should be well insulated. To reduce the effects of friction loss and elevation differences, the storage tank should be placed as close as possible to the pressure switch. Check the water pressure and also see if the tank is large enough to provide sufficient water to the house during peak load periods. In the summer, will sprinklers and swimming pools use water faster than your well can supply it?

Ask the owner or neighbours if, at any time during the year, the wells in the area have run dry. During a severe drought it is possible for the water table to drop and reduce the flow of water from your well. If the level of the well water is drawn down below the intake of the pump system, the pump will run dry. Since many pumps cannot reprime themselves automatically, they may have to be turned off manually to prevent the motors from burning out. When the pump is in operation, look and listen for unusual vibrations and sounds. An indication that the storage tank is "waterlogged" is when the pump starts and stops at very short intervals. This means that the tank cannot keep up with the demand for water, causing the pump to run more often. This will burn out the motor. Check the fittings and the air regulator. If you hear the pump starting at fairly long intervals while no water is being used, it may mean a pinhole leak in a rusty pipe or a leaky foot valve. Check the electrical ground, timers, filtering screens, sanitary covers, air volume controls, air valve and storage tank for corrosion.

Water Treatment

In rural areas drinking water may not pass through a sophisticated filtration system to remove bacteria, eliminate odours and improve the taste. Fortunately there are a number of water treatment systems available on the market that can treat the water supply for the entire house or be fitted under a sink to treat the water from specific faucets. While the methods of water treatment will vary, most types are equipped with a changeable filter system designed to eliminate debris from the water. The system should be chosen for its efficiency in removing particles and pollutants such as sediments, viruses, microbes, chloroform, formaldehyde, volatile chemical compounds and heavy metals like iron, lead and mercury. Filters should be easy and inexpensive to replace.

Water Supply Pipes

Water is delivered to the house under pressure along a 1-inch or 3/4-inch underground pipe. At the foundation wall, where the water line enters the house, this pipe may be reduced to a 1/2-inch pipe. Inside the house you will find a shut-off valve that controls the water for the entire house and a pressure regulating valve that reduces the incoming water pressure. Some plumbing codes require a backflow preventer, which prevents the backflow of contaminated water into the potable water supply lines of the house. Such a reversal of the normal flow is caused by a reduced pressure in the water supply piping. One homeowner, who left a garden hose lying on the lawn during a low water pressure situation, became quite ill when lawn fertilizer was inadvertently siphoned into the water system.

The pipes may be cast iron, galvanized steel, copper or plastic, or any combination of these if the house has been remodelled a few times. Bi-metallic connections should be avoided, though, as galvanic corrosion often occurs between pipes and fittings of different metals. For instance, brass or copper tends to attack galvanized steel. In older houses, where galvanized piping is in use, the same material should be used for all supports and connections. Use of lead pipes for plumbing systems (sometimes found in turn-of-the-century homes) has been discontinued as the lead will contaminate drinking water. Make note of the pipe markings that indicate its size, material, manufacturer's name, pressure rating and certification standard. As the type of piping varies, so will its method of connection. For example, copper is soldered, steel has threads, cast iron uses oakum, and lead and plastic requires a chemical solvent or metal connection.

Cast iron is one of the oldest materials used above and below ground for drains, vents, soil pipes and sewers. It is heavy, strong, durable and relatively inexpensive. It is also the quietest system available for drains and waste. Working with cast-iron pipe, though, requires specialized equipment, knowledge and skill. Plastic pipe is the newest material. It is flexible, lightweight, inexpensive, strong and resistant to corrosion, electrolysis and buildup of internal deposits. Minimal tools and skill are required for assembly. However, as plastic pipe is susceptible to permeation by fuels and other solvent-like chemicals found in contaminated soils, some types of plastic pipes have been banned, or restricted to cold-water use, by municipal authorities. Once the pipe walls have been contaminated, flushing will not solve the problem. The plastic pipes will have to be replaced with metal pipes.

Newer copper piping will be marked with a Type K, L or M stamp. Type K is the heaviest and is used for the main underground water line. Inside installations for hot and cold water lines should be marked with a Type L stamp. Type M, the lightest weight of copper, should be found only on indoor hot-water heating pipes. A DWV marking indicates a drain waste vent. When copper pipes are used underground, the connections are fitted with flare joints or are brazed to produce a durable structural bond. Sheathing around the copper pipe will protect it from acids within the cement of the foundation wall and allow for pipe expansion and contraction during cold weather.

Indoor Plumbing

Inside the house the pipes will branch off and be of smaller diameter yet large enough to deliver all the water needed at one time when all fixtures are operating. Horizontal pipes will be secured to floor joists by hangers or straps or recessed into notches. Copper pipes passing through heating plenums should be held in place by galvanized supports rather than iron nails, which would pose leaking problems. Some supply lines will have a slight pitch or slope towards the lowest point in the run. Here there will be a valve so that pipes may be drained easily in case of needed repair. Some pipes will lead directly to cold-water outlets while others make a stop at the hot-water heater. Then the hot and cold water lines go to each tap or fixture. (Hot-water heaters will be covered in Chapter 8.)

As most often the plumbing system is hidden between floors and inside walls, you will only be able to fully inspect the plumbing in unfinished basements and crawl spaces. When you look over each piece of piping, locate the hot and cold lines. The hot line is always on the left and the cold on the right. They should be at least 6 inches apart and insulated to prevent heat transferring from one to the other. Pipes next to exterior walls or subject to cold drafts will freeze if not insulated. Turn the taps on and off to check for leaking around the valve stems. If you notice that more water is coming out of one faucet than another, a valve may be partly closed or there may be a pipe obstruction. Check which fixtures and taps have individual shut-off valves. If a leaky tap requires fixing, you can shut off its valve without having to turn off the entire supply to the house.

Listen to the taps. When water flows through badly worn faucet stems or washers, the faucets may emit a "chattering" sound. Sometimes a resounding noise is heard when the taps are turned on and off quickly. This hammering noise may be caused by the sudden stop of the water travelling through the pipes. The longer the pipe, the greater the noise will be. Improper supports for the pipe may also be the cause. In extreme cases, where repeated hammering has occurred, the noise can be sufficient to break the pipes and rupture the valves and fittings. This problem can be eliminated by installing an 18- to 24-inch vertical length of capped pipe on the supply line, just ahead of the faucet. If a banging noise is heard, it can mean that more straps need to be added to the horizontal or vertical runs.

Check the water pressure by turning on all the faucets in the washroom. Then flush the toilet to see if there is a significant decrease in water running from the taps. If the flow of water is reduced to a trickle, it could be for a number of reasons. The following factors impede water flow: the city or well water pressure is too low; the supply line is too small in diameter; the supply pipe runs in a round-about route rather than directly to the outlet; the fixture is a considerable distance from the main water line; there are too many outlets on the line; there are too many elbows, valves and other fittings on the line. Another common complaint is the sudden temperature change to water coming from a shower faucet when a second faucet in the house is turned on. This can be remedied by installing a larger diameter pipe or a pressure balancing valve.

Outdoor Plumbing

The faucets on the outside of the house should extend a few inches from the wall so that a garden hose may be easily screwed on. They should be sloped downward so that when they are shut off during the winter months, water will drain out of the pipe and a freeze-up will be prevented. Check the location of the backflow preventer or antisiphon vacuum breaker. Turn on the taps to test the water pressure. The pressure should be consistent with that found inside the house. If there is an exterior door from the basement, there should be a floor drain in front of it. Using a garden hose, check to see if it drains properly. A non-functioning drain can cause water to flood the basement.

Water and Waste Drainage System

The purpose of the drainage system is to drain water, carry away wastes and vent sewer gases. The waste system consists of larger pipes than the supply system. The pipes are similar, though, in the type of material used and the manner in which they are fastened. Each fixture must have a waste line connection to prevent sewer gases from entering the house. These are P-, J-, U- or S-shaped bends of piping found under sinks. The toilet has one built into the system. Their position and shape serves as a trap to retain water and prevent sewer gases from rising.

The normal pitch from which drain pipes slope away from fixtures is 1/4 inch for every horizontal foot of pipe travel. If the slope is not very steep, water and waste will drain too slowly, causing a back-up into the fixture. A steep slope will cause water to run off so fast that solid particles are left behind and may empty water from the trap. For a trap to function properly, there must be a vent pipe attached to the system. This is a tightly fitted piece of pipe that goes through the roof and allows sewer gases to escape. It also prevents water from being siphoned off the traps by allowing air to circulate throughout the drainage system. Run your hand and mirror under each fixture in the house to inspect for discoloured wood, leaking water from connections and corrosion. Firmly push against the bottom of the trap to test for softness, an indication of deterioration. Often you will find electrical tape or window putty around joint connections in an attempt to seal leaks.

Every fixture must have a vent. Vents are often connected through a secondary piping system to a main vent. Sucking or gurgling noises heard when water is released into the drains could be evidence of inadequate venting. Another indication of improper venting is odour around the fixtures. From the attic, check to see that all vents and stacks pass through the roof to the outside. This pipe should be insulated where it goes through the attic. The main stack vent should be at least 4 inches in diameter and project no less than 4 inches from the roof in order to prevent frosting in below-zero weather (a condition that allows sewer gases to re-enter the house).

Waste branch lines from fixtures connect to a larger main drain that can measure up to 6 inches in diameter. This drain connects to a city sewage system or septic tank. The main sewer line should have a clean-out opening that is sealed by a threaded plug. Check the plug for signs of deterioration or thread damage. Provisions for cleanouts should also be found at the foot of secondary drains. Be suspicious of main drains wrapped with insulation or rags, or held together with clamps or wire. These are indications of leaks or other problems.

Some houses may have a sump that contains a back-water valve with a 90-degree "L" angle on the outlet of the sump. This is to prevent malfunctioning sewer lines from adjacent properties from backing up into your house or into the subsoil drainage system. Check to see if they work. Locate the sewer line in the yard. (One homeowner, when trying to repair a clogged sewage line, was faced with a major excavation and expensive repair when the sewage line was found under the centre of the concrete driveway.) When the sewer line outlet is higher in elevation than the basement floor, look for a sump in the floor at the lowest point. Sumps are typically covered, grated or open and are used only to accumulate water runoff during rains and floor drain input. Some sumps have a submersible pump and mtor. Check the motor, float ball, electrical connections and ground. Could the location of the sump be a health problem? Check the location of floor drains. Some plumbing systems will have a trap primer installed in floor drains to prevent their traps from losing their water seal by evaporation. Maintaining the water seal prevents the backflow of sewer gas into the area where the traps are installed.

Septic Tanks

A septic tank may be constructed of metal, fibreglass, concrete, cement block or pressure-treated wood. Unless the building site is remote, pre-cast tanks are the rule. A typical three-bedroom house should have a 1,000-gallon septic tank. Try to obtain a diagram of the septic tank's layout, showing the location of the tank, distribution box, pipes, manholes and disposal field. Also determine the level of the ground water and how deep below the ground the drain tiles are. Clogged pipes and saturated, poorly draining gravel beds can greatly shorten the life of a leach field. Make a note of any surface soil depressions over the field or recent digging. If there is both a well and a septic tank, determine the distance between them. Unless they are a considerable distance apart, there is a real danger that the septic tank and field could leach effluent into the well. Signs of a system failure are sluggish drains, foul water backing up from the ground floor drains into the house or smelly water surfacing around the leach field.

It is a good idea to inspect the tank by removing the cover. Look at the inlet and outlet devices. The inlet should be above the liquid level of the tank to allow for momentum rise in the liquid level during discharges to the tank. This drop prevents backwater and standing solid material from coming back into the house. The outlet opening should penetrate just far enough below the liquid level of the septic tank to provide a balance between sludge and scum. Inspect the sludge and scum accumulations with a long stick. When a stick test shows 1 foot of sludge in the bottom of the tank, it is time to have it pumped out. Normally a septic tank depends on gravity to work, although some have supplementary elements that can make them work more effectively. One such element is a grease trap. This plumbing fixture is located inside the house between the drain and the main waste line. The trap separates grease and oils out of water, collecting it for periodic removal by hand.

A common supplement to a septic system is a cesspool. Cesspools are meant to handle "grey water," which is waste water from tubs, showers, sinks and washing machines. This effluent contains no solid waste and therefore does not need as much treatment as "black water" from toilets. A cesspool can consist of a 50-gallon container with holes punched all over, filled with stones and buried several feet in the ground. A wasteline runs from the house and empties into the cesspool.

During your inspection it is a good idea to sketch a map of the plumbing system. This will help you analyze the potential for adding fixtures, finishing the basement or adding an outdoor hot tub.

CHECKPOINTS
✓✓✓✓✓✓✓✓✓✓✓

Supply System
____ well
____ underground pipe

Main Water Line
____ condition
____ meter
____ location
____ shut-off valve
____ age
____ size of pipe

Type of Pipes
____ galvanized
____ cast iron
____ copper
____ plastic
____ other
____ condition
____ insulation
____ sizes of pipe
____ plastic jacketed pipes
____ penetrating concrete
____ lead-free solder certification
____ how secured
____ shut-off valves
____ anti-siphon vacuum breaker
____ water hammer
____ unusual sounds
____ water pressure
____ outside plumbing and faucets
____ sweating pipes
____ pressure balancing valve
____ last updated
____ mechanical engineer approved
____ certified testing agency approved

Well
____ depth
____ hand-dug
____ driven

____ drilled
____ quality of water
____ condition of pump
____ pump type
____ water pressure
____ water storage tank size
____ well run dry
____ original well driller report
____ water sample after heavy
rainfall

Drainage System
____ galvanized pipes
____ cast-iron pipes
____ copper pipes
____ plastic pipes
____ other
____ pitch of drain pipes
____ condition
____ clean out openings
____ storm/sewage drain separation
____ pipe repairs
____ wall or ceiling access panels
____ distance of vents/stacks above
roof
____ soil stack
____ how secured
____ vent pipes
____ automatic air valves
____ traps under fixtures
____ sewage back-up valve
____ smell at drain
____ floor drain
____ trap primer for floor drain
____ radon trap
____ storm sump
____ grease and oil trap
____ sump pump
____ last cleaned
____ depth of sewage drain
underground

_____ certified testing agency
      approved

Septic Tanks
_____ location
_____ tank type
_____ distribution box
_____ manholes
_____ cesspools

_____ tank size
_____ ground water level
_____ soil condition
_____ last cleaned
_____ disposal tile location
_____ grease trap
_____ sewage pump
_____ certified testing agency
      approved

CONSUMER TIPS

- If you are buying real estate as an investment, it is a prudent to purchase within a geographic area of your principal residence that is within a four-hour drive. This is just a general guideline, of course. The point is that you want to be able to conveniently monitor and/or maintain your property.
- Ask the fire department for locations of fire hydrants and the time it takes for the fire truck to arrive at the location. Note a house on a hill may take longer for a fire truck to reach the site. Ask about the frequency of fires in the neighbourhood you are considering, relative to other areas in the general community. If there are a high number of fires, the neighbourhood could be a risk area, especially if arson is suspected. Also ask about the incidence of false alarms in the neighbourhood you are considering. This also gives an indication of potential problems.
- If you are interested in applying for rezoning, building a new house, or renovating an old house, ask for the following information as your circumstances dictate: zoning maps, zoning regulations, building codes, building permit application forms and instructions, municipal codes, regional master plans, soil conditions, etc.

- Check to see what restrictions on fire safety, security, noise, parking, and other matters may exist. For example, is there a community plan? What type of bylaw zoning is there, and is it changing. Is there a rezoning potential for higher or different use? Is there a land use contract? What about possible "non-conforming" status use of older or revenue buildings?
- What image does the media or the public in general have about a certain area? Is it positive or negative, and why? The perception of people as to the image of the area may have an influencing effect on rental or purchase decisions.

▼

CHAPTER 8

Domestic Hot-Water System

gas or ?
electric

THE PREVIOUS CHAPTER on plumbing reviewed the water system as a whole — how it flows in, through and out of the house. This chapter will take a look at the hot-water heating system as an appliance connected to the plumbing. The inner mechanisms and types of hot-water heaters are similar in many ways to heating systems discussed in detail in Chapter 6. The various types of domestic hot-water systems, their components, tank capacity and water quality will also be covered in this section.

Types of Hot-water Heaters

There are many types of water heaters, although natural gas, electric, oil and propane are the most common. Tank walls may be lined with glass, stone, copper, copper alloy or galvanized. Occasionally you will find a hot-water heater wrapped in an insulation blanket. The blanket should have a certified testing agency label. Make a note of the data on the manufacturer's label, which is usually found on the side of the tank. By contacting the supplier you should be able to identify the age of the unit, any warranties still in effect, the type of liner on the tank, its capacity and ratings.

Gas-fired

Natural gas water heaters have a quick recovery rate. They burn "clean," with no impurities such as smoke or other particle matters in the flue gas. The operation is quiet as it has no motor or pump. You may come across a high-efficiency gas hot-water heater where the exhaust gas is pumped out through the walls by means of a pipe. Here there is no need for a conventional chimney or chimney flue. However, the need to call in specially trained personnel may make it more expensive to service.

In a gas-fired heater, the gas supply line, insulation blanket and pipe installation must meet all requirements of the plumbing/gas code. A gas shut-

When is your turn for a hot bath?

A couple with a large family bought an expensive home that was finished with numerous amenities, including two whirlpool bathtubs. However, after moving in they discovered the hot water tank had insufficient capacity to keep up with the need for hot water, and there was no room in the house to add another tank.

off valve should be located near the tank. There should be no debris blocking the draft diverters over the flue opening at the top of the heater. The draft diverter chimney flue should have few elbows and should be pitched upwards toward the chimney. If the flue pipes drop downward, they can easily fill up with soot and prevent flue gases from escaping properly. Check the connections of the pipe at the chimney. Poorly fitted, corroded and loose fittings can cause the emission of toxic fumes into the house. To prevent the possibility of backdrafting down the chimney when the heater is in operation, the heater should have its own source of fresh air supply through a duct close to the burner area.

Place your hand near the diverter. There should be no downward movement of air on your hand. If you do feel air, there could be a chimney downdraft or pipe blockage. Note the colour of the pilot light in the burner area. If, instead of blue, it is yellow or orange, it is in need of adjustment. The smell of gas in the area should be reported to the owner. If you are familiar with the equipment, you may wish to turn off the flame and examine the burners with a flashlight to see if they are clogged. Note any large deposits of rust scale in the burner area.

Oil-fired

Similar to gas-fired units, oil-fired burners need their own air supply. These units are noisier and require regular cleaning of filters, fan blades and nozzle. They should be serviced twice annually. While in operation, check the burner flame. It should be a symmetrical bright yellow with no trace of smoke at its tip. There should be a foot valve to prevent oil from spilling onto the floor in case of malfunction. Check the fuel line and the fuel tank for leaks. If the fuel tank is buried, ask the owner its location and capacity. Check the exhaust flue and connections for corrosion. Ensure the draft regulator (usually found along the flue pipe) is operational and free of debris.

Electric

Electric hot-water heaters are quiet, require minimal maintenance and generally have a long life expectancy. The tanks have larger capacities because their recovery rate is slower than gas or oil units. They need a separate electric circuit and breaker, and do not need a flue or fresh air venting. No other appliance should be tied into this circuit. The heating elements inside the tank are of different types such as strap-on, immersion, in-tank or side-arm. Some electric heaters may be wrapped with a certified insulation blanket.

Built-in Tank System

You may find a water heater that is part of a boiler, which is also used to heat the entire house. There is usually an adjusting valve so that during the summer months only domestic hot water is supplied and not heat. A system using a hot-water boiler is usually inefficient and will require replacement after 20 years. Carefully look for any signs of corrosion or deterioration on bolts, pipes and connections. When inspecting this type of system, it is recommended that you let all of the hot-water faucets in the house run at the same time to observe the flow and clarity of the water at each faucet. If the flow is irregular, it is possible that the water lines or coils are obstructed by mineral deposits. Replacing parts can be expensive and servicing will be difficult if the boiler is under a stairwell or similar restricted area.

Tankless Water Heater

A tankless water heater is most often located at the point of water use—the kitchen, laundry or bathroom. The heaters are typically gas-fired or electric. An electric heater will have a separate electrical circuit and the gas model will require a flue. Both types should be professionally installed according to building code requirements. The electrical wiring or gas line and billing meter must be large enough to handle this type of heater. Tankless heaters will vary in their capacity and the degree to which they can regulate the outlet temperature. Check any unit accessories such as low-flow faucets and shower head restrictors. Repair costs for tankless water heaters are generally higher than for conventional storage water heaters. They are best suited to homes in which water use is infrequent and low flow rates are required.

Hot-water Tank Components

A water heater system consists of four basic components:
- an insulated sheet-metal housing containing the tank which stores hot water
- the heating source to produce the hot water
- the controls, which regulate water temperature, power input, safety devices and water circulation
- the plumbing, piping and valves, which transmit the cold water to the heater and the hot water to the points of use.

Water heaters of different sizes vary in power input and storage capacity. The greater the power input (kilowatt capacity), the faster the heat recovery (the time required to heat up a quantity of water to a predetermined temperature) and the less storage (tank size) is required. Where heat recovery time is not critical, a smaller power input and larger storage capacity may be an advantage. On the other hand, a large family or a family with infants may require a faster heat recovery time because of the increased use of clothes washers, dishwashers and showers.

40 gal tank min. (handwritten)

The number of occupants and their requirements will determine your water heater size. The average household uses 10 gallons of hot water per individual per day. Therefore, the minimum requirement for a family of four is a 40-gallon gas- or oil-fired tank. As electric tanks have a slower recovery rate, that same family will require a 55-gallon electric hot-water tank. The large volume of water used for a hot tub, for instance, may necessitate a second tank.

Hot-water Tank

The hot-water tank should be located in an area where leakage of the tank or connections will not result in damage to the surrounding area or to lower floors of the structure. Alternatively, there should be a drain pan under the heater that is at least 2 inches deep and 2 inches greater in diameter than the heater. The pan should be connected by a pipe to an adequate drain. The heater should be located close to the bathroom, kitchen and laundry areas. This will reduce the heat loss that occur in long runs of pipe and will shorten the length of time required to produce hot water at the faucets or appliances. Where long runs are involved, the pipes should be insulated to reduce heat loss and maintain hot water at the point of use. The heater should not be located where water lines could be subjected to freezing temperatures.

A drain valve will be located at the bottom of the tank. Open the valve and note the colour of the water. A sediment buildup is often present at the bottom of the tank. Too much deposit will act as an insulation and prevent the heat from reaching the water. With your ear against the tank, listen for any unusual rumbling, whistling, sizzling or cracking noises. This could mean a deteriorating tank. If the tank appears quite old, it may be best not to inspect the drain but to ask the owner when the tank was last drained or flushed.

Drain Valve. Listen to tank (handwritten)

Heating Source

As noted earlier, the manner in which the water is heated will vary depending on the type of heater. Examine the exterior and areas around the base of the water heater for signs of corrosion. Remove the metal service cover to inspect the inside walls, the burner, thermostat or element areas. Check for dampness and debris in the insulation. Condensation and rust on the inner tank are sometimes due to heavy hot-water draw-off (e.g., peak laundry days). The higher the water temperature, the greater the corrosive activity. For a tank to be completely free of rust is almost impossible. An anti-corrosion anode may be immersed in the water to provide extra protection against corrosive action.

Controls

On top or on the side of the tank, free from any obstacles, is the temperature/pressure relief valve. This spring-loaded device opens automatically when the temperature and pressure within the tank exceed the limit. Check the thermostat and control settings of the heater. Verify the actual temperatures by holding a thermometer under the hot- and then the cold-water faucets. For energy

~120 °F

efficiency and safety, hot water should not be more than 48 degrees C. Cold water temperature will fluctuate, depending on where it is coming from. Water temperatures should not be any higher than necessary.

> ## Have you tasted the water?
> After purchasing some property to develop a horse ranch, an Edmonton farmer discovered that the water was so iron-contaminated and unfit for human consumption, that it was necessary to have fresh water trucked in weekly.

Secure your water pressure gauge to a faucet and test for water pressure. Seventy-five

75 psi water press. req'd.

pounds per square inch (psi) is adequate for normal water use. Water pressure will vary throughout the day depending upon overall usage in the neighbourhood. Some appliances like dishwashers and toilets may not operate under low water pressure. Usually a pressure regulating valve is found at the main water line to reduce incoming pressure to the required service pressure and to maintain it at the point desired. High water temperature (caused by an improperly set or faulty temperature control) and high water pressure (caused by high incoming water line pressure) will shorten the life of the tank. In addition, an over-pressure condition may rupture the tank, and the steam and compressible gas generated by overheating can explode the tank. A combination temperature/pressure relief valve guards against the conditions of overheating and over-pressure.

Near the top of the tank is a vacuum relief valve. This device permits air to enter and prevents vacuum conditions that could siphon the water from the system and burn out the heater. The safety relief valve should be periodically tested by lifting the lever handle situated on top of the valve. If there is any persistent dripping after you have tested the valve, it may be due to some foreign material fouling up the valve seat. By lifting the lever again it should clear itself.

Plumbing

At the top of the tank you will see openings marked cold and hot. The cold water pipe enters the tank through the cold inlet and the water heated by the tank leaves through the line connected to the hot-water outlet. Check this out by touching the pipes. If the cold water line pipe is hot, the connections have been reversed. The relief valve should be piped to a sink drain, floor drain or out of the house. If the pipe leads to the outside, its size must meet the requirements of local plumbing codes so that it will not freeze up during winter use.

Check the floor under the heater and note any moisture accumulation. The moisture could be caused by leaks from element gaskets, the pressure relief valve or from threaded pipe connections. Excessively cold water from the source of supply can cause condensation on the pipes or the bottom of the tank.

Water Softeners

Some houses may be equipped with a manual or automatic water softener that removes the calcium and magnesium from the water. The simplest and most common type consists of a tank containing a thick bed of tiny synthetic resin or mineral beads, supported on a layer of gravel or other material. When the incoming water flows downward through this bed, the "hard" calcium and magnesium ions are taken up by the resin and "soft" sodium ions are released in exchange. When the resin has given up all its sodium ions, it must be recharged or regenerated with salt. Examine the tank and its valves for any signs of corrosion. Ask the owner for operating instructions and how often it requires recharging.

Water Impurities

There are a number of impurities in water that will affect its colour, smell and taste. The use of water filters, as mentioned in the previous chapter, can eliminate a good number of the offensive elements. If the water is sufficiently hard, it will promote the formation of scale and soap curd in the water. The scale deposits will accumulate on any heating elements within the tank, causing premature failure. Sometimes the scale will break off and fall to the bottom of the tank and cover the lower element. Should this scale harden, it cannot be removed and the water heater may become useless. The hard water conditions can also damage dishwashers, clog water pipes and make washed clothing appear dull and dingy.

Water Test !

Find a faucet over a basin. First let the cold water run and then the hot. Do you notice any discolouration or smell in the water? Taste the water. Does it taste bitter, fishy or earthy? Does the basin have coloured water stains around the drain? Rust-coloured water could indicate that old galvanized plumbing pipes are still in use. A defective pipe or damaged tank lining will also cause rust in the water. Black particles suspended in the water are usually the result of bacterial action. Although there may be no sign of discolouration at first, if left standing and exposed to air, or if it is heated, a reddish-brown rust precipitate will develop in iron-bearing water. This iron bacteria often gives an unpleasant taste and odour to the water. There are several methods of removing iron, such as iron filters, sand filters, chlorination and filtration of the hot-water tank.

Many types of odour develop in stored hot water. The most common and best understood is from hydrogen sulphide gas (rotten egg smell). Sometimes the gas occurs in the water as it comes from the ground, but the smell is not noticeable until it is heated. Heating water drives out dissolved gases. Hydrogen from an overactive anode inside the water heater helps to flush out other gases and can accelerate the odour problem. Removal of the magnesium anode may stop or reduce the odour, but if the system is infected with iron bacteria the problem will persist after the anode is removed. This removal may shorten the life of a glass-lined water heater, as the anode is a protection against corrosion and the manufacturer may void the water heater warranty.

Unpleasant odour or taste can also be attributed to an uncovered or poorly covered well, surface drainage into the source supply or a supply that is too close to a septic field or dugouts where algae are likely to form. If you notice a serious problem, check with the city to find out if the water is chlorinated or if fluoride has been added. You may wish to have the water tested at a certified laboratory.

DIAGRAM 5: Common Impurities in Water

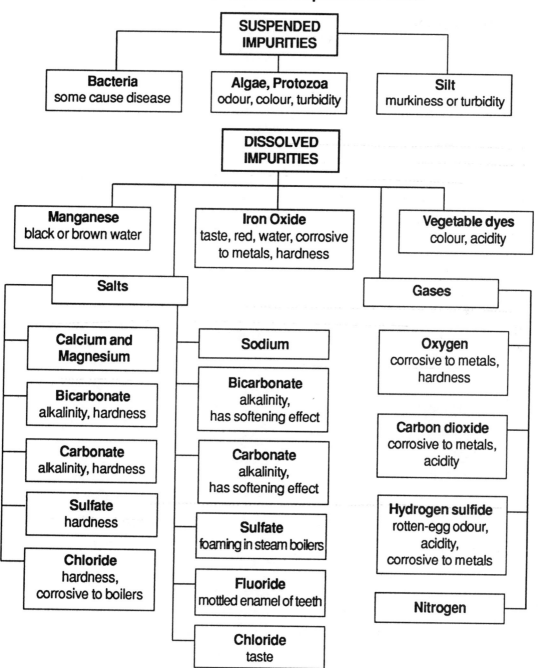

CHECKPOINTS
✔✔✔✔✔✔✔✔✔✔✔

Type
____ natural gas
____ electric
____ oil
____ propane
____ exhaust vent
____ fresh-air vent
____ main fuel shut-off valve
____ burner/element condition
____ manufacturer
____ model number
____ serial number
____ capacity (# gallons/litres)
____ condition
____ age
____ pilot light colour
____ last replaced
____ manufacturer's warranty
____ certified testing agency approved

Location
____ basement
____ crawl space
____ main floor
____ other

Other Features
____ drain valve
____ shut-off valve
____ floor drain
____ floor drain with radon trap
____ drain pan
____ floor drain trap primer
____ vacuum relief valve
____ backflow preventers

____ pressure regulating valve
____ hot and cold reversed
____ safety relief valve
____ anti-siphon vacuum breaker
____ water pressure at taps
____ pressure balancing valve
____ pipes insulated
____ water pressure
____ water temperature
____ thermostat setting

Water Condition
____ hard
____ soft
____ odour
____ discolouration

Water Treatment
____ filtration
____ chlorination
____ fluoridation
____ last serviced

Water Softener
____ manufacturer
____ model number
____ serial number
____ age
____ operating manual
____ condition
____ capacity
____ automatic
____ last serviced
____ manufacturer's warranty
____ certified testing agency approved

CONSUMER TIPS

- A prospective tenant or home buyer will want to have convenient transportation routes. Whether it is a bus, subway, rapid transit, freeway, ferry, or other mode of transportation, the quality of transportation will have a bearing on your rental price and prospects if you are buying the house for revenue purposes, or resale price when you sell it.
- Look at the size and shape of the lot. The issue has to do with subdivision or rezoning potential, resale marketability and general enjoyment.
- Look for trends in the community you are considering. Are people moving in or out, and why? What is the average age? Type of employment? Income level? Family size? If the population is increasing, it will generally create more demand for rental and resale housing. Conversely, if it is decreasing, the opposite will occur. If the population is an older population, people may prefer downsizing to condominiums rather than buying smaller houses. There are many variables to consider.
- The layout of the land is an important consideration. If there is a hill along the property, it could cause drainage problems in terms of water collecting around the house. Water could collect under the foundation of the house, thereby causing settling, assuming there is only soil under the foundation. Maintaining the property in terms of cutting the grass could be more difficult if the property is irregular rather than level. These are just some of the issues to consider.
- Are the parking facilities outdoors? Open carport or garage? Do you feel there is sufficient lighting for security and protection? Is it a long distance from the parking spot to your home? Is there parking space available for a boat, trailer, second car or recreational vehicle? Is there adequate visitor parking?
- Privacy is an important consideration and has to be thoroughly explored. For example, you want to make sure that the sound insulation between the walls, floors and ceilings of you're house is sufficient to enable you to live comfortably without annoying other family members, tenants or neighbours, or having them annoy you.
- Look at the exterior of the house and landscaping of other houses in the neighbourhood. Is there a mix of brand-new houses along with older ones? How many houses "look" tenant-occupied? How does the house you are considering purchasing look in relation to those around you?

• Check with your real estate agent to see what other houses are for sale in the same neighbourhood and ask what the asking prices are. Check to see which houses have recently sold and for what price. Ask how long those houses had been listed.

CHAPTER 9

Electrical Wiring

Y OU DO NOT have to be an expert to detect electrical defects in a house's wiring. However, you should know some basic terminology and safety facts about electricity, and the rest is mostly common sense. At the point where your inspection has raised considerable doubts about the wiring system, you may wish to consult a certified electrician or electrical inspector. They will be familiar with the electrical codes governing almost all aspects of wiring installations.

Electrical measurements are expressed in terms of volts and currents. The volt is the unit used in measuring electrical pressure, similar to the unit of "pounds per square inch" when measuring water pressure. The ampere is the unit used to measure electrical rate of flow. It is similar to the flow of water in gallons per minute. Resistance is measured by ohms. It is the property of materials to oppose the flow of current. The larger the wire (or pipe) the more current (water) it can carry. A current of electricity is a stream of electrons (negatively charged particles) moving along a conductor. A conductor is a substance that transmits an electric current. Most metals and watery solutions are good conductors of electricity. Since the human body has a high water content, it is also a conductor through which electricity will travel.

Grounding is the connection of the electrical service to the earth. A house's electricity is grounded to the earth through a wire. Should there be a malfunction or short circuit, electricity safely finds an easy route to the earth through this wire. Electrical grounding is an essential safety precaution to minimize shocks and prevent damage from lightning. Where electricity has not been grounded, the electricity is live and will transmit a fatal charge to a person who comes in contact with an electrical circuit. As electricity does not travel through rubber, this becomes a means of grounding yourself from electrical charges. Wearing rubber-soled shoes and using tools with rubber handles will provide you with the necessary protection to carry on your inspection.

Your inspection of the electrical wiring will be carried out primarily inside the house, although some examination from the outside is necessary as well. Make a list of all the electrical appliances, from the smallest to the largest, that you see in the home. Make allowance for future equipment you may purchase such as computers, welders, air compressors, hot tubs, etc. You will need to ensure that the electrical outlets, wiring and breakers are sufficient and accurate. A review of the electrical panel, lighting and outlets, size of the electrical service and the kinds of wire needed for different types of service will also be covered to guide you through your inspection.

Exterior Power Supply

Try to count the number of electrical wires coming from the utility pole into the house, making sure to separate out the telephone and cable wires for the television and radio. Generally three wires provide a 220-volt service and two wires indicate 110-volt service. If no wires are seen, the wiring may be entering the house through an underground service conduit. This conduit must be 3 inches in diameter, connected to a 200-amp meter base and a certified 200-amp service panel. This will be discussed further under the heading "service size." All electrical cable must be flame retardant as well as moisture, fungus and corrosive resistant. Its maintenance is the responsibility of the utility company. For safety reasons, wires should not be hanging in locations where they can be reached easily. A woman was electrocuted because she mistook the service wire on her balcony for a clothes line.

The service head, where the wires meet the house, should be no less than 15 feet and no more than 30 feet above the ground. Some exceptions of 11 feet have been made for low buildings where 15 feet is not obtainable. You should notice a drip loop in the wires to prevent rainwater from entering the house. Notice any frayed or bare lines, or deteriorating insulation and loose connections. The electrical meter and socket should be self-contained at a height of 6 to 7 feet above ground. A recessed meter may be positioned as low as 4 feet above ground if it is covered by a protective shield and is not more than 2 feet from a chimney or inside corner. Check the surface of the metal meter box for corrosion. If the meter is recessed, try to remove the protective shield. Often insulation is stuck behind this protection. As you separate the insulation, notice any dampness and wood deterioration. Notice if the meter wheel is spinning rapidly. This will indicate that an unusually high amount of electricity is being used at that time.

Check to see if the system is properly grounded. Find the main water meter and cold-water pipe coming in from the street. There should be a wire connection at the street side of the water meter. The wire will be a #6 or #3 gauge copper wire, depending on the amps of the main service wire. If it is found on the house side, removal of the water meter may break this ground circuit. To eliminate this problem, many older homes have a jumper wire clamped onto the house side of the cold-water pipe connecting over to the street side of this pipe. At the point where the ground wire touches the water pipe, see if the ground connection is properly secured. The pipe must be metal and not plastic. Sometimes you will see that

> **It's shocking!**
>
> One inspection revealed that live electrical wires were fed through heating ducts. From the ducts they fed into a homemade metal service panel box that had circuit breakers held in place with paper clips!

the grounding wire is attached to a rod extending several feet into the ground. Make sure that this rod cannot be pulled out of the ground. Some codes require a double ground, so you may see two rods.

Electrical Panel

From the meter the main power line is connected to the main service panel, which can be found almost anywhere in the house. It should be in a dry location as even a modest amount of moisture can damage the circuit breakers. The high humidity level in a damp basement will cause serious corrosion problems with the service panel. The inside of this box contains the main fuses, circuit breakers or branch circuit fuses. The circuit breakers may be the cartridge, toggle, or push-button-type switches or plug-type fuses. The purpose of these fuses and circuit breakers is to protect the wiring from overheating when too much current is passing through. These fuses or circuit breakers act as a safety device to shut off the current, thus preventing a fire. If the circuit breaker trips or the fuse blows in a branch circuit, the electricity will be lost to the room or rooms controlled by that branch. The switch-like circuit breakers should operate easily, and lock crisply into an on or off position. If corrosion has set in they will have a sort of mushy feeling when switching them on and off. As a cautionary measure, avoid touching anything in the box as it contains enough electricity to kill. Instead, turn off the main electrical power switch before testing fuses. If you must trip the breakers without turning off the power, do so with your left hand while keeping your right hand in your pocket and standing beside the service panel — never in front of it in case of an explosion. Before you test the main disconnect switch and the individual circuit breakers for the branch circuits, check with the owner. Some houses have sensitive electrical systems or appliances plugged into outlets that may require resetting after the power has been switched off.

All homes have three general types of circuits: lighting, small appliance (e.g., radio, television, vacuum cleaner) and individual appliance circuit (e.g., refrigerator, stove, dishwasher, etc.). On the cover plate all fuses or breaker terminals should be properly labelled. Hopefully there is space for adding more fuses or breaker terminals, as an adequately sized panel box will eliminate the need for costly rewiring. Unused breaker openings should be properly covered.

When you look behind the cover plate containing the circuit breakers and fuses, you will notice numerous wires of a variety of sizes, colours and arrangements. If the layout of these wires or their contacts are held in place with tape, or if they do not appear neat and consistent, some electrical work may have been done by a novice. Should this be the case, take a picture of the inside of the service panel and show it to a qualified electrician for examination. Make a general inspection of the wires and cables that leave the panel. Follow a few of them until they disappear into the ceiling, walls or floor. Notice whether the insulation around the wires is in tact. Look for evidence of arcing, overheating, burned insulation, loose connections and spliced wires. Transformers for low-voltage wiring may emit a humming noise.

Service Size

A house wiring system capable of handling immediate and future loads is essential for convenience and safety. This will avoid voltage drops, which impair the proper operation of most electrically operated appliances. The size of the service may vary from 60 amps in a small house to 600 amps in a large one. As the size of the service increases, so does the requirement for a larger-diameter conduit. If the size of the service needs to be increased, it can become a costly venture, especially if underground conduits must be excavated and replaced with larger ones.

If the house has less than 60 amps, you should check your present use to see if this will restrict your lifestyle. A modern home without electrical heating will have a minimum 100-ampere service, 1-inch conduit and an approved circuit panel box with a minimum of 30 circuit breakers. A larger home with electrical heating will usually have 200-amp service along with the required 3-inch conduit and an approved circuit panel with a minimum capacity for 40 circuit breakers. An electrically heated home with only 125-amp service, for instance, may prove troublesome and will limit the electrical supply.

The size of the electrical service can be determined by examining the size of the cable and the writing that appears on the sheathing of the cable. Examining the size of the cable alone may not give you an accurate assessment. Don't be misled by the electrical rating stamped on the metal surface of the distribution box. These readings are the manufacturer restrictions that indicate the maximum allowable service for the box and have no relationship to the size of the service or number of fuses. In the same way, the rating on the electrical meter is the maximum allowed by the manufacturer. In some cases you will find inappropriate fuse sizing, which also leads to misperceptions of the actual electrical capacity of the system.

VARIOUS HOUSEHOLD WIRE SIZES AND TYPES		
Wire Amperage Rating (amp)	Wire Size (Copper) (No.)	Wire Size Aluminum (No.)
15	14	12
20	12	10
30	10	8
40	8	6
55	6	4
70	4	2
100	2	0
200	000 or 3/0	250 MCM

Note: All wire guages are AWG (American Wire Guage) except 250 MCM, which stand for 1,000 circular millimeters.

Types of Wire

The size and type of household wiring will vary for proper protection and usage. You may wish to refer to an electrical wire gauge chart, which indicates the size of wiring used for different amperage ratings. You might find it helpful to visit an electrical supply store for samples of wiring for comparison. Note that the smaller the wire, the larger the gauge number. Now check the wiring for the breakers and fuses to ensure they are properly sized. Most modern homes have two basic kinds of electric wire: flexible armoured cable, called BX; and plastic-covered wire, known under such trade names as Loomex or Romex. If installed properly, they present no hazard. Knob-and-tube wire is old wire and you should plan for eventual replacement. You can inspect the wiring by looking inside electrical receptacle boxes, between open floor joists in the basement, in the attic or at the service panel.

If manufactured before 1977, some electrical wiring may consist of aluminum. The outer covering of the cable will be marked about every 12 inches with the word aluminum or an abbreviation such as "ALUM" or "AL." Some houses will have all aluminum wiring, all copper wiring or a combination of both. Unfortunately, when the insulation is stripped from aluminum and the wire is exposed to air, it begins to form a white-coloured oxide, which is a poor electrical conductor and causes a resistance to electrical flow. This, along with expansion and contraction, leads to a poor connection and overheating at the switch, receptacle or terminal. Overheating can be prevented when specifically designed and approved outlets, marked with CO/ALR, are used to assure a

DIAGRAM 6: Samples of Aluminum Wire

AL ACM NUAL NMD – 7

Manufactured after May, 1977 marked either aluminum ACM, ALUM ACM or AL ACM

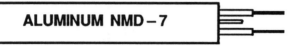

ALUMINUM NMD – 7

Manufactured before May, 1977

DIAGRAM 7: CO/ALR Wall Switches and Receptacles

NOTE: For devices other than standard receptacles and switches, the marking, which indicates that the equipment is suitable for use with aluminum wiring, is CU-AL.

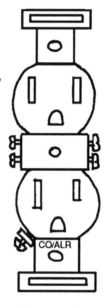

Receptacle

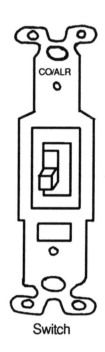

Switch

Note where the wires are connected to receptacles and switches. The wire shoud be formed in a clockwise direction around the screw into three-quarters of a complete loop.

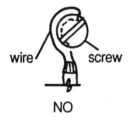

wire   screw

NO

NO

YES

"Special service" wire connector

good connection through the use of compatible materials and larger contact arcs. Check the switch and wall receptacle by removing the cover plates. Both must be approved for use with either type of wiring, which is indicated by the marking "CO/ALR" (copper aluminum revised). The aluminum wire should be wound around the screw in a clockwise direction into three-quarters of a complete loop. Inside the main service panel exposed aluminum connections should be covered with an oxidation-inhibitor compound to help maintain a solid connection. Note that electrical receptacles, wall switches and fuse boxes originally designed for use with copper wiring are not satisfactory for use with aluminum wiring.

Where solid aluminum wire has been connected to stranded wire, special service connectors should be present. These should also be used with hot-water tanks, baseboard heaters and similar types of cycling loads. For services other than standard receptacles and switches, the marking "CU-AL" indicates that the equipment is suitable with aluminum wiring. This marking would also appear on circuit breakers.

Go from room to room checking each outlet and switch for warm cover plates and strange or distinctive odours. Watch for intermittent flickering of lights that can't be traced to some external causes. Listen for any unusual static on the radio or television. These are all signs that the wiring should be checked by a qualified electrician. Note: some wire connections are covered with a paste-like oxide inhibitor to keep the air away from the aluminum.

Lighting and Outlets

Make a note of the location and the number of light switches and electrical outlets in each room and hallway. All outlets, switches and junction boxes should have covers to protect against an electric shock. Are all of the outlets functional and are there enough to meet your needs? Numerous extension cords or several appliances plugged into the same outlet shows a lack of sufficient outlets and the possibility of a circuit overload. Blackened faces on electrical outlets suggest there have been short circuits. Many times lights will dim before fuses blow. Do the kitchen lights dim when the refrigerator starts? This could indicate that the electrical circuit is close to being overloaded, or that the refrigerator needs to be plugged into a different outlet. When more than one appliance comes on at the same time, it usually results in a blown fuse. If the wiring is fairly new, the circuits are improperly divided and must be rearranged. Older wiring will have to be replaced.

Are the outlets the old-fashioned two-slot type or the newer grounded variety that will accommodate three-pronged plugs? A properly wired two-slot system will accept a three-pronged plug with an adapter that is fixed with a screw to assure grounding. You will notice that one of the receptacle slots is smaller than the other. This is the "hot" side. Take your electrical test probe and insert it into the small slot. Take the other probe and hold it onto the screw

[handwritten margin note: Enough outlets?]

[handwritten note at bottom: small slot + ground screw]

on the cover or the semi-circular ground hole. If it is designed for a three-pronged plug, a glow should be present at the test lamp. If not, then either the outlet is dead or it is not properly grounded. If you get current from the long slot and the ground hole or screw, the connection is not right and you have cross polarity. If you must pull out the switch or receptacle outlet to check its wiring, play it safe and first shut off the circuit breaker.

In newer homes some outlets are protected by a ground fault circuit interrupter (GFCI). These devices provide instant protection from a potentially fatal electric shock caused by a ground fault in an electrical tool or appliance. GFCI protection is usually found in laundry rooms, bathrooms, workshops and outdoor outlets. It can be recognized by a "test" and "reset" button built into receptacles, or the device can be found at the main service panel. These buttons should be tested once a month to ensure the device is operating properly.

Test and operate all light switches. Do the lights flicker? Do switches feel worn? Check the quality and condition of the fixtures and how they have been mounted on the walls or ceiling. Pay particular attention to exterior wall-mounted light fixtures that may have corroded internal parts.

Before completing your electrical inspection, check other wired items in the house such as telephone and cable outlets, door bells and intercoms, garburetor, sump pump and kitchen and bathroom fans to ensure they are functioning properly.

CHECKPOINTS
✔✔✔✔✔✔✔✔✔✔

EXTERIOR
Service Drop Wire
_____ location
_____ number of wires

Service Head
_____ location
_____ condition
_____ height
_____ service size

Electric Meter
_____ location
_____ meter condition

INTERIOR BASEMENT
Ground Connections
_____ grounded water pipe
_____ grounded to rod in earth
_____ other

Main Service Panel
_____ main fuse
_____ number of amps
_____ overfusing
_____ wire sizes
_____ separate circuits
_____ humming noise
_____ warm panel
_____ number of circuit breakers

_____ toggle switch circuit breakers
_____ pushbutton circuit breakers
_____ fuse circuit breakers
_____ room for expansion
_____ last updated
_____ electrical engineer approved
_____ certified testing agency
        approved

Kinds of Wire
_____ copper
_____ aluminum
_____ knob and tube
_____ wire sizes
_____ condition
_____ connections last tightened
_____ pigtailing of copper to
        aluminum
_____ paste-like oxide inhibitor

INTERIOR LIVING AREAS
Switches
_____ number of
_____ worn condition
_____ location
_____ warm switches
_____ single-pole switches
_____ double-pole switches
_____ three-way switches
_____ four-way switches
_____ timer switches
_____ rheostat switches
_____ dimmer switches
_____ photoelectric switches
_____ time clock
_____ other

Outlet Receptacles
_____ number of
_____ condition
_____ location
_____ three-prong
_____ two-prong
_____ warm receptacles
_____ ground fault circuit interrupter
_____ grounded
_____ open connections

Ceiling Light Fixtures
_____ condition
_____ location
_____ chandeliers
_____ decorative
_____ hallway
_____ entrance hall
_____ incandescent
_____ fluorescent
_____ recessed
_____ cornice wall brackets
_____ valance
_____ stairs
_____ closets
_____ other
_____ certified testing agency
        approved

Outdoor Lighting
_____ number of receptacles
_____ receptacles weatherproofed
_____ side wall lanterns
_____ area lighting
_____ ground fault circuit interrupter
_____ overhead wall
_____ porch
_____ garage

Low Voltage Wiring
_____ security alarm
_____ emergency lighting
_____ intercom system
_____ fire alarm
_____ remote control switching
_____ door bells
_____ TV and FM cable
_____ telephone cable
_____ other
_____ certified testing agency
        approved

CONSUMER TIPS

- Know the price range that you want when you are house searching, based on your available financing and real estate needs.
- Determine the type of ideal purchase package that you want (e.g. price and terms) as well as your "bottom line" fallback position. You want to know the maximum you are willing to pay and the terms that you can live with in your offer. Make sure that you don't compromise your own well-thought-out position.
- Real estate agents are a vital source of information about housing in the market you are considering. If the real estate board operates a multiple listing service (MLS) system, the real estate agent can locate a great deal of information for you through the MLS computer, such as price comparisons, historical data and trends, listing profile of property, etc. By doing that, you're better able to judge value and avoid overbidding.
- Check out the type of storage space available, including its location and size. Does there appear to be sufficient storage space for your needs, or will you have to rent a mini-locker to store excess items?
- If you are having a contractor do a remodelling job, rather than the whole house, ask the contractor for the following: plans and/or sketches of the work to be done; samples and literature showing different products that could be used; photographs of previous work completed, names of material suppliers, and subtrades used.
- Make sure if you have anyone to do renovation or repair on your house, that you have a detailed agreement in writing before you commit yourself and pay money. Never pay the whole amount at once, but in stages, as the work progresses, and the balance at the completion of the work, subject to holding back a portion of the project cost. In most provinces, this is referred to as a lien holdback for a period of time, to protect yourself from the contractor, workers, or suppliers filing a lien against your property for outstanding invoices. Ideally, have your lawyer look at the agreement before you sign it.
- Contact your local or provincial Home Builders' Association to see if they have sample contracts you can buy for contracting purposes.

CHAPTER 10

The Attic

THE DEGREE OF heat loss through a roof depends on the inside temperature conditions, ventilation of spaces between the insulation and the roof and the amount of insulation used. It is for these factors, then, that you will want to inspect the attic. You will find that most houses have an attic, although those with flat or vaulted cathedral ceilings with skylights do not. These types will be discussed at the end of this section as your inspection points will be different, although based on similar principles. The attics you do find will range from small finished or unfinished crawlspaces to full-sized lofts being used as an additional bedroom or hobby room. Of course, an unfinished attic is easiest to inspect as the ventilation openings, insulation and roof members are fully exposed. Again you will need your ladder, knee pads, notebook, thermometer, compass, awl, flashlight and face mask. Be cautious when walking in the attic to avoid damaging the ceiling below.

A frequent use of attics is for storage of outdated household items and keepsakes, seasonal clothing and sports equipment, etc. Be aware that items of considerable weight may cause the ceilings in the rooms below to crack. Stored boxes and furniture may have introduced active woodworm infestations that have spread to the sapwood in roof members. Also, flammable items such as stored household paints and exposed wiring become a fire hazard in attics where the ambient temperature is high. In older houses you may find a wealth of historical information buried under attic insulation. Such documentation can include drawings, specifications, photographs and other construction information that identify the architect, designer, builder and various trades. Notes on how many hours were spent by various contractors and how much they were paid can give you a real sense of the value of the house.

Moisture Problems

Moisture problems within an attic can be very complex and finding a solution may require considerable "detective" work. The most common sites for moisture to bypass into the attic are:

- floor or partitions intersecting exterior walls
- interior partitions intersecting ceilings
- ceilings above bathtubs that are adjacent to exterior walls
- areas above dropped ceilings
- oversized drilled openings in the ceiling for electrical, plumbing and heating connections
- recessed lighting
- attic hatch door.

Another cause of moisture buildup could be exhaust ducts that end in the attic, instead of running continuously to the outside through the roof. Exhaust ducts from clothes dryers and kitchen and bathroom fans can deposit large quantities of warm air containing water vapour and moisture. The duct joints and seams should be airtight and wrapped with insulation to reduce the possibility of condensation escaping.

If you are inspecting a house that has moisture problems in the basement or crawl space, the moist air will find a path that can lead directly to the attic. Leakage paths are created when the wooden framing dries and shrinks. Remember that the four basic means of moisture transport are gravity, capillary action, air transport and vapour diffusion. Wood has the ability to absorb large quantities of water vapour during cold periods and desorb (or diffuse) this moisture during warm periods. The moisture content of wood is far greater than what is noticeable on its surface.

By now you are probably familiar with the access openings into the attic or roof crawl spaces, since you have already come across these parts when you inspected the heating, electrical wiring, plumbing and domestic hot water. Review these notes along with those you made when inspecting the exterior and structure of the house. Follow up on those items you indicated needed closer review, such as a sagging roof and bird nest openings. Penetrations through the roof should be double-checked for potential water leakage from rain or melting snow. Always check under the valleys of the roof where leaks most often occur. Such deterioration in the supporting structure is likely caused by perforated acids from the accumulation of leaves, moss and lichen growth on the roof. Check purlin ends and rafter supports that have been built into solid gables. From the inside check for rotted wood and rusty nails. Can you see any daylight under the roof or around pipe penetrations through the roof?

In colder climates, many older houses experience water leaks caused by ice dams. Ice dams result from heat escaping from the attic, which warms the roof and causes the snow to melt. The water runs down the roof surface to the colder overhang of the roof, where it freezes. This causes a ledge of ice and backs up water, which can enter under the roofing shingles and drip down into the ceiling finish. A combination of proper ventilation and insulation prevents ice dams from occurring. Houses plagued with ice dams may be equipped with electrical heating cables around the exterior edge of the roof. Heat from the cable melts the ice so the water can run off. Check all electrical connections to ensure they are moisture proof and the outlets are in a dry place. All metal gutter downspouts and metal siding should be properly grounded. A short circuit could create a fire or shock hazard.

With your flashlight, check under the roof for dark areas of mildew, especially over kitchen and washroom areas. Does the underside of the roof sheathing feel soft? If so, rot could have set in. If the interior of the attic feels damp, humid and clammy, it could be a sign of inadequate ventilation.

Ventilation

The purpose of ventilation is to prevent an excessive buildup of winter frost and moisture condensation. It will also help to control snow melting on the roof's surface. During the summer months the attic ventilation will serve to keep the whole house cooler. It will also prevent heat buildup from solar radiation by replacing the warm air with cooler air and generally lowering surface temperatures. It is important to have a balanced ventilation, as too much can promote moisture decay and too little can reduce the pressure in an attic to a point that warm, moist air may be pulled from the living space into the attic. The arbitrary amount of venting for housing has been set at 1 square foot of unobstructed vent area for every 300 square feet of insulated ceiling. On low sloping roofs, air movement will be less and vent sizes should be increased. The greater the air space between the insulation and the roof sheathing, the more freely outdoor air can move through this space.

Ventilation openings should allow good cross-ventilation from end to end and from top to bottom. They should be located to limit the possible entry of wind-driven rain or snow, birds and insects. They should not be directly above a bathroom window that is frequently opened to let shower steam escape, as the wind will carry the moist air into the attic through the vent.

The most common vents are known as ridge, gable, roof, soffit and cupola. The primary purpose of soffit vents is to allow outside air to flow up into the unconditioned space and up to the highest portion of the ridge and out of the attic area through either ridge or gable vents. Soffit vents can be individually framed, continuously perforated or in long screened slots. Check the condition of the screens inside the vents. Gable vents should have slanted louvres. Inspect each vent carefully for any blockage, moisture, mildew and rot. The addition of attic insulation around soffit vents, for instance, may be blocking the movement of air. A baffle should be fitted between the rafters at the soffit to allow the air to be channelled into the attic.

Whole House and Attic Fans

You may find that an attic or house fan has been installed to alleviate uncomfortably hot temperatures in the house during summer months that is caused by inadequate attic ventilation. A whole house fan is centrally mounted on the attic floor and allows hot air to be drawn through a ceiling opening and exhausted through attic vents. Air exhausted by the fan is reached by cooler air coming from open screened doors and windows of the living quarters. At least two windows or a door should be open any time the fan is turned on. (Otherwise it can pull soot down the fireplace chimney or even through a furnace.) An automatic thermostat will turn on the fan when attic air exceeds a preset temperature, while a timer control will run the fan at fixed times of the day.

If the fan is positioned at a gable end (rather than in a central location), for it to operate efficiently all other attic vents must be closed off or a plenum must be connected from the fan to the opening in the living area. The fan should have an insulated cover to prevent heat loss through the fan during winter months. A safety component should be built into the switch that will shut off the fan and close the louvres during a fire or if the motor overheats. Find the switch and turn on the fan. Do you notice any noise or vibration? The fan may be stirring up loose fill insulation or fibreglass dust in the attic. While this type of fan can provide cooling to the house, it will not prevent the attic from overheating. Operational noise and unfiltered air drawn into the house are other disadvantages.

An attic fan should be mounted as high as possible in the roof surface or gable. This type of fan draws in outside air through vents in the soffits or eaves and other gables of the house. A properly located and working attic fan can prevent the attic from overheating and reduce attic temperatures by as much as 30 per cent. (It is not unusual during summer months for vented attics to reach temperatures above 180 degrees F.) An attic fan is smaller than a whole house fan and moves less air. The thermostat turns the fan on or off according to the temperature of the air in the attic. Notice the present temperature, and where the fan has variable speed controls. The fan may also be equipped with a dehumidistat to remove excess moisture from the attic. You will find the fan blades mounted directly on the motor shaft. Be careful not to put your hand in the fan area, as the motor can start at any time if it has a preset temperature setting.

You may come across a roof vent with a turbine wheel mounted on top of it. This device creates an updraft when the wind blows and helps to pull additional air out of the attic. Turbine vents operate best when air intake is provided by continuous soffit vents and wind velocity is up to 30 km per hour. The turbine's vent should be situated near the top of the roof ridge so that part of the turbine extends above the ridge. For proper movement of air to the vent, it should be clear of any obstacles such as trees or chimneys. On windless days, or if the turbine is worn out, this vent is no better or worse than an average roof vent. Because this type of fan may create negative pressure which will suck warm air and humidity through the ceiling leaks into the attic, there is a risk that more moisture than before will be brought into the attic. The noise of a worn-out turbine wheel fan may be bothersome.

How do I get into the attic?

A young couple bought a house which had an attic, but no attic access. They didn't think anything of it until one day, when inserting a hanging planter screw into the ceiling, water came running out of the hole. Moisture from a leak in the roof had collected over time and had rotted out the entire attic!

Insulation and Vapour Barriers

Insulation comes in a variety of types and thicknesses and serves the purpose of maintaining the house's ambient temperature—cooler in the summer and warmer in the winter. Does the insulation feel wet? Especially notice the areas around roof vents for signs of water penetration. What is the condition of the insulation throughout the attic area? It should be level and continuous, and come to the top of ceiling joists. (Inspecting insulation products will be covered in detail in Chapter 14 on energy conservation.)

In Canada vapour barriers are commonly used to resist diffusion of water vapour to protect the insulation and attic structure from moisture accumulation. A vapour barrier can be any material that is highly impermeable to water vapour. Some common materials are polyethylene, vinyl wallpaper, aluminum foil and asphalt laminated kraft paper. Joints and edges of the vapour barrier should be sealed. It is critical that the vapour barrier is located on the warmer side of the insulation—that is, between the heated living space and the insulation. Occasionally you will find the vapour barrier installed incorrectly, on the colder side of the insulation, where it can trap moisture. A vapour barrier in the wrong place is worse than no vapour barrier at all. If a vapour barrier is not present, you can purchase vapour barrier paints that can be applied to the ceiling and the inside surface of exterior walls. Vapour barriers should not be confused with air barriers.

Fire Safety

As none of the insulation products in use today will ignite spontaneously, fire safety normally involves minimizing the chances of any ignition source coming into contact with the insulation. All insulation should be kept at least 2 inches away from prefabricated insulated metal chimneys. The purpose of this air space is to prevent hot spots from developing in the chimney lining. A sheet metal barrier should be present to maintain the clearance extending at least 3 inches above the level of the attic insulation. Similarly, masonry chimneys should be protected with a sheet metal or fire-rated gypsum board barrier to maintain the minimum 2-inch clearance. This is absolutely crucial when polystyrene and cellulose insulations are used. The gap between the ceiling finish and a masonry or factory-built chimney should be filled with a non-combustible sealant or barrier.

Look underneath the insulation and inspect the electrical wiring for any missing sections of the wire covering. Examine electrical connections for signs of overheating, bare wire and looseness. If you come across electrical boxes, they should all have cover plates to prevent any contact with insulation. Check any recessed lighting fixtures in which the light bulb is wholly or partially above the ceiling level and where the fixture protrudes upwards into the attic space. You should see a clearance of at least 6 inches on all sides of the light fixture. A sheet metal barrier should be at least 3 inches higher than the level of insulation around the fixture and left completely open at the top. There have been cases where the intensity of the heat buildup has set unprotected insulation materials and joists on fire. Flammable materials like untreated sawdust, wood shavings, seaweed and horsehair should be removed the attic. Grease buildup on kitchen exhaust vent openings that terminate in the attic are a fire hazard.

If you are inspecting a townhouse, you will find that the units are separated with a firewall. These are continuous walls, usually supported directly from the ground, and are constructed with concrete masonry or fire-rated gypsum board that prevent fire within a structure from spreading to another structure. They must be able to withstand the devastation of prolonged exposure to fire and must be self-supporting, so that the collapse of the floor during a fire will not cause the collapse of the firewall. Make a note of how the firewall intersects at the roof.

Prefabricated Roof Trusses

Newer houses usually have prefabricated roof trusses. With excess insulation in the attic, these trusses have a tendency to lift up during the winter months, resulting in cracks to interior ceilings and wall finishes. High levels of insulation can cause the bottom cord to be dry and warm, while the top cord is wet with moisture. The expanding and contracting characteristics of some lumber and the changes in relative humidity can cause truss uplift every winter. The more unseasoned the wood and the younger the species, the greater the truss uplift. Long and low-sloped truss spans can increase the problem. During construction builders usually leave allowances for truss uplift by connecting the ceiling drywall to the partition wall top plates with drywall clips. The drywall is nailed to the ceiling at a certain distance from the wall partition, so that the drywall will only deflect in the event of truss lift, but will not cause ceiling and wall cracks.

Houses without Attics

Houses with cathedral ceilings or flat or mansard roofs are the hardest to ventilate because of the limited space between the insulation and sheathing. As in each case ventilation depends entirely on wind pressure, the best way to achieve it is by a continuous eave vent and a continuous outlet vent at the top of the roof. Poor ventilation causes prolonged drying of the wood when the weather warms, thus increasing the risk of moisture decay. It will also cause the living quarters below to become exceedingly hot in the summer and cold in the winter. Without going to great expense and modification to the roof structure, it is difficult to add more insulation, if required.

Cathedral ceilings or flat or mansard roofs are also nearly impossible to inspect for levels of insulation and moisture buildup. Roof leaks are difficult to detect, unless, of course, the ceilings and walls carry visible signs. The majority of serious roof condensation problems occur with flat roofs rather than roofs with attic spaces. This is because moisture is diffused over large surfaces before it condenses. In houses with flat roofs the condensing surface of the sheathing is close to the air leakage source. Moisture will concentrate near an air leak. As the weather turns warmer, accumulated frost melt will cause droplets to fall into the insulation below. Sufficient amounts of moisture will cause wet spots on the ceilings, stains and decay of the sheathing and joists.

During your inspection of the attic, you may wish to refer back to the notes you made regarding the roof's exterior and the structure. If you detected problems or stains visible from the outside, chances are these will also be evident from inside the attic. If they are not visible on the inside, then perhaps some early maintenance will prevent further damage. Unless the damage is extensive, repair costs may be minimal, such as the addition of adequate venting, insulation or vapour barriers.

CHECKPOINTS
✓✓✓✓✓✓✓✓✓✓✓

Type

_____ finished
_____ unfinished
_____ attic hatch or door
_____ hatch size
_____ hatch location
_____ insulation
_____ vapour barrier
_____ cathedral ceiling
_____ low-sloped roof
_____ fan exhaust ducts above roof
       level
_____ pipes insulated
_____ moisture signs
_____ possibilities for a fire
_____ possibilities for truss uplift
_____ mansard roof
_____ flat roof
_____ framing structual engineer
       approved
_____ other

Ventilation

_____ location
_____ ridge
_____ gables
_____ roof
_____ soffit
_____ cupola
_____ whole house fan
_____ attic fan
_____ two-speed motor
_____ turbine wheel
_____ manufacturer
_____ model number
_____ serial number
_____ thermostat
_____ dehumidistat

Snow Melting

_____ ice damming
_____ electric cables
_____ electrical grounding

CONSUMER TIPS

- Make sure that you have some familiarity with the renovation process, if you intend to repair or renovate. If you are not experienced in this area, consider taking courses, read books and magazines, and get expert advice.
- Be realistic and focused on the types of renovations and types of renovation properties you are considering. Certain types of renovations get a better return on your investment in terms of price and general saleability. The highest return generally comes from renovating the kitchen and bathrooms.
- Make sure that your personal goals and investment goals are clear; e.g., do you intend to purchase a property as a principal residence and then renovate it throughout the year and sell it? If so, you would normally be exempt from paying any capital gains tax on sale, because it would be deemed your principal residence.
- Be cautious when purchasing recreational, rural property, or property on leased land. Some potential limitations to consider include: degree of accessibility, lenders being reluctant to lend money in some cases, possible restrictions on use of the land, maintenance of the property could be limited due to distance, and vandalism is more likely if the property is in a remote location or only has seasonal usage.
- If buying recreational or rural property, water availability is a critical issue. Do you have well water? Is it safe to drink? Is it sufficient for your needs? Do you have a water system, either private or local, available to you? If you don't have a well, what would it cost to drill one, and is water available? Is there potential of contaminated water from creeks, high water table, or septic tanks? What are soil conditions like?
- Rural or recreational properties are particularly susceptible to the elements — wind, sun, ice, rain, snow — depending on the location. If the building is not regularly or properly maintained, it can deteriorate rapidly. Thoroughly check on the structural condition, and also check for insects, wood rot, etc.
- What type of waste disposal system is required or available? Is there a sewer hook-up? In more remote areas, is it a septic tank or other type of system? Is the soil suitable for a septic field? What about other types of waste disposal, such as garbage pick-up etc.?

- Check to make sure that the boundaries of your property have been clearly marked and pegged by a qualified surveyor. This is especially important with acreage or waterfront property. You don't want to have disputes with your neighbours. If you are buying in an urban or metropolitan area, a survey certificate is normally required for mortgage financing.

CHAPTER 11
▼
Interior
Living Areas

WHEN YOU FIRST walked inside the front door of the house, you
formed a quick first impression that persuaded you to pursue it
further as a prospective home for you and your family. Most first
impressions, however, are emotionally based and usually centre on one particular room or feature, such as a charming sun room, or a feature fireplace
and mantel in the living room or den. In conducting an inspection of the
home, however, you must try to put these emotional feelings aside and see the
house more objectively to get a true sense of its value.

Before you start the inspection of the interior spaces, quickly walk
through the entire house to familiarize yourself with it and gain an overall
impression. Draw some quick floor plans in your notebook and identify
each room on the plan. You may wish to review the notes you made in
Chapter 1 regarding the type of house well suited to your family needs to
ensure that the house you are inspecting is functional and meets the majority
of your lifestyle needs. This chapter will first review design and layout features, then take a more in-depth look at the placement and condition of the
entryways, stairs and interior finishings such as floors, walls, ceilings, doors
and windows. As you proceed with your inspection, notice any interior renovations or additions to the house, and whether quality materials and finishes
have been used.

Design and Layout

The size and shape of the rooms and their relationship to one another influence how well the floor plan will work. The size of a room will not indicate the
amount of useable space. Every room's usability is reduced by poorly located
doors, windows or closets. Study the plan carefully. An open plan can give a
feeling of spaciousness, but noisy activities may interfere with quiet areas.
Can walls be added if required? Closed plans will offer privacy and energy

efficiency but can also cause a feeling of constriction. Can walls be removed if needed? Are there various floor levels?

Your review of the design and layout of the interior living areas should follow six main criteria: traffic patterns, activity areas, room relationships, individual room details, storage spaces and lighting. Everyone will have widely varying opinions on these factors, just as everyone has a slightly different impression of what style of house to choose — bungalow, split-level or condominium, for example. Your opinions will be based on your background, lifestyle and the age and number of family members who will be living in the house. The following considerations primarily look at the functional use of the space.

Traffic Patterns

Traffic patterns relate to how you move through a room and from one room to another through the house. Are the hallways wide enough for two people to pass each other comfortably? Traffic flow between two or three levels in a house must be studied carefully. If the top floor is used for sleeping, can family members get to their bedrooms without crossing other rooms such as the living room? If you must travel through one room to get to another room, this greatly reduces the room's useable space and increases wear and dirt on certain areas of the carpet.

Activity Areas

Activity spaces focus on the working, living and sleeping areas. The work spaces are mainly the kitchen, laundry or utility areas. How is each part of the work area planned for efficiency? As these areas can be noisy and messy, are they located away from bedrooms and behind closed doors so that they can be at least partially hidden from guests? Are the sleeping areas quiet and private? Are they large enough so that you won't have to step aside to pull out a dresser drawer? Living areas can consist of the living room, family room, study or library. Are the living spaces flexible enough to adapt to a variety of activities and your changing needs?

Room Relationships

Room relationships considers how one room functions with respect to others. Are the bathrooms and showers situated within close proximity of the bedrooms? The dining room or barbecue patio should be within easy access of the kitchen to avoid unnecessary food spills en route from one room to the other. Will hot food become cold in transit before it gets to the table? In newer house designs you will find that the laundry facilities are located on the same floor as the bedrooms to save carrying heavy loads of bedding and towels great distances or up and down flights of stairs.

Individual Room Details

When you look at the features and shapes of individual rooms, consider their practicality in terms of placing furniture. Some condominiums, for example, have been designed with so many angled walls that they become almost totally impracatical for placing a bed or chesterfield against a wall, thus immensely reducing the living space. If the total area of the house is quite large, then such design creativity may be workable. Remember that it will also be costly when replacing the flooring of odd-shaped rooms.

Storage Spaces

Locate the storage spaces such as clothes closets, broom and linen closets, utility room shelving, basement and attic and other storage facilities. There should be a closet at every entryway into the house for storage of coats and footwear. Each bedroom should have a large closet. Some newer houses offer walk-in closets with space-saving shelves and rods, while in older homes the closet will be small or non-existent. Is there sufficient room for storage of off-season clothes and sports equipment?

Lighting

A room's lighting is usually a combination of natural and electrical light. It should provide background illumination and light for specific tasks, especially in work areas such as the kitchen and den. Light can also create a mood, define spaces and accentuate architectural details or decorative objects. The dining room, living room and family room are typical areas where you will find lighting used to create a mood. Many people favour an abundance of natural light through windows, doors and skylights. While this may be an attractive feature, it will also create greater heat loss.

Entryways, Stairs and Handrails

More than a point of coming and going, entryways are control centres for air circulation throughout the house. There should be sufficient space at the entryway to open the door easily and step back to take off your coat. The entryway should lead to various areas of the house without interfering with activities in any room. Measure the size of the entryway doors to ensure they are large enough to carry oversized items through them without taking the door off its hinges.

Staircases leading from the main entryway can have a definite personality and set a tone for the rest of the house. As for functionality, a central stair location is an integral part of a successful floor plan and traffic flow. Space is used more efficiently if the stairs are located above or below one another. Winding or spiral staircases can create impressive design features but can lead to tripping problems if the stair tread widths vary in size throughout the area of the wind. Sometimes an open riser is used in the main floor area to create an open design effect.

STAIRS

Proper stair construction takes a high degree of skill, and the workmanship should compare with that of fine cabinetry. Newer homes might have stairs that are prefabricated. The most important factor in stair design is the relationship between the rise (riser) and the run (tread minus nosing). When the rise/run combination is incorrect, extra strain will be placed on your leg muscles, which will promote fatigue. Stairs improperly measured are a hazard as they upset your natural posture and balance. For example, if the tread is too wide and the riser too short, your body will lean backwards when climbing the stairs. If the steps are too steep (narrow tread and high riser), your body will lean forward when going upstairs. There should be no more than 15 steps without a break for a landing. Are the stairs wide enough and the landing corners open enough to permit large items of furniture to be easily moved in?

Walk up and down the stairs to check for headroom clearances, slip resistance, steepness and uneven rises on steps. How is the lighting in the area? Did you hear any squeaks or feel any vibrations? Stairs will squeak for a number of reasons including poor gluing and nailing, shrinking lumber, or use of scrap lumber with splits and knots.

Examine the condition of all the stairs and handrailing, using the same method as for the exterior stairs as discussed in Chapter 3. Stairs that are open on one or both sides will have their handrailing enclosed by glass panels or have balusters and a newel. The newel supports the handrail, and may be the most decorative element on the stair. The starting newel must be securely anchored to the starter step or carried down through the floor and attached to the building frame. Push gently on the handrailing and the newel to ensure they have been fastened securely. Are the balusters secure? If they wobble when touched, you have a potential safety hazard. The handrailing should be comfortable and secure to grasp with your bare hands. Materials used on some handrailing may not be comfortable to grasp, such as a metal type with cold, sharp edges. Glass panels used between the balusters should be shatterproof.

Most interior stairs are open underneath so that you can see how they have been constructed. Often the "dead" space under stairways and landings is used for storage. Treads and risers are supported by stringers, which are fixed to the framework of the house. For wide stairs a third stringer is installed in the middle for stability. Quality treads and risers will be cut into the stringers and wedged from the underside. Examine how the stair is anchored. Stair components should be held together with wedges, screws and glue — not just nails.

Flooring

Walk on all the floor areas of the house to test for vibrations, squeaks or soft areas. Squeaks are usually caused by inadequate bracing of the floor joists, subfloor boards that have come loose or have cracked, or wood rubbing against nails that have pulled free. The problem can also occur when wood rubs against wood, where no room has been left for expansion or contraction due to a change in humidity levels. Warped joists or floor boards and improper gluing and nailing can also cause squeaking. Stand back and look at the floor to see if it is level. Take your marbles and let them roll on the floor to see if they all head in one direction. With your awl, examine all corners of the floor for moisture.

Floor coverings will vary depending upon the age of the house and its decor, and each house will probably have at least two or three different types. Carpeting, vinyl and hardwood floors are most common, although tile, marble and other specialty flooring will be discussed also. When inspecting the floor covering, be certain to check underneath loose floor mats and furniture. Often these have been conveniently placed to cover up damaged floor or serious burn marks in carpets. Make a note on your floor plan of the type of floor covering in each room and how badly it is worn in high traffic areas.

Carpeting

The advantage of carpet is that it provides warmth and absorbs sound. A disadvantage is that it hides dust and dirt and is more difficult to clean. It will also show signs of wear in heavy traffic areas sooner than other types of floor coverings, and areas around south-facing windows may look faded from the sunlight. Most house carpets are made of synthetic fibres such as rayon, nylon, acrylic, polyester. These will have a longer lifespan than others made of wool, silk, cotton, sisal and fur. Each will also have a different resistance to moisture, mildew, fading, abrasion, static electricity buildup, stains, shrinkage and burns. The textures will also vary as will the density of the yarn. A tightly woven yarn (dense pile) with multiple twists will be durable. A quality carpet will have resilience and bounce back after being crushed when its walked on. On the other hand, with a poorer quality, loosely woven carpet you may be able to see the jute backing through the pile. Shag or long-looped pile carpets (used extensively in homes built around 1960) may be a hazard, especially when used on stairs.

In a corner of the room or around a heat register, see if you can lift up the carpet for a closer inspection. Take the lifted piece of carpet and look at its profile. How high is the pile and how tight is the weave? How is the carpet held in place? You should find an underpadding (made of products such as rubber, foam or sponge), which acts as a cushion or shock absorber. it aids in insulation and acoustics and extends the life of the carpet. Rub the underlay with your finger to see if it disintegrates. This may indicate age or moisture problems. Now pinch the foam. With a good quality thick and spongy foam, your fingers will not meet. Check the seams of the carpet for separation and fraying. Outer edges may be secured with a strip of vinyl, aluminum or galvanized steel. Synthetic indoor/outdoor carpets are often used in damp areas such as porches or basements. Rubber and foam underlays will disintegrate with dampness so should not be used in these areas.

Lino

Check quality

Resilient Vinyl Flooring

Resilient vinyl floors are commonly used in kitchens, bathrooms, laundry rooms and other areas where water spills may occur and be easily cleaned up. They are manufactured in two basic forms — sheets and tiles. The newer types are exceptionally resistant to indentations, abrasions, scratches, staining, mildew and colour change. The wearing quality of different types of vinyl flooring is largely dependent upon the thickness. The rule is: "The thicker the vinyl, the better the wear; the higher the price, the better the quality." No-wax vinyl flooring has a natural high gloss polyurethane top coat that is applied at the time of manufacture. Older vinyl flooring is more subject to tears, blisters, scratches and stains. Check all seams of the flooring for separation.

Hardwood Flooring

Hardwood flooring comes in boards, planks, strips and parquet tiles. Strip flooring comes in different lengths, grades and appearance. Lower grades will be shorter and have more wormholes, knots and checks on their surfaces. The hardwood boards may be close-grain woods (yellow pine, maple, birch, beech) or open-grain woods (chestnut, ash, elm, oak, northern walnut or pecan). The natural colours of the wood will span from pale blond to ebony, and the application of different stains and finishes will vary the colour further. Water-based stains will not yellow or change the colour of the wood, whereas polyurethane finishes will.

Hardwood floors can be glued, blind-nailed or face nailed. In blind nailed flooring, the nails are concealed by the tongue of the next piece of wood. Face nailing occurs when square-edged flooring is used and the screws or nail heads are counter-sunk and holes filled with putty. With older installations, the nails may surface over time. In older houses it is not uncommon to find carpet and underlay over old hardwood flooring.

Around the heat register opening, check to see how thick the hardwood flooring is. Is there still enough wood left for future sanding or refinishing? Note that some pre-finished flooring is actually pine with an oak laminate. If any refinishing or sanding is done to this hardwood look-alike, the pine will show through. Some better installations have a layer of building paper under the hardwood flooring to prevent penetration of dust or moisture.

Cork floor tiles are compressible and have a good insulation value. The tiles are usually made from ground shavings, from cork oak in moulds, where baking along with mechanical pressure melts the natural resins in the cork and binds the shavings into one piece. Depending upon the temperature and the duration of the baking, the colour tones can be light, medium or dark. Cork crumbles quite easily, though, unless it has been sealed with many coats of varnish. A more resilient cork floor will consist of vinyl composition tiles that have cork sealed into the vinyl.

Ceramic Tile Flooring

Ceramic tile is one of the most versatile finishing materials and, if properly installed and maintained, will last a lifetime. It will bear such names as quarry tile, mosaic tile and glazed or unglazed floor tile. Unglazed tiles provide far better slip resistance. All tiles vary in their porosity, finish and strength. Thickness of ceramic tile is not an indication of its strength. Ceramic tiles come in a wide range of shapes and sizes from 1-inch to 1-foot and larger squares and hexagons. They will crack and chip if they don't have a stable base. They are also unforgiving — drop a jar or a plate and it will break. If you have back problems, you will find tiles tiring to stand on for long periods of time. Also, they can be cold to the eyes and feet. Some tile surfaces are smoother than others that can be quite coarse.

Each type of tile has its own standard trim pieces for finishing this work at joints around floors, doors, windows and counter edges. Make sure that tiles designed for walls have not been used for floors in high traffic areas. Grouts should be waterproof, mildew resistant and easy to clean. With your awl point check the grout between tiles. If it is soft, it is deteriorating. Put some water on the grout. Does it bead or is the water absorbed? Does the colour of the grout match the tile? If not, difficult-to-remove stains will be quite visible. Ask the owner if there are any leftover tiles to be used as replacements for scratched or cracked tiles. The underside of the tile may bear the manufacturer's name.

Specialty Flooring

You will also come across authentic and synthetic marble, terrazzo, terra cotta, slate, sandstone, brick, granite and travertine concrete flooring. Some of these materials, if stained, can leave permanent discolouration. Marble will scratch easily. Travertine is softer than marble. On a hardness scale of one to 10, travertine is about 3.5, marble is from 4 to 5, granite from 6 to 7, and diamond a little over 9. Granite is almost indestructible as a flooring material; it can have so much silica in it, it can be like glass and it does not stain easily when exposed to wine, vinegar and other common liquids.

Try to find out the weight of the material, its hardness and how it is adhered to the subfloor. Is the subfloor sufficiently stable and level to carry the weight of some of these heavier products? For instance, the subfloor to which the ceramic tile is applied must be rigid enough to prevent it from deflecting under load. Around the opening of the heat register, you should find a 3/4-inch sheathing material on joists spaced 16 inches on centres and a 1-inch thick mortar bed laid along the plywood along with wire-mesh reinforcement. Alternative construction practices have been used to hold the tile in place using thin mortar beds with no wire mesh reinforcements.

Most problems with ceramic tile and other heavier flooring materials are caused by incomplete bonding, grouting and differential movement between the finished floor and the subfloor. For instance, concrete mortar beds can shrink as they age while the finished flooring expands. In this case the finished floor can break, lift free of the subfloor or buckle in a ridge.

Walls and Ceilings

At the turn of the century it was a sign of elegance and luxury to have high ceilings. However, because of the high cost of heating these homes, more recent house designs including vaulted ceilings and sunken living rooms have combined the principles of heating efficiency with high-ceiling elegance. Rather than heat being trapped at the top of the room, it is channelled to another room, hallway or second floor above the living area with the featured ceiling. Some houses have beamed ceilings that are either embedded or span free across the space, supported at each end. Check the beam for sagging, and try to find out if it performs a structural purpose or is just there for decoration. In older homes tin ceilings, decoratively pressed from sheets of steel, were quite popular because they were durable, inexpensive and fire resistant and could be fastened over old cracked plaster without having to repair the original surface. The tin may be in its original matte finish or painted with a rust-resistant paint.

Interior finishing of ceilings and walls has changed considerably over the years. Old-fashioned plaster walls and ceilings were made by nailing a lath (thin strips of wood) to wall studs and covering the lath with three coats of plaster. Gypsum board or fibreboard lath with two coats of plaster were commonly used during the 1940s and 1950s. In the 1950s gypsum board was also applied as a double layer, with the second layer laminated crosswise to the first. By 1965 single thickness 1/2-inch to 5/8-inch gypsum boards were common, with only some custom homes using plaster as the wall and ceiling finish. (Note that gypsum board, drywall, plaster board and sheet rock are all basically the same material.) Perhaps when you were inspecting the attic, you made a note of the ceiling material that was underneath the insulation. Depending on thickness, plaster has better soundproofing than gypsum board. The most common problems with gypsum board are nail pops, cracking, visible joints, ridging, tape delamination covering the joints and waving or sagging ceilings. These may be due to improper ventilation or lack of heat during winter construction. Nail popping occurs when the drywall has been applied to wet framing and pulls away from the lumber as it dries and shrinks. The amount of shrinkage depends upon the species of the wood, moisture content, direction of the grain and relative humidity of the environment.

As discussed in earlier chapters, the purpose of the exterior walls and roof is to provide resistance to rain penetration, heat flow, water vapour diffusion, uncontrolled air leakage and, most importantly, to provide structural strength and rigidity. Interior walls and ceilings, on the other hand, perform insulative, acoustical and decorative functions. If, during your inspection, you notice

Nail popping [handwritten margin note]

major cracks and water stains, it is an indication that the outer walls or roof need attention. Minor cracks may be due to any number of reasons, such as settling of the house, age of the material or stress from the weight of a mounted fixture.

> ## Nice wallpaper!
> When a new homeowner started renovations to an old house, she found that the wallpaper was holding up the walls and ceiling — the plaster underneath had totally crumbled!

Cracking is most often seen over doorways, wall/ceiling intersections and around window openings, valances and stairwells. Here larger dimensions of horizontal pieces of framing lumber are found behind the gypsum board. Wider dimensions of wood have a larger cross grain, hence greater shrinkage factors. The lumber will shrink between 20 and 50 times as much in width as in length.

Glance over all wall and ceiling surfaces and make a note of crooked or bulging areas. Sagging or waving ceilings may be caused by inadequate securing or excessive humidity and moisture. Roof truss uplift can also cause ceilings to crack. Cracked and sagging ceilings are common with old plaster applications. Major cracks are seldom repaired, and instead the ceiling is replaced with gypsum board. With the palm of your hand, gently apply pressure over the wall surface. Does it feel soft and spongy, as if it is about to be pushed in? Look for holes behind doors where the wall has been damaged by a door handle. If the walls are covered with wallpaper or wood panelling, you can find out what is behind these finishes by removing the faceplate from an electrical switch or outlet. Check behind pictures on the wall to see if there are permanent dark silhouettes on the wood panelling.

You may be able to identify uninsulated walls by the unevenness of dirt on the wall. (Dust and dirt particles adhere more readily to cold than warm surfaces.) As the wall surfaces will be substantially colder between the studs, there may be lighter coloured streaks resembling an x-ray of the stud structure behind the wall. Make a note of all the walls and ceilings in the house that are washable.

As you walk about all the rooms, take the occasional deep breath to check for any suspicious odours. When high humidity prevails, mildew and moulds often develop, causing a heavy, damp smell. Check the exterior walls in corners, closets and behind heavy drapes or furniture where cold-weather condensation is greatest due to lack of air circulation. If you come across active moulds, it indicates a moisture problem exists, but it may not necessarily represent a decay hazard. For instance, it may be quite easy to eliminate the source of the moisture by using a dehumidifier, heating the area periodically with an electric light bulb, or installing a louvred door on a closet. To avoid excess moisture and possible indoor air quality problems, clothes dryers should always be vented to the outdoors. Chapter 14 on energy conservation will further discuss condensation and water vapour.

Baseboards and Mouldings

Mouldings are used around interior doors, windows and at the intersection of wall, floor and ceiling surfaces. Not only do they help to detail the style of the house, they also decorate, cover and finish off the seams, gaps and rough edges common to wall and ceiling finishing and door and window jambs. You will find mouldings made of wood, vinyl or aluminum. Inspect the mouldings to see how they are attached. They may be glued, screwed or nailed. Check how two separate parts are fitted together and how they are finished. The corners should be neatly mitred. Are the mouldings consistent throughout the house? Do all the rooms have baseboards? With your awl, check the mouldings for signs of rusted nails and rotted wood, especially at corners and below windows and doors.

Doors

Interior doors will range from the panel type of construction, with raised or sunken wood insets, to a French door with glass panels. Wood doors may be solid or panel veneer. You can tell by swinging it back and forth and tapping over its surface. A solid door, of course, will be heavier, and the panel door will give a hollow sound when tapped. The door should swing out of the way of traffic. Is the doorway large enough to allow furniture to pass through without removing the door?

Visually inspect the door and door casing for straightness, squareness and alignment. A well-hung door should close with a click. Is the gap between the door and its frame consistent? Hold the door by both handles and lift it up to see if there is play in the hinges. Are the door latches stiff and do the door hinges squeak? You will find that some wooden doors will stick only during humid weather. Look around the door casing for signs of rubbing. Examine the condition of doors on all six sides. Rub the surface of the door with your hand and use your mirror to inspect around the edges. Do you notice the doors delaminating at the edges?

Pocket doors, that slide out of sight behind walls, are sometimes found in kitchens, washrooms and closets. Slide the door back and forth. Do the rollers move smoothly along the track? Squeaks and rattles are usually caused by dirt in the rollers, a dented track or broken rollers. If the door binds, the door or the studs framing the pocket have warped. Sliding, bi-fold and louvre doors are also commonly used for closets or laundry rooms. Test the doors by opening and closing them to see how they fit their casings.

Check the locking hardware on doors to the bathroom, master bedroom, tool shop and basement. Quality hardware will have a brand name stamped into the metal of the face plate and hinges. Popular brands include Schlage, Yale, Weiser and Stanley. Does the finish and design of the hardware match that of other doors in the house? Are the door knobs and striker plates in good condition?

Windows

Look out each window to check for view, privacy, acoustics and safety. The higher the top of the window, the more deeply light will penetrate. The lower the sill, the better the light on horizontal surfaces near it. A horizontal window gives better light than a vertical window with the same glass area. While large and numerous windows will provide a lot of natural light, they will also cause the house to be less energy efficient. They will also limit your choices when placing furniture around the room. You may wish to refer back to the notes you made in Chapter 3 when you evaluated each of the windows in the house.

Make a note of all windows that can be opened. These help in cross-ventilating a house. Some wooden-framed windows may be painted shut. If the windows swing outward, can rain be brought directly into the house? Is there a fixed piece of hardware to prevent the wind from pulling the window open? Check the hardware and locking devices to ensure they function properly. Some may be difficult to replace. Windows in older houses occasionally have ripples or defects in the glass. Notice the thickness of the glass. Double- or triple-glazed windows have spacers between the panes around the frame. Butyl rubber or fibreglass spacers are better at reducing window heat loss, than wood, aluminum or vinyl spacers. This means less condensation on windows. If the glass rattles when you tap it, perhaps the glazing compound, gasket or seal around the frame has deteriorated or become loose. Seals provide tightness against air, water and vapour. Windows with metal mutins between their panes sometimes rattle when wind blows against the pane. Place your hand against the window. Do you feel cold air sneaking past the frame? Weatherstripping is designed to stop air leakage around the window openings. Check the condition of the weatherstripping.

Test for softness of the interior sills with the point of your awl to see if you can detect rot. Water often accumulates on the sill because of condensation, rain leaking through or an overwatered plant resting on the sill. A continuous problem exists if you find layers of paint applied over blistered surfaces where mildew has grown at the corners of the window jamb and sill.

Energy-efficient Windows

The energy efficiency of a window is dependent upon a number of factors, including the insulating qualities of the materials used for the frame and sash, the thickness and number of air spaces between the panes and special coatings applied to the glass during its manufacture. Special glazings applied to windows to improve energy efficiency may include low-E films and coatings, gas-filled windows, integrated blind systems and suspended and applied films. Each of these is explained below. If you encounter these energy-efficient windows, be certain to obtain from the owner all information regarding the manufacturer, installer and any warranties still in effect. If these windows do crack or shatter, they are non-repairable.

Low-E (low emissivity) "soft-coat" film consists of a thin layer of metallic coating, applied to a sheet of pre-cut glass. The coating can also be suspended on a thin plastic film incorporated between two panes of pre-cut glass. This can give an insulating air value of triple-paned glass without the added weight. The transparent material works like a two-way mirror. It reflects outdoor heat but not light in the summer, and reflects heat back inside in the winter. The coating will deteriorate rapidly if the seal is broken. Low-E "hard coat" coatings are sprayed onto window glass during the manufacturing process using various types of metal and oxide deposits. Unlike soft coat, hard coat sheets of glass can be cut to size as needed.

Some window manufacturers also insert a heavy gas (like sulphur dioxide, argon or krypton, etc.) between two panes of special glass. The gas conducts the heat less readily than air, resulting in less heat loss. Integrated blind systems are also used between panes of glass. These narrow blinds can be tilted at any angle by pressing a button near the window ledge. Operated from the inside, they shade the sun in the summer and block out the cold in the winter, as do interior blinds. Suspended films and applied films consist of polyester or mylar. The films are usually coated to either reflect solar heat back outside or internal radiating heat back inside, or to reduce the ultraviolet rays or transmissions of light. The suspended film must be used in a sealed unit and kept under constant tension to ensure that no ripples impair the visual performance of the glazing.

Glass Blocks

Some houses have glass blocks in areas of exterior walls, interior dividers, bathrooms or kitchen enclosures. Glass block has been used since the 1930s and is available in several different patterns creating distinct light transmission patterns similar to crystal. It offers insulating values similar to that of good-quality double-glazed windows. It is easy to maintain and gives a high-tech look. Glass-block walls are not structural, however, and need lintels and framing around them for support. In an inconspicuous area, touch the surface with your awl. If it scratches easily, the block could be made of plastic instead of glass.

Stained Glass

Authentic stained glass is a process by which pieces of coloured glass are fitted and fastened into leading. Examine the soldered connections for cracks or broken pieces of glass. Lightly press against the glass to see if it is loose. Over the years the sun's rays, street vibrations, polluted air and acid rain will cause the glass pieces to pull away from each other, causing gaps to emerge. If this occurs, the entire piece has to be releaded. However, not all stained glass is real. Stained glass overlay, an inexpensive look-alike, is a patented process whereby different colours of plastic film are applied to both sides of a sheet of glass. Once the film is in place, lead is applied around the outline of each piece of film. You may wish to contact the manufacturer for guarantees that the plastic film will not peel off, and heat and sunlight will not make it fade.

Skylights

The main function of skylights is to provide natural daylight and moonlight in central portions of the home. Interesting lighting and design effects can be created by the light that is cast upon interior features. Recognize, though, that this additional light may cause premature fading of your furnishings and floor and wall coverings in areas captured by the sunlight. If the skylights are facing south on a steeply sloped roof, there should be blinds, shutters, drapes or screens to prevent the rays from overheating the house in the summer months.

There is no doubt that skylights add extra costs to the home's heating bill. They lose more heat than similarly sized, double-glazed windows, because hot air rises and pools below the ceiling. To improve their energy efficiency, manufacturers now offer skylights with double, triple and even quadruple glazing. The layers of glass or acrylic are separated by an airspace and fitted into thermally broken frames. These factors reduce heat loss, condensation and frost buildup. The only place you should find a single-paned skylight is on an unheated porch.

Skylights may be constructed of acrylic or glass. Acrylic is lightweight and can be placed on either flat or sloped roofs. Glass should be placed on sloped roofs because it is heavy and breakable, but it is easier to clean, has better optics and doesn't scratch. Both can be tinted with various colours, reflective coating or film. You will see some acrylic skylights in such shapes as triangles, dormers, rectangles, bubbles, pyramids and ridge lights. Ridge lights are elongated pyramids that fit along the ridgeline of a roof. While domed skylights are more susceptible to surface damage by wind-borne sand, they have a larger surface area and pick up more light, especially when the sun is low in the sky. Some of the materials used in the older acrylic skylights had the problem of expanding and contracting, causing the surfaces to change colour or even disintegrate over time. Frames are made of aluminum, wood or vinyl. Vinyl relies on ultraviolet inhibitors to resist colour fading of its surfaces. Aluminum frames should incorporate thermal breaks to reduce heat loss and condensation. They can be caulked, welded or screwed together.

From the outside, notice how the skylight is mounted onto the roof. The flashing and curb around the flashing should be clear of debris to avoid deterioration and moisture penetration. On the inside, notice any old water streaks around the opening. The shallower this light shaft is, the more intense and unrestricted the light. Skylights positioned on top of a deep light well should have an extra sheet of double glazing at the bottom of the well, with gaskets and finishing moulding. The sealed air space will act to insulate the opening in the well and prevent air leakage and heat loss. Where there is air or heat leakage, there is moisture penetration. Leakage of whatever nature is usually due to a cheaper product line or inadequate installation. Check the manufacturer's warranty to ensure it has been approved by a certified testing agency.

Ask the owner if the skylight can be opened for venting and cleaning purposes. A properly installed skylight, when opened on a hot summer's day, can set up convection currents that pull hot air up to the ceiling and out of the skylight, while drawing in cooler air from outside. Because of the high moisture levels in kitchens and bathrooms, it is important that skylights in these areas can be opened. Skylights installed over a heating duct will similarly cause condensation problems and heat loss.

Clerestories are small windows usually found in a wall between two roof levels. Like a skylight, they bring daylight and moonlight into the centre of the house. Inspect them in a similar way. Will they be easy to clean?

Sun Spaces (Atriums, Greenhouses, Solariums, Sun Rooms)

An atrium might be located in the centre of a house to provide light, air and perhaps a garden view to the rooms facing it. Is there easy access for watering plants? Consider how moisture, acoustics, odours and air currents from the sun room might affect the rest of the house. From a fire safety perspective, it is wise to note that an atrium is a potential sun trap, and that air currents from this area may help to spread a fire.

Most of the sun spaces you come across will have been installed from prefabricated kits and made of aluminum, vinyl or wood. When attached to the house, they can become greenhouses, solariums, sun rooms or solar additions. They can enclose a kitchen or hot tub. In situations where they have been added as solar additions along south-facing walls, they are backed up with thermal mass-like brick or tile flooring, water tubes and brick facings, for purposes of supplying solar-heated air to other areas of the house. Ask the owner about the manufacturer and installer of the sun room and where replacement screens and glazing can be found.

Aluminum-framed systems are corrosion and maintenance free and should have thermal breaks consisting of gaskets that break the cold conductive path between exterior and interior metal. Vinyl and fibreglass frames also provide an airtight fit that acts as a thermal barrier against the cold. Vinyl never corrodes, rusts, needs painting or forms mildew. Wood frames are natural insulators but can cause problems in extremely high humidity areas. The frames will require attention when natural weathering causes checking and greying.

Numerous accessories come with installations, such as thermostatically controlled ventilation fans, interior and exterior open-weave fabric shading systems, backup heaters and movable windows and skylights. These give you greater control over the room's temperature during different seasons of the year. Sun space heating should operate as a separate zone with its own thermostat. A thermostatically controlled fan helps to regulate heat flow by removing hot air in the summer and cold air in the winter. Along with shading, ventilation and insulation, summer overheating is prevented by providing the warm interior air with ample pathways to the outside.

Examine the insulation and vapour barrier in all parts of the solar addition that aren't glass. This includes roof and wall sections, kneewalls, foundation and floor. Concrete foundation and floor insulation can consist of rigid foam, which will help to reduce heat loss. The most important factor affecting the transmission and storage of heat energy is the type of glazing and framing used. During the winter some materials will gain enough heat that will be gradually released when the sun goes down. The density and colour of stone, slate, tile and concrete will determine how much time it takes to absorb and radiate the heat that is generated in a solar sun space. Quilts, blinds, shutters and insulated panels are designed to cover cold glass surface areas for night-time insulation.

Inspect the glass panels, glazing bars and gaskets for flexing and distortions. Is the glass broken due to structural movements? Single glazing has a very high heat loss and in humid situations tends to result in condensation. If there is double glazing, make sure the units have been sealed to avoid condensation between the glazing. Most problems with sun spaces result from leaks and fogging of insulated glass units. The thickness of the air space between the panes determines the insulating value. Most manufacturers leave a space of about a half inch between the panes of glass. If you come across triple glazing, note that the added pane's insulation value is offset somewhat by reduced light transmission and additional weight. The glass should bear certification that it has been tempered for safety. Acrylic panels may be used instead. The double-skinned sheets should be separated by an air space and supported by a network of ribbing. The acrylic is shatter resistant. Check for condensation in the air space. Condensate channels help to drain water down to the sill, where it is collected in trays and drained outside. Look around the frame of the glazing to locate the drain channels. Glazing that stops a foot or two above the foundation serves as a backsplash on the outside, preventing the buildup of dirt, and reduces the danger of the glass being accidentally kicked and broken.

Study the location of the sun space. Does it really have a solar-heating function? Will you have maximum shading during the summer and minimum shading during the winter? Has care been taken with the finish materials and roofing to match with the rest of the house? Check the sidewall flashing where the sun space joins the house. This is an area most prone to leak. The metal flashing should tuck up under the existing siding and extend over the sloped glazing. There should be a perimeter drainpipe around the footings to prevent water from getting under the structure. Notice the condition of the doors leading into and out of the sun space. Is the hardware lockable?

Like the rest of the house, a sun space requires good glazing and insulation to provide comfort and energy efficiency.

CHECKPOINTS
✓✓✓✓✓✓✓✓✓✓✓

Living Areas
____ number/dimensions of bedrooms
____ number/dimensions of kitchens
____ number/dimensions of bathrooms
____ number/dimensions of hallways
____ number/dimensions of closets
____ number/dimensions of living rooms
____ number/dimensions of dining rooms
____ number/dimensions of entrances
____ number/dimensions of stairs
____ accessible to disabled
____ wheelchair accessible
____ whole house air circulation
____ ceiling heights of rooms
____ other

How Finished
____ bedroom floor, walls, ceilings
____ bedroom doors, windows, trim, lighting
____ kitchen floor, walls, ceilings
____ kitchen doors, windows, trim, lighting
____ bathroom floor, walls, ceilings
____ bathroom doors, windows, trim, lighting
____ hallway floor, walls, ceilings
____ hallway doors, windows, trim, lighting
____ closet floor, walls, ceilings
____ closet doors, windows, trim, lighting
____ living room floor, walls, ceilings
____ living room doors, windows, trim, lighting
____ dining room floor, walls, ceilings
____ dining room doors, windows, trim, lighting
____ entrance floor, walls, ceilings
____ entrance doors, windows, trim, lighting
____ stair floor, walls, ceilings
____ acoustical control
____ other

Stairs
____ type (straight, spiral, etc.)
____ head-room clearances
____ slip-resistant treads
____ number of steps
____ length and width of landings
____ tread and riser dimensions
____ steepness
____ unevenness
____ width
____ number of stringers
____ open or closed stringer
____ handrailing type
____ height of handrailing
____ balusters
____ newel
____ landings
____ graspable handrail
____ number and height of handrails

Floors
____ age
____ type
____ squeaks
____ condition
____ thickness
____ texture
____ colours
____ patterns
____ shapes
____ sizes
____ uneven surfaces
____ slip resistant
____ how maintained
____ wear
____ stain resistant
____ sound insulated
____ manufacturer's warranty

Interior Doors
_____ condition
_____ brand-name hardware
_____ door stops
_____ undercuts for ventilation
_____ warpage
_____ fit against frame
_____ door thickness
_____ how finished
_____ manufacturer's warranty

Windows
_____ sill width
_____ condition of sills
_____ number of panes
_____ missing hardware
_____ thermally broken
_____ special glazing
_____ glass thickness
_____ condensation
_____ loose windows
_____ special coatings applied to glazing
_____ air leakage
_____ curtain rods
_____ glass block

Skylights
_____ location
_____ tinted
_____ blinds
_____ acrylic
_____ glass
_____ other
_____ thermally broken
_____ flashed curb
_____ size/shape
_____ number of panes
_____ shutters
_____ condensation weep channels
_____ clerestories
_____ other
_____ manufacturer's warranty
_____ certified testing agency approved

Sun Spaces
_____ type of glass
_____ blinds
_____ wood construction
_____ aluminum construction
_____ vinyl construction
_____ combination construction
_____ wood preservatives
_____ glazing type
_____ hot stale air
_____ thermal shades
_____ number of panes
_____ shutters
_____ temperature controls
_____ ventilating fan
_____ moisture problems
_____ floor material
_____ foundation type
_____ slab on grade
_____ framing of structure
_____ corrosion of components
_____ manufacturer's warranty

Ceiling Fans
_____ make
_____ serial number
_____ reversible fan
_____ vibration
_____ model number
_____ any special features
_____ length of fan blades
_____ number of fan blades
_____ wobble
_____ number of speeds
_____ manufacturer's warranty
_____ certified testing agency approved

CONSUMER TIPS

Be aware of the various forms of legal restrictions that could affect the house you buy, whether you are buying in rural, urban or metropolitan areas. Your lawyer can search the title of the property to see what encumbrances or restrictions are on title, as a condition of any offer you make. Some examples are as follows:

- *Right of way.* This generally means a statutory (legal) right for certain companies, crown corporations or government departments to use or have access to part of your property. Examples would be for hydro, telephone, sewer, drainage, dike, public access purposes.
- *Easement.* An easement is similar to a right of way, but normally is the term used when one neighbour gives another neighbour the right to use or have access to a piece of land; e.g., permission to reach a waterfront by crossing a neighbour's land. This agreement is put into writing and filed in the closest land titles office.
- *Restrictive covenant.* In this situation, a developer in a subdivision could make any purchase subject to ongoing in certain areas; e.g., requiring that all roofs be covered by shakes rather than shingles. The purpose would be for aesthetic uniformity. Another example could be a restriction prohibiting operating a business from your home, part-time or full-time. Even if municipal bylaws might permit you to do so, the restrictive covenant would normally prevail.
- *Zoning.* There could be restrictions on the type of use of your property, e.g., in the case of rural property — only seasonal use, no mobile homes on the property, no other buildings to be constructed, etc. In the case of urban or metropolitan property — single family usage only, no rental accommodation technically permitted (e.g., suite in basement), no additions to the house possible, etc.
- *Leasehold interest .* In this example, the holder of the interest in land has the right to use the land for a fixed period of time — for example, 50 or 99 years. The owner of the property (landlord or lessor) signs an agreement with the holder of the leasehold interest (tenant or lessee) setting out various terms and conditions of the relationship. The leasehold contract would set out such conditions as maintenance requirements, restrictions on use of the land, building construction or renovation requirements, and other matters. A leashold situation can cover condominiums or houses.

▼
The Kitchen

CERTAINLY THE KITCHEN is a room that commands major attention when a house is being considered for purchase — and for good reason. It is the most complicated area and one of the most expensive to renovate. Because of its mixed use as a work, storage and sometimes eating area, numerous features should be combined to enhance its appeal. But do not be influenced by good looks alone. The kitchen's size, layout, lighting and cupboard space will have helped to create your first impression. On a closer look, the basic principles of design such as line, style, form, texture, harmony and proportion used in the original planning will be evident. Any kitchen should have a common look that co-ordinates the different elements in it and makes it uniquely personal.

The kitchen's location in relation to the rest of the house also will be important. It should be proximate to the dining room and family room for ease in serving prepared food. Ideally it should be located near an outside entrance, such as the patio. This will have the added advantage of helping to balance the heat, humidity and air quality characteristics caused by food preparation, cooking and clean-up. A kitchen that gets the direct sunlight may become overheated during the summer months. This chapter will review the design and functionality of the kitchen, as well as cabinets, countertops, sinks, flooring, appliances and other considerations.

Space, Size, Shape and Function

You will find that most older houses tend to have larger kitchens than newer ones. This is because it used to be a room where a family and neighbours would engage in conversation, light meals and joint food preparation. With the advent of the busy lifestyle and dual-career families, time-saving kitchen appliances and instant meals became necessary. Thus, less counter and work space is necessary in modern kitchen design. However, this is not to say that all lifestyles follow this norm. If you enjoy cooking, have a large family or prefer to use the kitchen as an informal eating area, then a spacious kitchen will be critical for your enjoyment of the house. Take an objective look at all the activities that occur in your present kitchen. Will you be able to accommodate these activities in this kitchen?

Informal eating areas within a kitchen may include space for a table and chairs, or it may have built-in seating and counter. If the main dining area is an extension of the kitchen, is there a visual barrier to block the sight of the

DIAGRAM 8: KITCHEN LAYOUT AND EFFICIENCIES

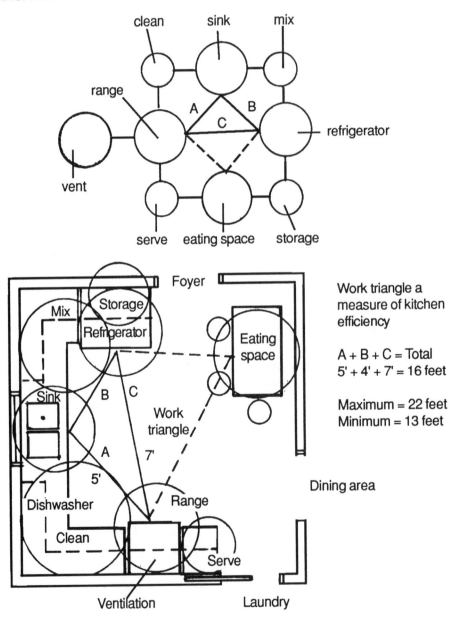

Work triangle a measure of kitchen efficiency

A + B + C = Total
5' + 4' + 7' = 16 feet

Maximum = 22 feet
Minimum = 13 feet

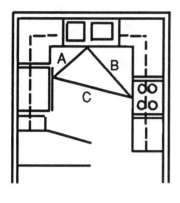

Peninsula

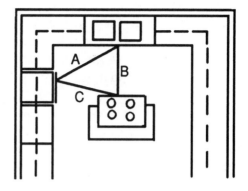

Island

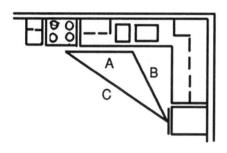

L-shape

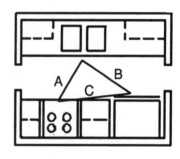

Corridor shape

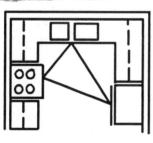

U-shape

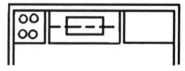

Single wall shape

kitchen sink and counters while dining? Some kitchens offer a partial wall with a pass-through counter between the kitchen and dining areas. Besides saving your legs when serving and clearing tables, pass-throughs can open up an otherwise small room. Notice the shape of the kitchen. Is it like a peninsula with only one entrance? Or is it more like an island with more than one access from the hallways and other rooms? If your lifestyle is such that more than one person will have regular use of the kitchen, then additional entrances will provide more freedom of movement in and about the room.

Draw a plan of the kitchen, noting the location of the range, sink, refrigerator, dishwasher and any other free-standing appliances. Measure the floor area and notice the space required for opening cupboard, refrigerator and range doors. Is there room for bending, crouching and a second person to pass by while the doors are open? Sketch circles or ovals onto your plan to represent the various activity centres such as cooking, eating, cleaning up, baking, serving, laundering and so on. Now walk about the kitchen to these activity areas. The imaginary line — when you walk to the refrigerator/dishwasher/ sink and range — should form a triangle. This represents a path that is followed during meal preparation and clean-up. In an efficient kitchen, to avoid an overcrowded work pattern, the sum of the three sides of the triangle should not exceed 22 feet and should not be less than 12 feet. The distance between either of the appliances and/or the sink should not be less than 4 feet or greater than 9 feet. Too large an area between work centres would mean a waste of time and energy. Refrigerator doors should open away from the work triangle, and away from the traffic path. If you are a left-handed cook, you will no doubt find the majority of kitchens designed for right-handed use.

Wiring

A clear sign of the age of a kitchen is with the wiring. Unless it has been remodelled, an older kitchen will have few electrical outlets compared to today's standard. Count the number of outlets and mark them on your plan. Are they proximate to the activity centres you outlined earlier? Appliances like food-waste disposers and dishwashers are permanently connected and wired. Electrical ranges are connected by a special power cord and receptacle. Appliance circuits must have only one outlet per circuit to safeguard against overloads.

Electrical outlets along the counter, where small appliances will be used, must be located in such a way that no point along the counter is more than 36 inches from an outlet, excluding the sink and range. Make a note of receptacles mounted flush on the surface of counter tops or those that are mounted in such a way that they could fill up with water and debris. For instance, it is dangerous to let steam from a frying pan or boiling electric kettle discharge onto an outlet. Check the outlets for certified electrical ground fault interrupters.

Kitchen outlets are required to be on three-wire branch circuits and may have one receptacle or two "split-type" receptacles per circuit. Split-type receptacles have the top halves of two receptacles on one circuit and the bottom halves on another. Adjacent outlets may not be wired together. By splitting a receptacle, you can plug in two high-wattage appliances (a frying pan and kettle) without the inconvenience of blowing fuses or tripping circuit breakers. To find out which kitchen receptacles are split, plug in your tester at the outlet, go to the main service panel, find the kitchen fuses and turn them off. You may have to go back and forth numerous times to see which tester light is on and off. With the electrical current off, check the duplex receptacle by removing it from the outlet box. Look for a metal fin, located in either side of the outlet, connecting the two terminals on that receptacle. If the metal fin is broken or removed, the outlet has been split and there is no continuity within both ends of the duplex receptacle. Check with the owner to find out if the circuits have overloaded when two or three appliances have been in use in the kitchen.

Lighting

Fluorescent fixtures will provide three or four times more light than the incandescent type. They also produce less glare, spread the light better and help to eliminate shadows. Almost no heat is produced, whereas incandescent bulbs are a definite heat source. Fluorescent lamps are named after the colour of light emitted, for example, cool white or warm white. You will usually find a central ceiling fixture or a luminous ceiling. Counter-top lighting, along the wall of overhead cupboards, is often found in modern kitchens.

Turn on the light switch. Do the lights flicker or hum? This may indicate an overloaded circuit. Open the cupboards. Can you see inside them, or is it dark inside? Is your shadow cast over work areas? Do surfaces glare in your eyes? Built-in over-counter lighting should cover all work surfaces with a strong, even light. For maximum reflection, a flat white paint finish is essential on the underside of the cabinets on which fluorescent strips are mounted. Check luminous ceilings for broken covers. Are they easy to remove for cleaning or replacing light fixtures? Kitchen lighting should be functional, attractive and easy to clean.

Cabinets

The style of the entire kitchen is set by the cabinet doors, drawer fronts and counter tops. Cabinets come in a variety of styles, finishes, materials, colours, shapes and sizes. They will be either custom or factory built. You may be able to locate a manufacturer's stamp inside the cupboard, which will assist in identifying its construction. Old cabinets that may soon need replacing may in fact be built into the wall itself, as part of the structure. Better-quality cabinets should be screwed, rather than nailed, into the wall to provide greater sup-

A shattering experience!

A new homeowner carefully unpacked her expensive china (which she received as wedding gifts) into her new kitchen cupboards. During the night she was awakened by a loud crashing noise. She discovered that all the kitchen cupboards had pulled loose from the wall!

port. Wood, pressboard, plastic or steel may used in cupboard construction. Use of solid hardwood such as oak offers an attractive appearance and long life. Softer woods will warp over time due to excessive moisture in the cooking areas. While older, steel cabinets are durable and warp free, corrosion of the metal surfaces is often a problem. Inexpensive plastic-laminated finishes will scratch easily. The vinyl material may shrink, leaving edges and corners of wood exposed. Are the surface areas thick with old paint?

The main components of all cabinets consist of the counter top, front frames, drawers, doors, end panels, backs, bottoms, shelves and hardware. At the base of the cabinets there should be a recess for your toes. Measure the height, width, length and depth of the cupboards. How does this compare with the amount of storage area you have at present? Are overhead shelves placed within easy reach for storage of daily-use items without use of a stool? Is there space for storage of large pots and baking pans? Is there room under the sink for storage of a trash can and cleaning supplies? Measure the thickness of shelves and check how they are finished along the edges. Can the shelves be easily cleaned? Do they sag from the weight of heavy objects? Are the shelves adjustable? Some cupboard shelves may be equipped with rails and glides so they can be pulled out for easy access to hard-to-reach corners or deep areas. Check that the glides work smoothly. Modern kitchen cupboards have numerous accessories that add function, organization, utility and convenience. Examples include slide-out cutting boards, microwave openings, lazy susan assemblies and pan and lid racks.

Notice the mouldings on the face of cabinet doors and drawer fronts. Are they real mouldings or have the grooves been router-cut? For comfort and safety the edges of doors and drawers should have rounded corners. Check the swing of all of the cupboard doors. Do they feel heavy and large? Do they shut by themselves forcefully? This may mean that they have been improperly mounted, or a hinge has become loose. Stand back to see if the doors look warped and out of alignment with the floors and walls. Where doors slide inside rails and glides, check the door for looseness and ease of movement. Rails and glides, if worn, can be expensive to replace. The doors should open away from the work area, and not into another's path. Unless there are adequate clearances for corner cabinets, the hinges, knobs and door pulls may interfere with each other. When checking the hinges, keep in mind that worn-out hinges may no longer be manufactured and finding replacements may be impossible. Over time the inexpensive variety of spring self-closing hinges will break and the door will no longer close by itself.

Take the drawers out and look at the sides. Sturdy construction will be evident by multiple dovetailing or a rabbeted joint used to connect the sides to the front and back. Likewise, the drawer bottom should be "dadoed" into the sides, front and back. You may come across one-piece moulded polystyrene drawers with rounded corners for easy cleaning. If the drawer is held together with glue, staples or nails, it may not be capable of holding much weight before the bottom loosens and falls out. Examine the drawer slides. On well-worn older drawers, where wood slides on wood, deposits of fine sawdust can be seen piled up at the end of the worn grooved slides. Newer slides will consist of nylon sliding on nylon or ball-bearing wheels in metal channels.

Countertops will take as much abuse as the kitchen floor. Most are constructed of pieces of plywood, oriented strand board or particleboard fastened to the base cabinets with a finish surface glued or laid on top. The finish surface may consist of stainless steel, plastic-laminated wood, tiles, real or synthetic marble or stone slabs. Harder surfaces are noisier, and dishes will break more easily on them. With your marbles, check if the countertops are level. Run your hands over the surface to check for smoothness. Do you notice any cracks, scratches, burn marks, fading or uneven or bulging surfaces? Are the corners and edges seamless? The front of the countertop should be finished with a slightly raised no-drip edge to prevent spilled liquids from running into the drawers or over the front face of the cupboards. Countertops should be of similar height and finished with a backsplash at the back. Ideally the backsplash will rise all the way to the bottom of the wall cupboards, making the surfaces easier to clean. Gaps between the counter surface and the splashboard will allow water to seep through and provide an entrance for small insects.

Sinks, Garbage Disposers and Faucets

The sink is the start and finish for all kitchen functions. It may have single, double or triple bowls. It may be of stainless steel, ceramic, porcelain or fibreglass construction, and quality sinks will have a brand name fixed near the faucet. Stainless-steel sinks come in 18 and 20 gauge. The smaller the number, the thicker the gauge. Also, a mix of alloys may be used. For example, an 18—8 mix means 18 per cent chrome and 8 per cent nickel content. Chrome allows the sink to keep its finish and resistance to stain, wear and abrasion over the years. Nickel gives the steel the ability to withstand corrosion under all kitchen conditions. Good-quality stainless-steel sinks are undercoated with sound-deadening material. A porcelain sink will chip if heavy items are dropped into it and will show more wear over time than a good-quality stainless-steel sink. Porcelain and fibreglass sinks come in a wide range of colours that can enhance the kitchen decor. Some sinks have accessories such as built-in cutting and drainboards, colanders and coated-wire utility baskets.

Check the inside of the sink for wear and scratches. Notice how it is finished around the edges. Most have a built-in extended rim that fits over the countertop. Examine the sides and bottom of the sink for corrosion and wood rot. Water leakage is often found under the drain trap, beneath the faucet areas, where the sink is sealed to the countertop.

While under the sink you might see a garbage disposer connected to the sink drain. A manufacturer's label and model number should be evident. Most models are insulated and have rubber-cushioned mountings to reduce vibration and noise. Top-quality models have stainless-steel parts and have at least a 3/4-horsepower motor. The shredding compartment capacity and the rate of disposal will vary between models. Some will jam if the garbage is fed too fast. All disposers are equipped with protectors that shut off the unit automatically when the motor becomes overloaded.

If the house has a septic tank, the municipality may require that a larger tank be installed for use with a garbage disposal unit. This is because solid wastes will be introduced into the septic system at a greater rate than would be the case under normal conditions. Also, the tank will require cleaning at more frequent intervals.

There are three basic types of faucets, classified by their shut-off action: conventional washer, washerless and single-lever faucets. Better quality units are constructed of cast brass with a plated finish. Some newer faucets are raised, which makes it easier to work in and around the sink. Turn the water on to check the water pressure under both the hot and cold water. If there is a sluggish flow from the faucet, the aerator (located at the tip of most spouts), which mixes air and water, may be filled with dirt particles. Press down on the handles and move the spout back and forth. Make a note of any water seepage around the handles or spout. If there is a vegetable sprayer, test to see if it is functional. How long does it take water to drain out of the sink? Ask the owner if any chemical drain openers have been used.

Ventilation

Since most kitchens open directly into other living areas, they must have adequate ventilation to carry cooking odours, moisture, smoke and heat to the outside. Look for an exhaust fan installed directly over the range or inside a hood or mounted in the ceiling or wall in the cooking area. For best results, the duct should be made of metal and be short and straight with a minimum number of elbows. There should be no changes in duct size as this will waste fan power and create a place for grease to collect. Wall-mounted fans will not have a duct. If the fan has no duct, it could mean the fan is venting into the cupboard space above — in other words, the contractor never got around to finishing the job! When outside venting is not possible, a ductless fan is installed and an activated carbon filter is used to absorb cooking odours. The disadvantage of a ductless fan is that it does not remove excess heat and moisture from the air. Be aware that a built-in range-grill exhaust fan is strong enough to depressurize an airtight house, and cause backdrafting of air and gases down the chimney.

Switch on the fan. You should hear a slight "ping" indicating the heat-saving damper inside the vent has opened. It will close when the fan is shut off. Does the fan operate quietly? Turn the knob to various speed settings and see if you notice significant air speed changes at each position. The fans located over ranges should have hoods as wide as the range and should project forward as far as possible without interfering with cooking. Check under the hood for a washable one-piece aluminum mesh grease filter. Usually these filters have never been washed and are filled with grease. Without this filter the vapours from cooking and frying will accumulate on the inside of the ducts, resulting in a fire hazard.

Appliances

With appliances like ranges, microwaves, dishwashers and clothes washers, you will not have enough time to check each appliance individually, or to run them through their entire operating cycles. Therefore it is best to get the seller to warrant in the contract that the appliances work. Copy down the name, model and serial number of each appliance. Later contact the manufacturer for details about the age, warranties still in effect, service and operation manuals. Your local library may have appliance manuals of older models.

Check whether the appliances are powered by natural gas, electricity or propane. Keep in mind that if the appliances are included in the sale, they may not be worth much unless they are new. For example, a refrigerator (the largest user of household electricity) that is 10 years old will consume more electricity than a newer one. A modern dishwasher will have added features to handle specialized jobs such as heavily soiled pots and pans.

Floors, Walls and Ceiling

Kitchen flooring material will range from asphalt tile, asbestos vinyl tile, vinyl, linoleum carpet to clay tile and other varieties. It is available in literally thousands of designs, patterns and colours. For comfort and a long lifespan, the material should be water and stain resistant, easy to clean and walk on and free from static electricity buildup. It should aid in sound control and provide resistance to indentation. Some better-quality vinyl flooring is soft to walk on and easy to clean. A clay tile floor is cold and hard to walk on, and unforgiving when dishes are dropped onto it. Tiles easily crack.

Firmly walk about the entire floor. Do you notice any squeaks? Kneel down and have a closer look at the floor around the stove, sink and fridge areas. The more expensive coverings give higher wear resistance. If you discover slightly damaged tiles, perhaps the owner has some replacements or a patching kit. Can the present flooring be removed? If so, look underneath to check the condition of the floor beneath it. One prospective purchaser found three completely different types of worn-out floor coverings under the carpet. If a heat register is near the sink, there may be corrosion in the ducts.

Some wall coverings are both decorative and functional because they are fire resistant and act as a noise barrier. Materials like ceramic, glass or metal wall tiles will be more durable than wood panelling, wallpaper and paint. To prevent mildew and wear, ceramic tiles should be finished with a grout sealer. Semi-gloss paint is the most common material for kitchen walls. A high-gloss enamel paint will add glare and show wall imperfections, while flat finishes are difficult to wash. If it is an older home, you may find boarded-up openings that are no longer used. Check these for signs of mildew.

Most ceiling tiles sold for kitchen use are vinyl coated and resistant to grease, dirt and smoke soiling. Some are impregnated to aid in acoustics when there is another floor above the kitchen. Where suspended ceiling tiles have been used to lower a ceiling, take a tile out of its support to examine it. A good paint job will last two or three years. Textured plastered ceilings are most difficult to clean and repairs to damaged surfaces are difficult to disguise. Notice any cracks in the ceiling. One homeowner noticed suspicious cracks on her lath and plaster kitchen ceiling. Shortly after occupancy, when sitting at the breakfast table, she was showered in ceiling material and debris!

To familiarize yourself with various kitchen products, you may find it helpful to first visit a kitchen showroom at a building supply or plumbing fixture store. Keep in mind that the inclusion or removal of major appliances from the Offer to Purchase is often a negotiable item. If you wish them to be included in the price, be certain you know their present value and working condition.

CHECKPOINTS
✔✔✔✔✔✔✔✔✔✔

Kitchen
____ location
____ size
____ shape
____ layout
____ odours
____ natural light
____ natural ventilation
____ mechanical ventilation

Electrical
____ number of outlets
____ split receptacles
____ overloaded outlets
____ certified electrical ground
____ fault interrupters
____ last updated

Lighting
____ type
____ fluorescent
____ incandescent
____ track
____ recessed
____ shadows
____ glare

_____ valence board
_____ other

Cabinets

_____ manufacturer
_____ height
_____ width
_____ length
_____ depth
_____ age
_____ condition of doors
_____ condition of drawers
_____ condition of countertop
_____ condition of back splash
_____ adjustable shelves
_____ accessible shelves
_____ cutting board
_____ manufacturer's warranty

Hardware

_____ condition of knobs
_____ condition of pulls
_____ condition of hinges
_____ child safety features
_____ certified testing agency approved

Sink

_____ age
_____ size
_____ shape
_____ stainless steel
_____ porcelain
_____ fibreglass
_____ how secured
_____ other
_____ vegetable sprayer
_____ garbage disposer
_____ condition
_____ last replaced
_____ manufacturer
_____ certified testing agency approved

Faucets

_____ manufacturer
_____ age
_____ corrosion
_____ water pressure
_____ drains work
_____ last replaced
_____ adjustable faucet heights
_____ manufacturer's warranty
_____ certified testing agency approved

Appliances

_____ fridge
_____ stove
_____ other
_____ features
_____ energy-efficiency labels
_____ manufacturer
_____ model number
_____ serial number
_____ age
_____ certified testing agency approved
_____ manufacturer's warranty

Flooring

_____ type
_____ condition
_____ age
_____ last replaced
_____ wear
_____ stain resistant
_____ polishing or waxing required
_____ manufacturer's warranty

Walls and Ceilings

_____ finish
_____ moisture stains
_____ washable surfaces

CONSUMER TIPS

As mentioned earlier, if you are buying a new house, ask if the builder is registered with the New Home Warranty Program in your province. If the builder is registered with the NHWP, in some provinces the deposit funds are protected up to a maximum amount. If the builder is not registered with NHWP be very cautious, and don't pay any money or sign a builder's contract without your lawyer's advice. The NHWP of each province is similar but has some differences. The builder adds the fee for NHWP coverage onto the house price or builds it into the price. NHWP coverage generally includes buyer protection for the deposit, incomplete work allowance, warranty protection up to a year, basement protection for two years, and major structural defect protection for five years. Although the NHWP was designed to protect purchasers of newly constructed houses against defects in construction, there are limitations in coverage. These limitations and exclusions could cost you a lot of money. That is why you need to check out the NHWP and builder thoroughly.

If you are buying a house with others, in a non-personal relationship situation, for example, as an investment, make sure that you set out the arrangement clearly in writing beforehand. The agreement would cover such issues as: what if a partner dies or wants out of the agreement, under what circumstances would the house be sold, who looks after the bookkeeping and has cheque writing privileges, who pays what position of the monthly and annual expenses etc "Falling-out" with investment partners can and does occur, with frequency. Speak to a lawyer to get advice to protect yourself.

Factors to consider when buying real estate with others include:

- goals and objectives
- expertise of the other owners
- liquidity that is, how quickly you can get your money out of the investment
- potential personal liability
- legal structure of property ownership who has control
- tax considerations
- compatibility with other owners
- risk assessment
- contribution of owner in time and money
- percentage of investment for money
- management responsibility
- how profits and losses are dealt with
- getting out or buying others out.

CHAPTER 13

The Bathroom

LTHOUGH ONE OF the most basic rooms in the house, bathrooms can be a key decision-making factor as to whether the house is suited to you and your family. As with kitchens, your choice will depend upon lifestyle, convenience, luxury and style considerations. Modern bathrooms that offer extra amenities and space may appeal to your love of luxury. On the other hand, the traditional style and charm of an old-fashioned tub and pedestal sink may strike your fancy if you enjoy antiques and country-style homes. For everyone, though, the number of bathrooms, their size and location are the main convenience factors that will be addressed. For instance, a family home may ideally have three bathrooms: a powder room close to the living area for guests, an en suite off the master bedroom for the parents, and a bathroom used mainly by the children. Some houses come completely outfitted with a master suite bath, garden bathroom, powder room, a children's bathroom, sauna and steam bath rooms. This chapter will review each of these as well as the fixtures, accessories, lighting and floors.

As you walk through each of the bathrooms in the house, consider your lifestyle needs. If you will not need each of the rooms, will they end up being a nuisance rather than a convenience factor? Regular upkeep and repair may be time-consuming and costly. Will the added rooms enhance the resale value of the house? Adequate ventilation is a prime concern for bathrooms. Notice any musty or stale odours in the bathrooms. Also important are provisions for natural light, privacy and acoustics.

Test to see if there is enough room to start and finish an activity with ease by going through natural simulated hand, elbow, arm and body movements at each fixture. Especially if the bathroom is small, you will want to know that you could dry yourself after a shower without hitting your arms on fixtures or walls. Will the tissue paper become wet when you shower? The angle at which the door opens is an important privacy consideration. Walk out of the bathroom, leaving the door open, and stand in the hallway or room adjacent to ensure the fixtures are shielded from view. The door swing should not interfere with cupboard doors or towel racks.

Vanities, Countertops and Basins

Look at the vanity and countertop in the same manner in which you inspected the kitchen cupboards. Do the same for the cupboard construction, drawers, doors and hardware. You will find a greater variety of bathroom ceramic tile countertops than you will in kitchens. The most common are glazed, quarry, crystalline and scored, mosaics and decorated tile. Check the condition of the grout with your awl. Also look at the construction of the backsplash. Depending on the construction of the vanity, caulking should be used along the crevice between the wall and edge of the countertop backsplash in order to waterproof the area.

Basins come in different colours, styles, shapes and sizes. They can vary from vitreous china, fibreglass or plastic to formed steel or cast iron. Look around the edge of the basin to see how it is mounted. It may be a pedestal, wall-hung or a one-piece type where the entire unit rests on the cabinet framework. This type is commonly made of synthetic marble or plastic. The basin may also rest inside a ring on a rim or clamped under the opening provided by the countertop. If a wall-hung basin has not been properly secured by hangers, it will pull away from the wall. This and the pedestal type takes up the least amount of space and is least expensive. However, it also leaves the plumbing pipes exposed and provides no storage. Any visible pipes should be chromed for an improved appearance. Check the condition of the hangers for anchorage ability and corrosion.

Look inside the basin for chips and cracks and how well water is kept out of the seams and joint lines. With your flashlight and mirror, explore under the basin as you did under the kitchen sink. If you do find that the basin must be replaced, how easily and inexpensively can this be done? When basins are used in pairs in a countertop, there should be "elbow room" between the two. Is there an overflow edge around the rim to collect water in case the sink is filled to capacity? Does the basin have a self-draining soap rest? The brand name and colour of the basin should match that of the toilet and tub.

Toilets

All toilets do not work or look alike. Some are less prone to clogging up, quieter and more energy efficient than others. Notice the design and profile of the toilet, and whether it is a one- or two-piece unit. Good-quality toilets are made out of vitreous china. In a basement with a concrete floor, you may find wall-hung off-the-floor toilets. These are designed to discharge above the floor directly into the drainage line fitted in the wall. Another type of toilet you may come across fits into corners and is triangular in shape. The Victorian pull-chain toilet has a floor-mounted bowl and an elevated tank. Other names you may hear to describe toilets are siphon action, siphon jet, reverse trap or wash-down. The only difference between these is their flushing action. The toilet seat should match the bathroom decor and fit the shape of the toilet bowl — either oval or round. It is usually made of solid or moulded wood or plastic. The hinge posts should be secured tightly without a trace of metal corrosion. Some seats have an easily removable hinge to simplify bowl and seat cleaning.

With a mirror, check the underside of the bowl for cracks and stains. Similarly, check the underside of the toilet tank for dripping water. Sweating occurs when cold water in the tank cools the porcelain and warm moist air condenses on the outside. Some tanks are lined with foam insulation to reduce condensation and sweating. Water dripping from the tank will cause mildew and floor rot. To eliminate this problem, some owners have installed a tempering valve at the toilet shut-off valve that mixes hot and cold water entering the tank. With both hands, try to move the toilet. Is it loose and not secured properly? Is there a gap between the base of the toilet and the floor?

Look into the bowl and see how much of it is covered with water. Place a piece of tissue paper in the bowl and flush the toilet. Monitor how long it takes the tissue to disappear. How close does the water come to the rim of the bowl during the flush? Did the toilet completely shut off the water flow at the end of the flushing action? Now remove the lid from the tank and check underneath. Here you will find the model, style and manufacturer's name. By contacting the manufacturer you will find out the age of the unit and how many gallons of water are used per flush. Flush the toilet again and study the tank mechanisms including the handle, arm, chain, float ball and closing valve. Does the water refill the tank to the necessary depth and then shut off in the supply line? How close does the water come to the overflow mark inside the tank? If the water level is too low you will get an incomplete flush and the bowl will not cleanse properly.

Bathtubs

Like the other bathroom fittings, bathtubs come in many sizes, shapes, styles and colours. The five main types of tubs are enamelled cast iron, enamelled steel, acrylic, press-moulded fibreglass and gel-coat fibreglass. Gel-coat fibreglass is the most difficult to repair should a scratch penetrate the surface colour coat. Acrylic and press-moulded fibreglass are more durable and the colour is an integral part of the material — therefore it doesn't scratch easily. However, they have a tendency to flex during use because they are lighter. As a support there should be sand or plaster of Paris under the tub. If concrete has been used, you will never be able to remove the tub in one piece.

Enamelled cast iron and enamelled steel will draw heat faster from the water if the undersides are not insulated. The high-gloss finish is durable, but it will chip if a heavy object is dropped into it. Keep in mind that neutral

What's behind those soft, bulging bathroom tiles?

On looking behind some tiles that had fallen off the shower wall, a new owner was surprised to find old, rusted licence plates and delaminated real estate signs that were nailed to the wall and covered with ceramic tiles!

colours are easier to repair and don't show water or dirt marks as readily as bolder colours. These tubs are quite heavy, and the weight of the tub filled with water can add substantial pounds per square foot to the load of the floor structure. If a recently renovated upper floor bathroom has a cast-iron tub in it, ask the owner if the existing floor joists were doubled to support the extra weight. The manufacturer's specifications should indicate the tub's capacity and installation requirements. The water capacity can range from 17 to 40 gallons, and the weight of an empty tub is usually about 8 pounds per gallon capacity.

Whirlpool and Jet Tubs

Some tubs have the added feature of whirlpools or jets. In a whirlpool tub, air and water enter through large end jets which push water along your body. In jetted tubs, air and water are injected through matched pairs of ports on each side of the tub. Some tubs have tiny holes in the floor that create a bubbly turbulence, but they don't provide as fast a current as the side-mounted jets. More expensive whirlpools come with built-in arm rests, sculptured edges, moulded back supports, underwater lights, grab bars, angled sides to help splashes run back into the tub and slip-resistant textured floors.

A greater quantity of jets does not necessarily mean higher quality. The important consideration is jet size and location. Fewer but larger jets can move over 25 gallons of water per minute. More circulation of water throughout the tub causes a greater whirlpool action. Jets placed high and low are ideal for massage, as well as helping the tub to drain more easily. Small tubs with high-velocity jets can cause water to sting the body. The jets should rotate through at least a 60 degree arc. See if you can adjust the direction of the jets. Check also how the air/water mix adjustments are made.

You may wish to visit a bathroom plumbing display store to investigate the whirlpool tub's brand name, construction and circulating pipes. If the pipes are angled and lie flat, the tub may drain poorly and be noisy. Sloped and curved piping helps water drain out of the system to prevent it from stagnating and smelling. Examine how the pipes are held in place to prevent sagging. Measure the size of the supply lines. Larger models should have two sets of piping or the water will be cold when the tub is full. Check for certified testing agency labels (such as Underwriters' Laboratories or Canadian Standards Association) to prove that there is no chance the electrical current can reach the water.

Remember that each time you fill the tub you will use a lot of hot water, so check the capacity of the hot-water heater with this in mind. Depending on the size of the house and the number of occupants, some reserve of hot water should be left for other demands. Larger models have in-line heaters that warm the water as it circulates. If you find in-line heaters on smaller units, be aware that bath soap can damage the heater.

Check all timers and switches. To prevent electrocution, they should be mounted at least 5 feet from the tub. Find the whirlpool's motor and pump. The access panels should be easy to remove. There may be a trapdoor through the ceiling of the room below or in the bathroom floor. Most tubs have a to 1-horsepower motor with two speeds. The larger the motor, the more voltage is required. Take note that some motors will burn out if they are started before the tub is sufficiently filled with water. The pump should be wired to a separate ground-fault circuit interrupter and any copper pipes must be grounded. Ask the owner if there are any warranties on the tub, motor and pump.

Soaking Tubs

You will sometimes see the Japanese-type soaking tub, which is jetless and fills to chin depth. Check to see where the fittings are mounted and make sure the floor is well constructed to withstand the heavy load of water when the tub is in use.

Showers

You will find tub/shower combinations as well as single and double shower stalls. They may be fabricated during construction or factory made. The materials used in factory-made or one piece tub/shower combinations are the same as those discussed in the section on tubs. One-piece units come with unbroken surfaces and no joints or grout lines to prevent leaks. Floors in some shower stalls are reinforced plastic or pre-cast to provide a threshold and curb. Check for non-slip surfaces.

Pay particular attention to the waterproofing of the joints and the opening of the shower enclosure. There may be a curtain rod or glass door. You will find that neither will keep water away from the floor at the threshold. Look around the floor and wall on the outside of the shower stall, and test with your awl for soft, moist areas. Often water seeps under the bathroom flooring material. You might want to plug the drain in the shower-stall floor and let water flow from the shower for a few minutes. Do you notice any water seepage around the floor?

Firmly press your hand against all surfaces of the shower wall areas, especially those that have been fabricated during construction. Notice soft or bulging areas. This is a sure indication of water leakage and rot behind the wall. Check the condition of the caulking where the fittings penetrate the wall areas. If there is a window along the shower wall, water that collects along the sill will promote mildew and decay.

Fittings

Fittings include all devices used to control and direct the flow of water. They include faucets, taps, shower heads, centersets and so on. The durability of the fittings depends upon the internal operating mechanisms and the quality of brass used under the chrome, gold, ceramic or plastic finish. Brass workings are not affected by alkalinity, corrosion or strong detergents. Cheaper fittings will wear out sooner and can prove to be more expensive over the long term. By familiarizing yourself with low, middle and luxury lines of fixtures on display at plumbing supply stores, you will be able to recognize the quality differences.

Faucet controls for hot and cold water will range from single-handle, two-handle, twist-handle, to push-pull or single-lever types. Internal valve operations can include compression valve, ball and socket, cartridge, tapered cam or disc to disc. Turn on the water at all faucets and flush the toilet. Do you notice a reduction in water pressure at the faucets? Did you get splashed when you turned on the water? This may indicate an inexpensive installation.

Check the shower heads. Do the ball joints and swivel head connections leak? Some shower installations will have various types of hand-held shower heads. More expensive models will have automatic flow controls to adjust the force of the flow to give a water massage, for instance, and scald prevention valves. What fittings must be activated to get water out of the shower head? Put your hands on the levers and knobs to check for looseness. Is the location of the shower head high enough so you won't have to duck under it when showering? Check for blue-green stains near the drains. These can be caused by copper salts deposited by a dripping tap and are difficult to remove.

For servicing or emergencies, you will need to know where the shut-off valves are for each of the fittings. These are most often found under the toilet tank, sink and tub. Some are under the floor coverings. Water pipes for fittings found in uninsulated exterior wall cavities run an extreme risk of freezing or bursting in cold weather.

Check the bathrooms for the number of certified ground fault interrupters and their location. Will these meet your needs for plug-in shavers and hair drying and styling equipment? You may find a variety of built-in accessories such as telephone, intercom, heat lamps, mirrors, medicine cabinets, etc. Examine each for wear, discolouration, looseness, corrosion and consistency in design. Some of these devices may be mere gadgets rather than being functional or practical.

Ventilation

Bathrooms need exhaust fans to remove or reduce the odours and high humidity caused by excessive moisture. Locate the fan and ductwork. Similar to the kitchen fan, the duct should be as straight as possible, with a minimum number of elbows. The location of the bathrooms will determine which way the vent blows — down and out or up and out through a wall or the roof. In single-storey houses or top-floor bathrooms, the duct should pass through the attic and vent to the outside above the roof level. The duct connects to a roof vent with a heat-saving damper, which opens only by the force of the fan. From outside of the house, observe how the vent is capped. Does the metal around the vents look corroded?

Remove the grill cover to see if it is an axial or centrifugal (squirrel cage) type. The centrifugal fan is more effective in removing air quickly. Check for dust inside the fan. Turn on the power and listen for grinding noises. If the fan blades turn slowly, the motor may need replacement.

A wall-mounted fan on an exterior wall can move more air faster because there is no ducting to slow down the air flow. It is, however, prone to air leakage and heat loss when the fan isn't operating because the louvres don't shut tightly. The uninsulated wall space also increases heat loss. An overhead infrared lamp is a popular method of reducing condensation in bathrooms. These lamps are sometimes combined with a blower to help circulate the warm air. While they remove the visible signs of condensation, heat lamps do not remove moisture.

Lighting

Determine the types of activities that will take place in the bathrooms and the lighting level that has been provided. The light level should increase near the sink to assist with hair styling and makeup applications. The toilet and tub area should have a dimmer and more relaxed lighting. Sometimes dimmer switches are provided to allow a range of lighting moods. Most bathrooms have flush-mounted wall or ceiling fixtures or recessed downlights. Hanging fixtures are often prohibited in building codes. Any light fixtures in the shower area must be a waterproof variety. For shadow-free light around the mirror, you may find theatre-type strip lights or warm incandescent bulbs are used. White or warm-toned fluorescent tubes have quite different distorting effects on skin and decorative wall finishes. Do the fluorescent tubes have an electronic ballast? You may find a "humming" noise from lower-quality tubes.

Floors

Identify the floor material used. It should be water resistant. A vinyl, cushioned type of flooring will feel the softest to walk on. Note that ceramic, brick and stone finishes will feel hard and cold to the feet. Polished natural stone, granite, marble and slate can be slippery and therefore are better suited for walls or countertops. Also, to support the weight of these materials, floors should be specially reinforced. Conventional carpet will rot unless it has a waterproof backing and is made of synthetic fibres. Check if it is tacked down or laid loose. Can it be removed easily for drying or cleaning? Examine the floor areas for "wet" zones around the shower, sink and tub. Make a note of any discolouration of floor surfaces and lifting tiles. There may be serious rot and decay underneath. Also check around and inside the heat register for signs of rust.

Walls and Ceiling

Walls and ceilings must be waterproof, as must any wooden wainscoting. Run your hands over the wall surfaces and check the corners for mildew. Pay particular attention to large outlines of dried drip marks along walls and ceilings or blistered paint and moisture stains around the bottom of window walls. These are all signs of inadequate ventilation.

For acoustical privacy, good wall insulation and sound-proofing construction should be in place. Bathroom noises should be isolated from the rest of the house, and vice versa. To test if this is the case, let some water run from the tub faucet, then leave the bathroom and close the door. Poorly insulated walls will allow sounds to transfer to other areas of the house, which can be a nuisance.

Saunas

The sauna is a high-temperature, low-humidity treatment used to relax muscles and produce a cleansing of the pores through the promotion of excessive body perspiration. While a sauna can be found almost anywhere in a house, ideally it should be located close to a swimming pool or bathroom so you can have a cold-water dousing as a final step.

Ask the owner if the sauna came in a kit form and enquire about the name of the manufacturer. Observe the construction materials and detailing used in the sauna. The wood must be able to withstand extreme temperature changes, and act as a floor, wall and ceiling insulator. It must also diffuse the heat so that the surfaces remain warm but not hot to the skin. Aspen or kiln-dried clear all-heart and A-grade redwood are commonly used. For adequate air convection, the ceiling should not be less than 7 feet in height.

The heater size should correspond to room size and may be electrical, natural gas, free-standing or wall-mounted. Examine the controls. Saunas must contain a "manual reset over temperature protector" to automatically shut off the sauna if it becomes too hot. This is actually double-protection that takes over if the room temperature control thermostat fails. All controls and heaters must be rated by a recognized testing agency such as Underwriters' Laboratories or Canadian Standards Association.

Behind the interior walls you should find metal foil insulation, approved by a certified testing agency. Above the insulation in the ceiling there should be adequate air circulation space. Check the condition of the light, vent window, benches, backrests, doors, hardware hinges and trim. See if the slatted platform floor can be lifted out for cleaning.

Steam Baths

Unlike a sauna, a steam bath has a high moisture content with an average humidity level close to 100 per cent. As steam can penetrate tiny crevices and damage walls and ceilings, the enclosure must be vapour-tight. The walls and ceiling should be lined with an impervious material applied over waterproof gypsum board. The floor must also be waterproof and have adequate drainage. Check if the door is vapour-proof and shatter-proof and seals tightly.

A steam generator boils water and sends the steam through tubing into the stall. The system should consist of a timer control and anti-scald steam outlet head. Refer to the operating instruction manual for built-in safety features. Check the condition of the enclosure for mildew, dampness and rotting materials. Examine areas along the bottom of walls and at the ceiling edges and corners with your awl.

A word of caution is necessary on the use of spas, whirlpools, hot tubs, saunas and steam baths. These devices can cause high blood pressure, increased heart rate and decreased muscle tone, and therefore are not recommended for use by people with such medical conditions. Play it safe and have a medical checkup beforehand.

CHECKPOINTS
✔✔✔✔✔✔✔✔✔✔✔

General
____ location
____ size
____ privacy
____ odours
____ acoustics
____ natural light
____ condensation
____ natural ventilation
____ mechanical ventilation
____ wheelchair accessible

____ fibreglass
____ other
____ edge finish
____ age
____ leaks
____ corrosion
____ condition
____ loose basin
____ last replaced
____ certified testing agency
        approved

Basin
____ manufacturer
____ vitreous china
____ cast iron
____ plastic
____ formed steel

Countertop
____ finish
____ caulked joints
____ backsplash
____ last replaced

Toilets
____ manufacturer
____ age
____ vitreous china
____ other
____ seat and lid
____ condition of internal components
____ tank insulation liner
____ leaks
____ loose toilet
____ flushing ability
____ condensation
____ water used per flush
____ bidet
____ last replaced
____ certified testing agency approved

Bathtubs
____ shape
____ enamelled cast iron
____ enamelled steel
____ cultured marble
____ press molded fibreglass
____ gel-coat fibreglass
____ acrylic faced
____ hard or soft surfaces
____ manufacturer
____ age
____ how cleaned
____ gallons of water required
____ jets
____ motor
____ pump
____ timers
____ switches
____ leaks
____ shower
____ caulking
____ grout
____ grab bars
____ other
____ certified testing agency approved

Faucet Fittings
____ manufacturer
____ age
____ last replaced
____ brass
____ plastic
____ other
____ corrosion
____ leaks
____ water pressure
____ drains work
____ adjustable-height faucets

Accessories
____ rod hooks
____ soap holder
____ paper roll holders
____ grab bar
____ mirror
____ shower curtain rod
____ sliding shower doors
____ lockable medicine cabinets
____ child safety features
____ certified testing agency approved

Lighting
____ fluorescent tubes
____ recessed
____ strip lights
____ incandescent
____ dimmer switches
____ timer switches
____ heat lamp
____ other
____ certified testing agency approved

Electrical
____ number of outlets
____ certified electrical ground
____ fault interrupters

Floor
____ type
____ condition

_____ age
_____ wear
_____ stain resistant

Walls and Ceilings
_____ finish
_____ moisture stains
_____ shower walls
_____ acoustics

Sauna
_____ manufacturer
_____ age
_____ type of wood
_____ heating source
_____ benches
_____ manual reset over temperature

_____ protector
_____ light fixture
_____ window
_____ backrests
_____ manufacturer's warranty
_____ certified testing agency
　　　 approved

Steam Baths
_____ vapour tightness
_____ timer control
_____ enclosure condition
_____ age of generator
_____ anti-scald outlet
_____ manufacturer's warranty
_____ certified testing agency
　　　 approved

CONSUMER TIPS

There are some classic pitfalls when people buy real estate that you should avoid. People who have real estate problems generally succumb to a combination of the following common traps:

- Not having an understanding on how the real estate market works.
- Not having a clear understanding of personal and financial needs.
- Not having a clear focus and lacking a realistic real estate investment plan, with strategies and priorities.
- Not doing thorough market research and comparison shopping before making the purchase.
- Not selecting the right property considering the potential risks, money involved, and specific personal needs.
- Not verifying representations or assumptions beforehand.
- Not doing financial calculations beforehand.
- Not buying at a fair market price.
- Not buying real estate at the right time in the market.

- Not buying within financial debt servicing capacity, comfort zone, and skills.
- Not understanding the financing game thoroughly, and therefore not comparison shopping and not getting the best rates, terms, and right type of mortgage.
- Not making a decision based on an objective assessment but on an emotional one.
- Not determining the real reason why the vendor is selling.
- Not having the property inspected by a professional building inspector before purchase decision made.
- Not selecting an experienced real estate lawyer and obtaining advice beforehand.
- Not selecting an experienced professional tax accountant when selecting real estate investment property, and obtaining advice beforehand.
- Not selecting an experienced realter with expertise in the type of real estate and geographic location you are considering.
- Not negotiating effectively.
- Not putting in the appropriate conditions or "subject clauses" in the offer.
- Not buying for the right reasons, in other words buying for tax shelter inducement reasons rather than the inherent value, potential, and viability of the investment property.
- Not independently verifying financial information beforehand.
- Not obtaining and reviewing all the necessary documentation appropriate for a given property, before making a final decision to buy.
- Not selecting real estate investment partners carefully.
- Not having a written agreement with real estate investment partners, prepared by a lawyer.
- Not specifically detailing what chattels are included in the purchase price.
- Not seeing the property before buying it, but relying on pictures and/or the representations of others or model show homes or suites.
- Not managing property well, or not selecting the right property management company.
- Not selling the property at the right time in the market or for the right reasons.
- Not buying another house before you sell the one you own. That is if you only want one house and are not speculating.
- Not looking at long-term value but only a good price.

CHAPTER 14

Energy Conservation

TO THIS POINT in your inspections you have been carefully monitoring the quality and durability of construction materials used in the house. Now it is time to focus on how comfortable you will be in the house. The way your family uses a house will greatly affect its energy consumption. Therefore, because of widely varying lifestyles, you should not assume the previous owner's heating bills will be the same as yours for the same house.

The variables affecting energy consumption will either relate to lifestyle or house construction considerations. Lifestyle factors include the number of hours the house is occupied, the size of family and conservation habits of each individual in the house. For example, a typical family may produce 2 to 3 gallons of moisture per day, solely from breathing and bathing.

The age of the house and its method of construction is the largest factor affecting the effectiveness of the heating, insulation and air circulation. Of course, as mentioned earlier, the number and age of the occupants (including pets) and their lifestyle habits will also be a factor. Increased attention is being drawn to reducing consumption and raising awareness of energy conservation. Governments, schools, corporations and the media have begun a concerted effort in this regard.

House Construction

To best ascertain the real age and method of construction, ask the owner for all construction documentation, plans and specifications for the house. Careful review of this documentation will take away a lot of the mystery and worry of whether you will have a comfortable and trouble-free existence in the home. Once you have moved into the house, the documents will assist you and any tradespeople you may hire to solve problems or nuisances as they arise. As well, this information will be invaluable when making additions or renovations or for resale of the house. In many cases, depending on the age of the house and the number of times it has changed ownership, the necessary documents will be no longer available. Even without the paperwork you can inspect for type of construction, air leakage, insulation, wall and ceiling type, as described below.

Type of Construction

Earlier, in Chapter 4, construction techniques such as platform frame, balloon frame and solid brick were discussed. If the house was built after 1982, specific performance standards for energy efficiency may have been a requirement. Depending upon the climate of the region and the size of the dwelling, the house may have been built to specific technical requirements of the R-2000 Home Program. This program was designed to ensure the method of construction met certain standards for heating, lighting, ventilation, insulation, and quality of door and window products. One such requirement is the use of Air Drywall Approach (ADA). This system uses sealants, adhesives, caulking and gaskets in various combinations to provide air-barrier continuity between various framing components of the building's construction. The major function of the continuous air barrier is to prevent air leakage and control moisture movement through the building envelope.

Air Leakage

Air flow is extremely important in a house, since it carries moisture, heat, pollutants and odours throughout the house. The continuous exchange of air between the interior of the house and its exterior surroundings is through controlled mechanical ventilation and uncontrolled air leakage.

Air leakage, in fact, is the most serious energy loss problem in any house. It will affect comfort, energy costs and ventilation. The rule is: *If you want to make your house more energy efficient, seal before you insulate.* Types of sealant include caulking, weatherstripping, tapes and foams.

Caulking is used where two materials meet but do not move relative to each other. An example is where a vent pipe penetrates the wall. The caulking should be uniform and durable, and still adhered to its surface. Often new applications of caulking have been applied on top of old, especially around exterior window/door frames and over masonry cracks, stucco or wood siding. This is reason enough to suspect there is water penetration into the house. Notice any dried caulking that can be easily lifted with the point of your awl.

Weatherstripping should be found wherever one surface moves relative to another. It should be found around the outer edges of doors, windows and attic hatches. Door weatherstripping comes in two forms: magnetic and compression. Magnetic weatherstripping will work only on steel doors. It behaves like the seal on your refrigerator door. It is installed around the top and lock side jambs, where it seals against the flat door surface. The compression type is used on the hinge side. Compression weatherstripping is squeezed between the door and jamb to create a seal. After being compressed it should spring back to its original shape. Lower-quality brands can become permanently deformed and no longer effective.

Weatherstripping along the threshold of the door is thicker, often with multiple flanges or lips making contact with the threshold. Thresholds are made of rigid vinyl, wood or aluminum. The aluminum type should have a thermal break consisting of a thin layer of insulating material between the inside and outside parts of the threshold. This prevents conductive heat loss as well as condensation forming inside the threshold.

As discussed earlier, the quality, location, size, shape and number of windows will have a significant impact on energy costs. Fixed windows need no weatherstripping, but the edges may be caulked. Hinged windows should have compression weatherstripping between the sash and frame at each side, top and bottom. Double-hung windows or sliders should also be weatherstripped. Metal and vinyl sliding windows and sliding doors have a specially fitted pile-type weatherstripping. Inspect the pile-type weatherstripping in its track to see if it has resisted mould, mildew, corrosion and damage from ultraviolet light. Notice its density, width and thickness. The most difficult windows to weatherstrip properly are the jalousie type, often used in living rooms, kitchens, bathrooms and bedrooms. Sealant tapes are also used to join the edges around windows. Fillers, such as oakum, polyurethane foam or loose glass-fibre insulation, are used for larger openings.

Walk around the house and note all air-leakage areas. Hold your hand over an opening to feel for cold air drafts, or hold a feather and watch for the fluttering of the plume. Start at the openings around doors, windows and mail slots. From the inside looking out, is there any daylight visible around the edges of the weatherstripping? Do you notice any black streaks inside the door jams? This is from air infiltrating and exfiltrating the house. Check around electrical outlets and switches and everywhere there are electrical wires, plumbing, stacks or chimneys penetrating the ceiling. Are there foam gaskets behind the electrical face plates? Check the fireplace damper and seal of the glass doors. Other areas to check include the joints between the walls and ceiling, the sill plate and foundation wall area, around the attic hatch and vents in the kitchen, bathroom and laundry room. Dirty patches on the undersides or along the edges and joints of insulation batts indicate extreme leakage.

While checking the house for air leakage, be aware of the windward and leeward sides of the house. If most of the openings you find are on the windward side, inside air pressure will increase. Walls on the low-pressure or leeward side of the house may show more signs of moisture because the warm, moist air is being drawn to the outdoors through those openings.

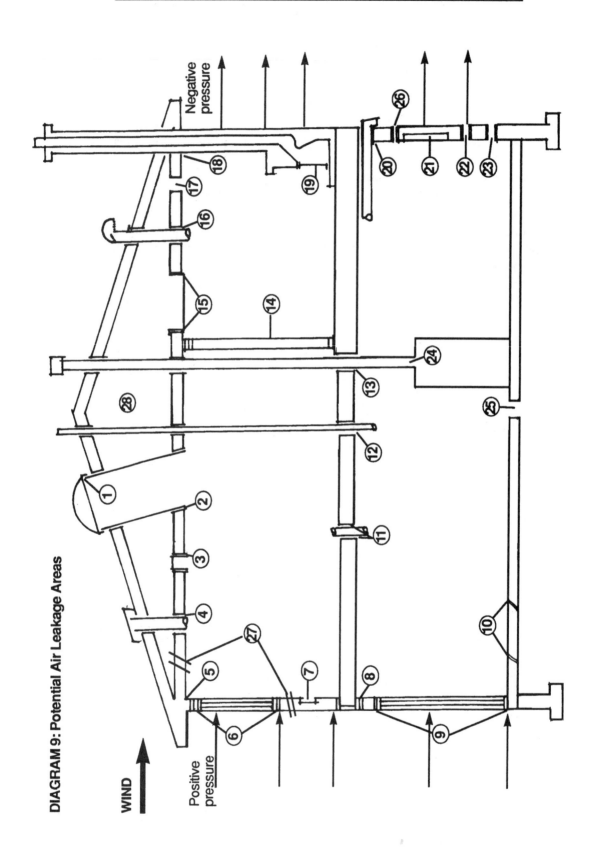

DIAGRAM 9: Potential Air Leakage Areas

AIR LEAKAGE AROUND:
1. Skylight
2. Skylight lightwell
3. Electric light fixtures
4. Exhaust vents from bathrooms and kitchen
5. Joints between ceiling and walls
6. Window frames and panes, deteriorated weatherstripping
7. Electrical boxes
8. Sills and floor
9. Door frames and door threshold, deteriorated weatherstripping
10. Concrete floor cracks
11. Pipe and wire penetrations through floor and ceiling joists
12. Plumbing vent stacks penetrating through floor and ceiling joists
13. Chimney penetrations at floor and ceiling areas
14. Interior wall partitions
15. Attic hatch poorly fitted
16. Kitchen exhaust vent and damper door
17. Recessed lights
18. Fireplace chimney penetration of ceiling
19. Leaky fireplace glass doors, fireplace damper and fireplace clean-out door
20. Exhaust ducts penetrating walls and dampers
21. Electrical panel
22. Natural gas pipe penetration
23. Water faucet on exterior wall
24. Chimney continuously leaks air from house
25. Floor drains; air enters from drain tile
26. Cable television, telephone and electrical wire wall penetrations
27. Ceiling and wall cracks, broken vapour barrier
28. Humid air in attic

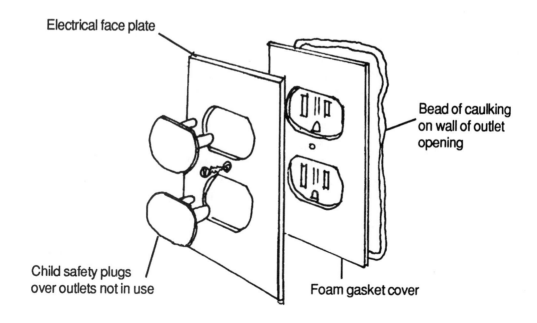

Electrical face plate

Bead of caulking on wall of outlet opening

Child safety plugs over outlets not in use

Foam gasket cover

Insulation Materials

Insulation may be attached to the framing of the house or placed inside the framing. The six major types are flexible, fill-type, rigid board, interlocking panels, foamed in place and reflective. Each has different uses, which are described below.

Flexible insulation materials are made of mineral wool, rock wool or glass fibre and are compressed into batts or blankets. Available in several thicknesses, it is installed in the hollow cavities between framing members in walls, ceilings and floor joints. Older blankets and batts will have a heavy paper covering, often asphalt-impregnated. It may be covered on one or both sides with a metal foil or metal foil paper, which serves as a vapour barrier and as reflective insulation. There should be at least 3/4 inch between the reflective foil and the nearest facing surface.

Fill-type insulation is made of the same material as batts and blankets but comes in loose form and is poured or mechanically blown into place. It is used most commonly between the joists in unfinished attics and less frequently in walls because of its tendency to settle, which destroys its effectiveness.

Rigid board insulation is applied directly to the studs, either on the inside or outside, or both. Glued or mechanically fastened, it can be applied horizontally or vertically. The joints are taped where the panels meet. The board is commonly manufactured in 4' x 8' sheets in a variety of thicknesses. You will normally find rigid boards in tight spaces such as under basement ceilings. It is also applied over cathedral ceilings and concrete foundations in basements and crawl spaces.

Some houses are built out of solid interlocking insulation panels that provide both structure and energy efficiency. The panels snap together to form foundations and walls that are reinforced with steel rods and concrete. When inside the house, check the perimeter walls with the palm of your hands for any movement. As acoustics are sometimes a problem in homes with this type of insulation, you may wish to test for sound travel by playing a radio in one room while you walk through other rooms.

Since 1980 the use of Urea Formaldehyde Foam (UFFI) foamed-in-place insulation has been banned because of the severe health hazard. Gases emitted from UFFI have caused throat, eye and nose irritations, coughing, headaches, dizziness, insomnia, skin rashes, sneezing and nausea. It was commonly used in attics, ceilings, interior partition walls, basements, floors over unheated spaces and under bathtubs. None of these areas allow for air circulation and the formaldehyde gas released from the foam gradually infiltrates the living areas. Besides the health risks, improper installation of UFFI can physically damage homes because of its chemical reactions and deterioration. Electrical fittings and mortar may corrode and walls may mould and rot.

Reflective insulation differs from other types of insulation in that the number of reflecting surfaces, not its thickness, determine its insulating value. The reflective materials require an air space to be effective, and their efficiency is determined by the amount of still air between the insulation and the building material — both on the inside and outside. For example, an aluminum-foil insulation (with two bright faces), installed with air space front and back is considered more effective than a foil insulation with a single bright face installed directly touching the

> **Energy conservation**
> A house was sold under the pretense that it had met all energy efficient standards of construction. After moving into the house and meeting a few of the neighbours, he learned that the house had been slapped together using recycled wood.

sheathing in a wall. Reflective insulation reflects radiant heat waves in the same way a mirror reflects light. It is more effective in blocking heat from entering the house than in holding heat inside. The surfaces must be free from dust to work effectively. When installed properly, the metal foil is also a good vapour barrier. However, in an attic with a pitched roof and conventional mass insulation, the reflective material must never be found on top of the insulation, as this will create a vapour barrier on the cold side of the insulation. Some 30 years ago multi-layered foil insulation was used in the walls and it was found that the foil layers proved ideal channels for convection currents, causing the walls to cool the house rather than contribute to the insulation properties.

Inspecting the Insulation

Throughout the earlier sections of this book, regular reference has been made to insulation, especially with respect to moisture or air leakage. In particular, a review of the notes you have made during your earlier inspection of the attic, roof, structure, floors, walls, windows and doors will assist you in your overall assessment of the insulation. A few additional comments will be made here to tie the picture together.

The purpose of insulation is to reduce convection, conduction and radiation heat losses. Most types have acoustic principles as well. As previously discussed, insulation materials vary in their effectiveness in serving each of these functions. Therefore, you should find a variety of types used throughout the house. Insulation should be found in virtually every wall, floor and ceiling, with special emphasis on the exterior walls. It is not uncommon, however, to find an older wood-frame house with no insulation around its perimeter walls. In such cases, convection air currents carry moisture within the wall cavities, promoting wood rot and creating an extreme fire risk. A key concern for all materials is that the insulation has been kept clear of heat sources to avoid temperature buildups and resultant fire hazards.

It is easiest to start your inspection of the insulation in the attic. Try to lift up or dig under the insulation to see what is underneath. It is not uncommon in older houses to find four layers of insulation, ranging from cellulose and glass fibre to rock wool. The insulation should be consistent, level and continuous. Measure the thickness and take a small sample of each for later identification and determination of its "RSI" or "R" value. You may be able to locate an old insulation package in the attic that will indicate its rating. RSI (Resistance System International) values indicate thermal resistance in metric terms, while R values represent imperial measurements. Thermal resistance value is a measurement of the insulation's resistance to heat flow. The higher the resistance, the less heat will escape through the insulating material.

When collecting samples of the insulation, notice if it feels wet from condensation or a leaky roof. Water penetration will damage the insulation. As humid air rushes through a poorly insulated ceiling, it is quickly chilled and the moisture condenses into dew or frost on the roof sheathing and structural supports. This moisture will greatly lower the insulation's R value and further promote mouldy rafters and rusty nails. It takes only a small gap in insulation or a tear in the vapour barrier to create a heat loss, draft or moisture problem. Attic hatches should be insulated and have weatherstripping to seal the edges tightly over the opening. Finished crawl-space doors, sometimes found behind closets, should be similarly insulated.

Older homes with flat or cathedral ceiling roof structures may not have sufficient space between the top of the insulation and underside of the roof sheathing to allow for adequate ventilation of moist air. At certain temperatures, water vapour condenses and moisture causes rot, water leakage through ceilings, deteriorated interior room finishes and decreased thermal resistance to insulation. Newer houses should have an increased depth of the flat or cathedral ceiling roof by use of a truss system or deeper joists. Some roof structures will have a combination of deeper joists and cross purlins to permit a continuous flow of air.

Inspect areas over stairs, dropped ceilings of the kitchen and washroom, and walls around skylight wells. When batt insulation has been used in walls, the weight can loosen the insulation over the years, causing it to fall down from its original position to the ceiling below. This exposes the interior walls and results in heat escape. In some houses you can see into the wall cavity from the attic. You might want to check the space more carefully by lowering a weight on a string down inside the wall from the attic. How far does the weight go down? Another way to inspect wall insulation is to look behind a light switch. After turning off the power, remove the outlet cover and, with your bent wire hook, try to reach into the opening to pull out a bit of insulation. Shine your penlight into the hole. Is any insulation visible? Is there a vapour barrier behind the electrical switch or outlet box? In places where the wall finish is so tight that it is impossible to get access to the inside of the wall, you can drill a small hole in the back wall, under a sink or inside a closet. Again, reach in with your wire hook and see what insulation can be pulled out. Later plug the hole with putty.

Every perimeter wall should be inspected for insulation. There should be a vapour barrier between the insulation and the inside wall. Place your hands over the interior wall surfaces. Do they feel as cold as ice? In some cases this means the absence of insulation or simply inadequate construction. Poorly fitted pocket doors, recessed light fixtures, built-in wall cabinets and pull-down stairs leading to attics can also cause cold air to move within wall cavities. Often, when insulation is added to the exterior walls, holes are drilled and the material is blown in. The holes are patched or openings enclosed with miniature 3/4-inch circular ventilators. Side wall ventilation, to be effective, requires openings in the bottom and top of the wall — one to let air in and the other to let it escape. All such vents open to the outside. Touch the vents to ensure they are firmly held in place. Houses that are not of wood-frame construction should have insulation sandwiched between the different building materials.

Floors above any unheated spaces should be insulated. Examples include under cantilevered bay window areas in living room or bedroom floors, living area floors above an open garage, etc. Where houses have electric floor drop-in heaters, wall heaters or baseboard heaters against exterior walls, there must be adequate insulation within the wall cavities.

If the basement or crawl space is finished, check it for insulation in a similar way as you did the perimeter walls of the house. Measure the thickness of the insulation and check for a vapour barrier to prevent moisture from getting into the basement. Look for peeling paint and efflorescence — sure signs of excess moisture. If the house is in a poor drainage area, the foundation walls should not be insulated on the inside. Because of its exposure to outside temperature fluctuations, it could suffer from freeze/thaw damage. Houses built on a flat concrete slab on the ground should have insulation applied outside the floor slab and footings. A bit of digging will be necessary to check this insulation. Above-grade insulated sections must be covered with protective covering and flashing.

How energy-efficient are the furnace and hot-water tank? If you decide to purchase the house, perhaps one of your first household expenses will be to replace them with more efficient models. Are the hot and cold pipes insulated? Are there open seams and joints around heating ducts?

After you have finished inspecting the house for insulation and air leakage, you might want to note areas that require upgrading. Will this be easy and relatively inexpensive? Is there much accumulated deterioration that will require replacement of some of the wood framing? Treat the house as a system. Whatever you do to change one element in the system causes changes in others, as it tries to establish a new equilibrium. The house must be seen as a total environment made up of the building envelope, the occupants, mechanical systems and surrounding soil conditions and climate. The aim is to have comfort and balance between air quality, temperature and moisture levels within the environment.

CHECKPOINTS
✓✓✓✓✓✓✓✓✓✓✓

Attic
____ attic stairways
____ ceiling holes
____ ceiling light fixtures
____ top of interior/exterior walls
____ access hatch or door
____ heating duct work and pipes
____ passing through attic
____ around plumbing stack
____ around chimney

Living Areas
____ windows
____ window casings
____ exterior doors
____ door casings
____ exhaust vents/fans
____ interior trim
____ storm doors
____ storm windows
____ under window sills
____ electrical outlets
____ plumbing holes
____ electrical holes
____ fireplace dampers
____ mail slot
____ recessed light fixtures
____ dropped ceilings
____ cracks on walls/ceilings
____ baseboards and moldings
____ under door thresholds
____ recessed cabinets
____ pull-down stairs
____ pocket doors
____ wall ironing boards
____ under sinks
____ behind bathtubs

Basement or Crawlspace
Areas to be sealed:
____ service entrances

____ foundation cracks
____ frame cavities
____ sill plate
____ concrete block openings
____ heating/cooling ducts

Sealants
____ caulking
____ tapes
____ foam
____ oakum
____ glass-fibre insulation
____ foam rope
____ rope caulk
____ condition
____ bondability
____ life-span
____ paintable

Check sealing of:
____ plumbing pipes
____ electrical wires/pipes
____ ventilation system pipes
____ dryer vents
____ heat lamps and fans

Weatherstripping Doors and Windows
____ magnetic
____ compression
____ threshold
____ pile-type
____ condition
____ durability
____ rubber
____ plastic
____ foam
____ felt
____ other

Furnace

_____ air filter cleaned
_____ duct connections sealed
_____ ducts or pipes insulated
_____ asbestos
_____ thermostat efficiency
_____ furnace efficiency
_____ heater insulated
_____ pipes insulated
_____ last drained

Insulation

_____ flexible
_____ fill-type
_____ semi-rigid
_____ batt or blanket
_____ rigid board
_____ interlocking panels
_____ reflective
_____ foamed in places
_____ thickness
_____ R value

_____ walls
_____ basement
_____ crawl space
_____ slab-on-grade
_____ evenness of insulation in attic
_____ exterior insulated ceilings
_____ cathedral ceilings
_____ attic vapour barrier
_____ wall vapour barrier
_____ vapour barrier location
_____ wall vents
_____ wet insulation
_____ cold walls

Overall Comfort Rating of House

_____ poor
_____ average
_____ good

Overall Annual Energy Costs of
Heating and Cooling this House
$_____

CONSUMER TIPS

Real estate is a cyclical industry, depending on various factors. It is important to know where the cycle is, relative to the exact location you are considering. It is also important to appreciate that different provinces, regions, cities and communities can be in different parts of the economic cycle. Awareness of the cycle is important when making buying/selling decisions.

Cycles are reflected in the description given for the market at any point in time. The most common terms to describe the three types of real estate markets are as follows:

- *Seller's Market.* In a seller's market the number of buyers wanting homes, for example, exceeds the supply or number of homes on the market. This type of market is characterized by homes that sell quickly, an increase in prices, a large number of buyers, and a minimal inventory of homes. These characteristics have implications for the buyer, who has to make decisions quickly, must pay more, and frequently has his conditional offers rejected.

- *Buyer's Market.* In a buyer's market the supply of homes on the market exceeds the demand or number of buyers. Characteristics of this type of market include: homes being on the market longer, fewer buyers compared to availability, higher inventory of homes, and a reduction in prices. The implications for buyers in this type of market are: more favourable negotiating leverage, more time to search for a home, and better prices.
- *Balanced Market.* In a balanced market, the number of homes on the marked is equal to the demand or number of buyers. The characteristics of this type of market include: houses selling within a reasonable period, demand equalling supply, sellers accepting reasonable offers, and prices generally stabilized. The implications for the buyer of this type of market are that the atmosphere is more relaxed and there is a reasonable number of homes from which to choose.

There are many factors that influence real estate prices. You need to understand what factors are present that are impacting on the market, so that you can make the right decisions at the right time in the right location. Many of the following factors are interconnected:
- position in the real estate cycle, e.g., country's political climate, e.g., elections
- interest rates
- taxes
- rent controls
- economy
- population shifts
- vacancy levels
- location
- availability of land
- public image of area
- political or regulatory policies of provincial or municipal government
- seasonal factors.

CHAPTER 15
▼
Security

S ECURITY IS ONE aspect of the home that is usually overlooked when prospective purchasers inspect a home. For example, a purchaser may be attracted by the privacy and seclusion afforded by tall hedges and trees surrounding a home without realizing that this also provides a burglar with equal privacy. A charming old Victorian-style home is more likely to have a high fire risk, due to the building methods and materials used 40 to 50 years ago. Once you move into the house, though, security will be of prime importance in enhancing your enjoyment and feeling of comfort and safety. Burglary and fire are the two most common risks that a homeowner will want to protect against, and both will be covered in this chapter. While neither is totally avoidable, there are certain precautions one can take to reduce their likelihood of occurrence. This starts with having a general awareness of the concerns.

Burglary Protection

A survey of the neighbourhood is the best place to start your investigation. Talk to the occupants of the houses next door and across the street. Ask if they have experienced a break-in or are aware of any recent break-ins in the neighbourhood. The local police department or sheriff's office may offer a free home security survey. They will be able to inform you of any "operation identification" or neighbourhood "crime watch" programs that are in place, and indicate if the neighbourhood has experienced a low or high crime rate relative to other areas. An area with a high percentage of renters as opposed to homeowners is often the target of vandalism and theft by young offenders. Perpetrators more skilled at their craft prefer well-to-do neighbourhoods.

Exterior and Property

Take a look at the house and property from a burglar's perspective. The following factors make the house an easy target:

- dead-end street with minimal traffic
- bushes that cast shadows on the property from the street lights at night
- shrubs and trees planted too close to doors and windows providing a visual shield during both day and night
- tall, enclosed fences with more than one gate (escape route)
- sliding glass patio doors.

Time, noise and light are a burglar's greatest enemies. Noise and light from in and around the home may be enough to deter the onset of a planned theft. Factors that will slow or impede the intruder's entrance into the home will frustrate and deter most inexperienced burglars. Doors and windows should be visible from all angles, and the house and grounds should be visible from the street and neighbours' homes. You should be able to see over and through the fence. Fence gates may be wired to a warning device in the house. The hinges should be attached with bolts rather than screws.

Effective use of lighting can counter most of the above risk factors. Ensure that all entrances, back porches, patios, driveways and balconies are well lit. Install floodlights on all sides of the house. The light switch should be in a convenient location and the bulbs should have a tamper-proof cover for protection. For extra security the lights can be controlled by an electric eye or photoelectric switch. With the use of automatic timers, interior lights and radios can be turned on and off at certain times to create the impression that people are in the home while you are out of town or arriving home late. In fact, the simplest security system against burglars is a watchful dog with a ferocious bark!

The garage is usually the easiest target for break-ins. Besides finding valuable tools and sporting equipment stored here, a burglar will also find ladders and garbage pails that will help in gaining access to a balcony or unlocked window. Where the garage is attached to the house, this is usually the burglar's entry point into the house. Once inside the garage an intruder is able to work privately at gaining entrance by picking the lock or cutting a hole through the door or gyproc wall. Will it be easy for someone to gain access to the garage through the door or windows? You should note that many automatic garage door openings may be opened by stray radio frequencies, although there are devices available to filter unwanted signals.

As you walk around the house, make a note of all openings including doors, windows, air conditioners, solariums, stairwells, crawl spaces, pet doors and mail slots. How visible are they from the street or neighbours' homes? Can someone gain access to upper floors or low roofs by far-reaching tree limbs and trellises? Some older houses still have milk and pantry openings. If these are no longer in use, they should be sealed shut to prevent access by a burglar or arsonist, not to mention other considerations such as heat loss and wood decay.

Windows and Skylights

After the garage, the next best target for entry is through windows. Jalousie windows offer the least security as they are fastened on vertical ends only and do not have an all-round frame for the glazing. Note the windows within a reasonable reach and easiest to pry open. What has the owner done to improve security around window openings? Check the durability of the locking hardware of every window. Can the sliding sash be removed from the frame in a locked position? If the house has skylights, how easy is it to climb the roof and remove fastenings around the skylight? Check if the unit is made of tamper-resistant materials.

Some types of glazing and window films make the glass shatter resistant. The following varieties offer resistance to breakage: polycarbonate plastic more than 1/2-inch thick; acrylic plastic more than 3/8-inch thick; wired, plate, conventional float or sheet window glass more than 1/4-inch thick; and tempered plate glass more than 2/16-inch thick. Some basement windows will have metal bars or mesh screens in place over the openings which can provide the greatest security if properly designed and installed. Windows should not be permanently sealed, as this would prevent access in case of a fire.

Doors and Locks

Re-examine all the exterior doors, frames and hardware. Doors should fit tightly in their frames. Steel, plank wood and solid-core wood doors that are at least 1 3/4-inches thick offer the best resistance. Hollow-core doors can be easily broken, and sliding glass patio doors are easily lifted out of their tracks. A door with a glass sidelight panel may also provide easy access unless the glass has security features and is on the opposite side from the door lock. Otherwise the glass can be broken by a thief who can then reach in and open the door. Similarly, the mail slot should have a deflecting baffle to restrict access to the door's locking device. If the door is equipped with an optical viewer, check from the inside to see if the visibility is wide and clear. It should provide a 180-degree viewing area.

The frame also should be made of solid reinforced wood or sheet steel to prevent potential intruders from wedging a crowbar between the door and frame and damaging the frame to free the lock. Some frames have a piece of countersunk angle iron in the area of the strike, so that the tip of a screwdriver or crowbar will not reach the latch bolt. Whenever you see the exposed heads of screws on locking hard-

How well do you know your new neighbours?

A young couple who bought their first home on a corner lot well-sheltered by trees and hedges did not realize that a local gang took advantage of the secluded property as an escape route for their midnight escapades. After only one year (and three break-ins) they decided to sell because of their constant state of fear and the face that the insurance companies would no longer provide them coverage for theft.

ware, make sure that the heads are tamper resistant, making the screw impossible to remove. The same rule applies to outside hinge bolts. They should be held in place by set screws or other non-removing methods. Some hinges come equipped with pins so that the door will be harder to lift out, even when the hinge bolts are removed. Check areas of the frame around the hinges and hardware for any damage that could suggest a previous break-in.

The best door locks are only effective if properly installed and placed in doors and frames that are suited to preventing an attempted entry. In other words, an expensive lock on a solid-core door will offer no additional security. Every exterior door should have a dead bolt. The type offering the highest degree of security is the tubular dead bolt which is mounted in the door. When in the locked position, it should project at least one inch from the face plate. It should have a freely rotating, hardened steel rod insert that rolls under a hacksaw blade and prevents it from being cut. The case of the lock should be made of steel and not die-cast metal. The lock cylinder should have a tapered, freely rotating cylinder guard to protect against pulling and twisting attack.

The most commonly used residential lock is the key-in-knob type with a spring latch or dead-latch plunger. However, the latch bolt on these locks often engages the strike plate by as little as 1/8 inch, making it easy to force a softwood frame apart enough to disengage the latch. In addition, the door knobs can be easily gripped with a tool and twisted off, thereby allowing access. You may come across auxiliary locks or home-made security devices. Often used over basement doors, they may consist of tubing, metal bars or wood bracing placed under door knobs.

The strike plate screws should penetrate through the door frame and into the wall framing. If you look inside the strike plate opening you might see a strike box. This too allows screws to penetrate deeper into the wall framing and prevents the door frame from splitting or pulling away.

A well-made, pick-resistant key will have varying key cuts. The more expensive variety, and the hardest to pick open, have varying cuts on both the top and side edges. Newer homes may have push-button keyless locks which are operated by pressing the correct combination numbers. The more numbers used in the combination, the more difficult it is for an intruder to match the combination. Of course, it is advisable to change the locks when you take possession of the house.

Alarms, Intercoms and Safes

Where an alarm system is in place, there should be warning stickers on windows and doors. This in itself may be a deterrent for inexperienced thieves. Alarm systems may have perimeter or interior sensors. Perimeter sensors guard exterior doors and windows, while interior sensors detect movement inside the home. If separate surveillance zones have been installed, perimeter sensors may remain active when the interior motion detector is shut off while your family is in the house. This allows the alarm system to be designed to accommodate the lifestyles of your family and pets.

It is not unusual for alarms to be tripped by stray light, humidity, curtains blowing, the sound of heavy rain on the roof and noises from aircraft, vehicles, thunder and certain metallic household fixtures. In fact, one police officer estimated that 97 per cent of all alarms are false alarms, primarily due to faulty installations. Ask the owner for the name of the manufacturer, installer and operating instructions. Find out how effectively the unit can discriminate against random movement and transient noises. The unit should have an approved ULC label and certificate to verify that the installer is a member of a provincial alarm association and that the alarm has been properly installed and inspected. The system should work if there is a complete power failure. Wireless units should have an indicator to alert you when the batteries are low. If there are wires connecting various components, are they exposed where they can be cut? Will the sensor be triggered if a burglar used a glass cutter? Check where the sirens are located. Enquire about the monthly fees for monitoring the system, which need to be paid to the police, fire department or security company. Also, check the distance from your home to the security personnel to get an idea of the response time you can expect.

Additional features offered by some alarms include medical alert, alarm sirens, smoke and fire detection, built-in telephone dialler to summon help, and monitors for room temperature, freezer temperature, power failure, flood detection, gas pressure and water pressure where fire sprinkler systems are used in the house. Some homes have an audio intercom system near the door that prevents opening of the door until the occupant permits the caller to enter. Check with the owner for operating instructions. In older homes you may find a built-in strong room or safety deposit box. Some newer homes are equipped with in-ground safes. Examine the door, walls, hinges and locking hardware. If the unit is factory built, look for the certified fire resistance label. Is the installation explosion, fire and burglar proof? Check with your insurance company if belongings stored here require special insurance coverage.

Fire Safety

Fire safety begins and ends with you and your family. Every house has combustibles, so personal care and precautions can prevent most household fires. Flammable liquids such as gasoline and cooking oil are the most common materials that ignite. Upholstered furniture, bedding and mattresses are next on the list, frequently ignited by cigarettes, candle flames and sparks from fireplaces. The third most common class of fire is due to building elements such as electrical, structural components and finish materials. Leaking gases, heat or moisture, as discussed in earlier chapters, may be the cause of such fires. Wherever there is movement of air within the wall structure, there is sufficient draft smoke, flame and fire to funnel through the house's structure.

Check where the nearest fire hydrant is located on the street, and the distance to the firehall. How many potential fire areas can you identify in the house? If fire were to engulf the house, how long would it take you and your family to get to safety? If the house is equipped with safety escape ladders for the upper floors, test them to see if they function properly. It is important that the house be protected in two locations: where the fire starts for quickest response, and wherever the occupants are to warn them of the danger. Household fire warning devices may include heat detectors, smoke alarms and sprinkler systems. Check with the fire department in the community for different types of fire extinguishers your house may need.

Heat and Smoke Detectors

Heat detectors are sometimes found in kitchens and furnace rooms. These devices only measure heat and are set to go off at predetermined temperatures or rate of temperature rise. Locate the smoke detectors. Test them by lighting a match near the unit. The most common causes of smoke detector failure are dead or missing batteries, ineffective locations, dirty or defective components and incorrect wiring. Some detectors are powered by electric household current. Others are a combination electric wired unit with a back-up battery. The detectors should be interconnected so that when one goes off, they all do. They should not be installed around corners of rooms, in areas with dead air pockets, or bathrooms and kitchens where steam and cooking fumes will set them off. The ionization type of smoke detector uses a small amount of radioactive material to make it work. The photo-electric type, which operates by a small light source, is more reliable and sensitive to slow, smouldering fires.

Sprinkler Systems

A value-added feature in some newer homes is a fire sprinkler system. It will prevent the rapid spread of fire and contain the fire in its room of origin, and can protect lives and property immediately adjacent to the fire room. There are wet-pipe and dry-pipe sprinkler systems. A wet system uses automatic sprinklers attached to a piping system containing water and connected to a water supply so that water discharges immediately from sprinklers opened by a fire. This system is installed in areas not subject to freezing. The dry system also uses automatic sprinklers but they are attached to a piping system that contains air under atmospheric pressure. Loss of pressure from the opening of a sprinkler or detection of a fire condition causes the release of water into the piping system and out the opened sprinkler. Where this system is located in an unheated area that is subject to freezing, an antifreeze solution is held within the pipe and connected to a water supply.

Some installations use plastic piping, which is lighter in weight and resistant to corrosion and scale buildup. There should be an approved testing label on the product. Notice the layout of the piping. The sprinkler heads should be located away from heat-producing sources such as light fixtures and ventilation grilles. Check how the sprinkler head piping is braced. During operation, bracing prevents upward movement of the sprinkler through the ceiling. The materials used for piping connections should be consistent. Who installed the sprinkler system? Ask the owner how often the sprinkler heads must be tested and how the tests are performed. Will the piping layout interfere with any future renovations to the house?

If you decide to purchase the house, such awareness of security concerns, and regular communication with neighbours can establish an effective team approach for your new neighbourhood. Inside the home, proper care and precautions offer the best prevention along with regular maintenance checks. And, of course, for those unfortunate situations that do occur, carrying appropriate insurance policies will secure your family against a total disaster.

CHECKPOINTS
✔✔✔✔✔✔✔✔✔✔✔

Yard Landscaping
- _____ trees
- _____ bushes
- _____ shrubs
- _____ fences
- _____ gates
- _____ shadows
- _____ yard light
- _____ street light
- _____ photoelectric switch
- _____ electric eye
- _____ neighbours' visibility
- _____ street visibility

Garage
- _____ exterior doors
- _____ exterior windows
- _____ locking devices

Exterior Doors of House
- _____ solid core
- _____ metal
- _____ safety glass panes
- _____ reinforced frame
- _____ side-light windows
- _____ door thickness
- _____ door intercom
- _____ doors with glass panels
- _____ sliding patio doors
- _____ damaged frames
- _____ optical viewer in door

Hardware
- _____ hinge bolt location
- _____ hinge bolt secured
- _____ hinge pins
- _____ dead bolt
- _____ pick resistant
- _____ strike box
- _____ home-made locks

_____ any locks changed by owner
_____ door opener type
_____ tamper resistant screws
_____ screw length
_____ push-button key-less
_____ double cylinder deadlock
_____ cylinder deadlock with thumb turn
_____ spring latch
_____ deadlocking latch

Exterior Windows
_____ ground floor
_____ basement
_____ upper floor
_____ shatter-resistant films
_____ vertical sliding
_____ horizontal sliding
_____ pivoted
_____ hinged
_____ sashless
_____ jalousie
_____ semi-sashless
_____ side-light adjacent door
_____ distance from ground
_____ windows locked
_____ ease of window removal
_____ homemade locks

Safety glazing types:
_____ polycarbonate plastic
_____ acrylic plastic
_____ wired glass
_____ plate glass
_____ float glass

Other Burglar Entry Areas
_____ solarium
_____ stairs
_____ window wells
_____ stairwells
_____ low roofs
_____ crawl spaces
_____ skylights
_____ milk openings

_____ other openings
_____ ventilating fans
_____ air conditioners
_____ balconies
_____ mail slots
_____ exterior attic hatches
_____ trellises
_____ pantry vent openings
_____ wood/coal shutes

Interior Safety
_____ strong room
_____ burglar resistance rating
_____ safety deposit box
_____ fire-resistance rating
_____ explosion resistance rating
_____ certified testing agency approved

Burglar Alarms/Sensors
_____ photoelectric
_____ magnetic contacts
_____ audio detectors
_____ ultrasonic
_____ microwave
_____ passive infrared
_____ smoke/fire detectors
_____ telephone dialer
_____ room temperature monitor
_____ water pressure monitor
_____ perimeter sensors
_____ interior sensors
_____ manufacturer
_____ installer licensed
_____ quality of components
_____ wireless unit
_____ monitored by security
_____ surveillance zones
_____ operation manual
_____ police station location
_____ audible alarm
_____ silent alarm
_____ manufacturer's warranty
_____ certified testing agency approved

Smart House Monitors
- ____ computer
- ____ model number
- ____ guarantees/warranties
- ____ noise problems
- ____ make
- ____ serial number
- ____ service contract
- ____ electromagnetic interferences
- ____ certified testing agency approved

Fire Safety
- ____ escape routes
- ____ escape ladder
- ____ last fire safety inspection
- ____ fire protection for vents/ chimneys
- ____ combustible materials
- ____ fire hydrant location
- ____ firehall location
- ____ fire detectors
- ____ certified testing agency approved
- ____ other

Sprinkler System
- ____ wet system
- ____ dry system
- ____ antifreeze
- ____ plastic piping
- ____ metal piping
- ____ bracing

- ____ corrosion
- ____ pipe freezing
- ____ water pressure
- ____ maintenance requirements
- ____ backflow preventers
- ____ metal sprinkler head
- ____ plastic sprinkler head
- ____ number of sprinkler heads
- ____ location of sprinkler heads
- ____ sprinkler coverage
- ____ sprinkler alarm
- ____ manufacturer
- ____ installer's name
- ____ last inspected or serviced
- ____ inspection fees
- ____ pressure gauges
- ____ valves and drains
- ____ manufacturer's warranty
- ____ certified testing agency approved

Smoke Detectors
- ____ ionization
- ____ photo-electric
- ____ combination
- ____ heat detector
- ____ number of detectors
- ____ location
- ____ audible trouble signal
- ____ last tested
- ____ manufacturer
- ____ certified testing agency approved

CONSUMER TIPS

Mortgage lending has become very complex, with constantly changing rates, terms, and conditions. Each lending institution has its own criteria that apply to potential borrowers. Some insist on a particular type of property as security, while others require a certain type of applicant. In this latter case, factors such as type of employment, job stability, income, and credit background are weighed. There is a broad range of philosophies and policies held by the various lending institutions on the issue of security and applicant qualifications in order for a lender to advance mortgage funds.

Look in the weekend real estate section of your local newspaper to see mortgage rate comparison charts.

Other factors also impact on mortgage approval. Availability or shortage of funds, past experience in a specific area, perceived resale market for a particular property, and the attitude of the lending committee (if a credit union) are all factors that could affect approving a mortgage.

Mortgage brokers make it their business to know all the various plans and lending policies, as well as the lender's attitude on various aspects of mortgage security and covenants. A mortgage broker is in effect a matchmaker, attempting to introduce the appropriate lender to the purchaser.

Mortgage brokers have access to numerous sources of funds, including the following:

- Conventional lenders such as banks, trust companies and credit unions
- Canada Mortgage and Housing Corporation (CMHC)
- Pension funds
- Insurance companies
- Private lenders.

The broker knows all the lenders' objectives; the broker is therefore capable of matching the applicant and his or her property with the appropriate plan and lender. Alternatively, the broker can offer several mortgage plans from which the borrower may select the one that best suits his or her needs.

Mortgage brokers basically offer two types of services:

- They arrange a simple mortgage that will get automatic approval in your particular circumstance. As a consequence, this saves you a lot of time searching. The broker generally receives a commission directly from the lender, as a "finder" or "referral" fee. You don't pay any extra money or higher interest. Lenders do this because the mortgage market is so competitive.

* They arrange a more complex mortgage that would not be automatically approved. This takes more time, skill, and persuasion on the part of the broker to source out a lender or number of lenders who will provide the funds you need. For example, if you did not have the normal amount of down payment required, had a negative credit rating, were highly leveraged already, or did not have the normal income required, you would probably be turned down by a conventional lender such as a bank, credit union, or trust company.

If a mortgage broker succeeds in arranging your financing, given the above types of factors for a more complex mortgage, you would pay a commission. The commission could be between 1% and 5% of the amount of the mortgage arranged, depending on the degree of difficulty, the urgent need for funds, etc. In some provinces there is legislation that prohibits a mortgage broker from charging an advance fee (application fee) if the mortgage amount is below a certain figure.

To find a mortgage broker, look in the Yellow Pages of your telephone directory, under that name, ask your real estate lawyer, or your realtor. As with any decision involving a service, you should consider a comparison of a minimum of three lenders/mortgage brokers before deciding who is offering the best deal and who you would like to deal with. Remember, it is a very competitive market place.

NOTES

CHAPTER 16

House Care
and Annual Check-up

A HOUSE IS PROBABLY the largest investment in most people's lives, yet often it is an investment that is cared for inadequately. General upkeep of the home and property is sometimes overlooked. When soot and moisture are allowed to build up on housing materials, decay will commence and so will repair bills. When preventive maintenance items are overlooked the repair bills can escalate quickly. It is a known fact that home buyers usually base their choice of home on aesthetic features rather than on its soundness of design and construction. Frequently a combination of a poor maintenance program with inadequate design and construction reduces a home's useful life and therefore its value. The intent of this book is to help you to use sound judgment in the choice of your home, reduce the need for extensive maintenance and to protect your investment.

Once you have purchased the house, it is important to maintain an annual inspection program so that most problems can be identified before they cause considerable damage. An annual review will help you to plan and budget for maintenance and repairs on an ongoing basis. If it does not eliminate them, it will drastically reduce the number of unexpected "surprises" and major repairs that then need immediate attention. It is recommended that you set up a filing system to document and store details on the house, its age and construction, materials used and warranties on appliances. File your thorough initial house inspection as well as your annual maintenance inspections and repair inspections performed by tradespersons such as plumbers, electricians, etc. These reports will then be handy to refer to from time to time as the need arises.

Climatic conditions will dictate the best time for inspections of different parts of the house. For example, an inspection of the roof, gutters, downspouts, perimeter drainage and chimneys is best carried out after a heavy rainfall. The cause of excessive wetting of any wood or concrete surfaces in a house should be investigated and measures taken as soon as possible to prevent further wetting.

Exterior

Look at the chimney for loose mortar joints, missing bricks and cracks. The masonry chimney should be cleaned annually and exterior surfaces should be waterproofed at least every five years. If a factory-built metal chimney is present, check the top and connections for corrosion. Metal liners and metal outer shells are susceptible to corrosion, and inner shells are subject to buckling. Deterioration of metal chimneys is often covered by warranty. Check the flashing around the chimney and roof. Rust on roof metal, ventilator covers and flashing warns you that a leak may develop. Cover rust spots with a rust-inhibiting paint. This can prevent serious damage and prolong service life substantially.

Perimeter roof edges are always subject to decay, especially where fascia boards and eave mouldings are attached. If rain seepage is not corrected, rot will extend into the rafter ends. With unboxed or finished eaves, watch for wetting of rafter and fascia board ends and sheathing edges. A dirt streak down the fascia boards often indicates a gap where water is penetrating through openings or under shingles. Check the overall roof surfaces for accumulation of moss, algae growth, leaves and wind-blown debris. Any debris will shorten the service life of a roof. This is particularly true of wood shingles and shakes, which are subject to rot. Remove old bird nests and wasp hives as you find them.

Roof leaks tend to develop over long periods of time. The sheathing around chimneys, vents and skylights often decay, leaving no evidence on the outside or inside. The best way to determine if a roof is rain-tight is to inspect the underside in the attic after a heavy rain. Any leaks found there can be stopped by caulking the area. While in the attic, look for evidence of condensation and fungal growth under the roof sheathing along the soffit areas. Evidence of moisture can also be seen on exposed nail points protruding under the attic sheathing. Check the attic for moisture problems during or just after a cold period in January or February. If there is a heavy frost buildup on all surfaces, there are venting problems that must be solved. Locate and seal all air leaks to reduce humidity levels in the house.

Eave gutters and downspouts can be a problem to keep clean. Sagging or clogged gutters and rusted-through downspouts cause wetting of the fascia boards and walls, and lead to extensive hidden damage. Excessive ground splash to the lower walls caused by inadequate drainage or rain runoff can result in wood decay and paint deterioration on surfaces. After a heavy rain, walk around the foundation walls of the crawl space, slab-on-grade foundations or basement. Determine if water accumulates adjacent to the foundation or is able to drain away from the house. The most obvious warning sign is a strong musty odour due to mould development. The areas most vulnerable to decay are the bottoms of wood columns, stairs and partitions in contact with the concrete floor, cupboards or panelling on exterior walls and wood floors. A common source of dampness in crawl spaces and basements is excessive ground water and a periodic high water table. Check the drain areas to ensure they have not become clogged with leaves and debris. With a garden hose, let water into the perimeter drainage system.

Inspect all wall surfaces for signs of moisture damage. When wood surfaces contain too much moisture they have a tendency to buckle. Alternate shrinkage and swelling may result in splitting of the wood through which large amounts of water can enter. Nail pulling is most common on walls with wetting and rapid drying between rain showers. If wet lumber is used in construction, nail heads may protrude after the wood dries. Look for rust developing around nail heads. Absence of rust does not always mean absence of decay. If galvanized nails are used, wetting of the wood can occur without rusting of the nails. Wood species that hold paint poorly have paint failure with much less wetting than that needed to promote decay. General paint peeling can be the result of severe rain seepage and condensation within walls or incompatible paints. Always check with a reliable paint manufacturer for proper surface preparation techniques. Where decay is in its early stages, the wood should be stripped of its paint, then sealed and repainted or stained. Exterior wood surfaces usually require repainting approximately every five to 10 years.

Often you will notice black or grey discolourations and streaking over the wall surfaces that are not directly exposed to the sun's rays. These moist surface stains occur without rain seepage and should be washed off. Also inspect wood areas for damage caused by pests or termites. You will need to investigate further from the inside to see how extensive the problem is. Remove all pest-infested and rooted wood and replace with new materials. If the holes are evidence of a problem that no longer exists, caulk them to prevent moisture decay.

Exposed wood columns, wooden stairs, steps, landings, handrailings, balustrades, exposed beam ends, porches, balconies and decks are areas subjected to a high decay hazard. When watering your lawn, ensure the sprinkler spray does not reach these areas. If caught in time, some areas of decay may be treated with a water-repellent preservative. Avoid poor soil drainage. Around the base of the house wall be sure that there is no wood/soil contact. If necessary, regrade the soil so that it is at least 8 inches away from wood framing and basement doors. Avoid piling wood and other materials against the sides of the house.

Look for loose mortar in masonry walls. If water has entered any cracks and frozen, some of the mortar will have come loose. Inspect your driveway, patios and sidewalks for similar frost damage. Freezing water can turn hairline cracks into wide crevices. If snow melts quickly from your roof and near the basement and crawl space walls, or if the flowers seem to come up sooner at your house than they do at other houses facing the same direction in your neighbourhood, then chances are you are losing heat through the wall and ceilings. Check the amount of insulation in these areas and plan to add insulation and eliminate drafts as soon as possible. The reduction in your heating bill should offset the cost of the insulation.

Interior

After taking possession of the home, you will undoubtedly find a number of maintenance tasks to perform. It is recommended that you live in the house for a year, especially during a winter season and monitor what needs to be done. During that time make a note of insulation, caulking and weatherstripping that may be required. Check the weatherstripping around doors and windows to prevent water, dust and air infiltration. Corners of door and window frames, joints and trims are rot problem areas. Most seepage is found at the bottom of building components. See that these vulnerable points are particularly well treated or that the decayed wood is replaced. So often drying and decayed wood shrinks and collapses beneath old hard paint surfaces. The damage is not usually discovered until the decayed wood breaks as it is being repainted. Lubricate all door and window hinges, glides and locking hardware.

Window and door frames should not be in direct contact with soil. Examine the caulking between frames and where there is a change of wall materials. Old caulking compounds become hard and cracked and allow for water seepage. Depending upon the amount of moisture the caulking is exposed to, you can expect it to last anywhere between five years for surfaces exposed to prevailing winds and rains, to 10 years for drier areas. For best results, old caulking should be removed before applying a new coat.

Check for plumbing leaks under kitchens, utility rooms, bathrooms and where the main water line comes into the house. Fix all leaking faucets. Periodic inspection of joints around shower pans, bathtubs and basins will tell you when it is time to recaulk the joints to prevent water from seeping into the framing members and causing rot. A common way of introducing fungus and pests into the structure of the house is through decaying wood. Clean any grease traps in the lines between the house and septic tank. Grease traps should be cleaned annually and a septic tank generally needs to be pumped every two to three years.

Check all appliances and special fixtures in the house. The information you gathered from the previous owner and the notes you made during your initial inspection will now become useful. Review the model and serial numbers, the manufacturer's name, operation manuals and any guarantees and warranties still in effect. You may want to refine your list of appliances, making notes of those items that require monthly, quarterly or yearly servicing.

Your list may include the following:

- refrigerator
- humidifier
- swimming pool
- range
- dehumidifier
- sauna
- freezer
- heat-recovery ventilator
- hot tub
- dishwasher
- exhaust fans
- fire sprinkler heads
- garburetor
- air conditioner
- smoke detectors
- washer/dryer
- electronic air filter
- burglar alarm system
- furnace
- hot water heater
- thermostats/controls
- ventilation fans
- built-in vacuum system
- water softener
- sump pump
- well water and pump
- water shut-off valves.

Home maintenance of each of the above items will vary and can consist of the following:

- check belt tension
- lubricate oil ports
- wipe away any accumulation of lint and dust around mechanical housings
- wash fan blades or impellers
- clean or replace grills, air or oil filters and screens
- check barometric damper doors and nozzles
- clean burners and ports
- check all fresh air or exhaust openings for any obstructions
- test temperature and pressure relief valves
- check gaskets, seals and connections for leaks
- test electrical ground fault interrupters
- check or replace batteries (use only replacement batteries specified by manufacturer)
- test water pressure and temperature
- drain water from hot-water tank or heating pipes to flush out scale, rust and sediment
- analyze water for bacteria, chemical and mineral contamination
- take water sample in sterilized bottle to your public health office; ask for it to be checked for lead, copper, cadmium, phenolics, formaldehyde, chlorinated phenolics, hydrogen sulphide, xylenes and refinery hydrocarbons.

Before inspecting, cleaning or making repairs to anything electrical, shut off the power. For maintenance or repairs to plumbing or gas items, you may need to shut off both lines. Remember, if in doubt, call in a professional. If any features or appliances need upgrading or replacing (such as a wood stove), check with local building authorities to see if a permit is required. Also consult with your insurance company to find out if your insurance rates will be affected.

Who else has a key?

A busy new homeowner forgot to change the locks. One evening he came home to find all his belongings had been stolen. The neighbours informed him that the house had been previously occupied by numerous tenants over the years.

It is very important to conduct a regular fire inspection. Is the number of the nearest fire department and other emergency services posted near the telephone? Your family should have a practised plan of action if fire breaks out. Windows and doors should be burglar proof, yet be unobstructed to serve as emergency exits. Check where oily rags and flammable liquids are kept. Do any stove pipes run through attics or concealed spaces? Have approved fire extinguishers been checked and charged? Is the electrical wiring properly grounded, with no loose connections or frayed wires? If is recommended that you contact your fire department for further helpful hints on fire safety. Hundreds of lives — most of them children — are lost each year as the result of house fires.

Finally, remember that no house will be perfect. But the careful choice and care of the house will affect its eventual resale. Proper maintenance of the house becomes an investment, appreciating its value. Your file containing all the documentation on your house, warranties, repairs and expenses involved will be invaluable to you and a new owner.

CHECKPOINTS
✔✔✔✔✔✔✔✔✔✔✔

Every Month
____ Ground fault circuit interrupters
____ Kitchen fans
____ Bathroom fans
____ Other mechanical ventilation
____ Fire extinguishers
____ Smoke detectors
____ Well water
____ Door/window hardware
____ Plumbing system
____ Security
____ Insects
____ Appliances
____ Water pressure
____ Energy-saving devices

Every Six Months
____ Electrical wiring
____ Paint condition
____ Electric motors
____ Drain traps
____ Floor drains
____ Hot-water heater
____ Skylights
____ Structural foundations
____ Plumbing fixtures

Every Fall
____ De-icing systems
____ Heating system(s)
____ Thermostat(s) control(s)

_____ Fireplace(s)
_____ Chimney(s) and ashpit(s)
_____ Air filters
_____ Weatherstripping
_____ Attic ventilation
_____ Roof
_____ Flashing
_____ Gutters and downspouts
_____ Perimeter drainage
_____ Window/door storm covers
_____ Fire sprinkler heads
_____ Exterior siding
_____ Sump pits
_____ Exterior caulking

_____ Septic tank
_____ Drain lawn faucet(s)

Every Spring
_____ Window/door screens
_____ Air conditioner
_____ Roof
_____ Attic ventilation
_____ Crawlspace ventilation
_____ Gutters and downspouts
_____ Perimeter drainage
_____ Exterior siding
_____ Landscaping
_____ House paint

CONSUMER TIPS

When you are selling the property, you want to be ready for the home inspection by the potential buyer, as well as a professional home inspector hired by the buyer. First impressions are lasting, so there are things you can do to enhance the image of the home and thereby add a marketing edge to its sale. Both the inside and outside of the home must make a positive feeling with the prospective buyer in order to obtain a quick sale and the highest price.

Ask yourself objectively what your perceive a prospective buyer's first impression would be of the outside of the home and the inside. If you feel you cannot be objective or want a second opinion, have a relative or friend look at your home with a critical eye and ask them to tell you all the negative aspects.

Another important step, once you have completed all the home improvement procedures, is to prepare a list of things about your house that you like, e.g. special or unique features such as a workshop or solarium, or a beautiful garden. Do a list of the key selling points about the house, in your view. For example, if you have repainted the house, inside or out, replaced the carpets or had new landscaping done, those are key points to make your home attractive. Finally, do a list of the main points that you like about the neighbourhood, such as convenient shopping, transportation, schools, parks, or playgrounds. In addition, such factors as a quiet neighbourhood, friendly and helpful neighbours, lots of babysitters nearby, and a community spirit are important points to note. If you are using a realtor, give this list to your agent.

The following points highlight the main interior features that you should concentrate on, in the process of getting your home ready for the market. If you are buying a home, look for the absence of these points that could give you a basis for coming up with a more negative visual inspection report and therefore negotiating leverage to lower the price:

- keep appliances, floors, etc, clean
- make the interior decorating attractive
- unclutter the premises
- clean up all closets
- make kitchens and bathrooms inviting
- tidy up the garage
- make necessary repairs
- make the interior environment as peaceful and comfortable as possible
- keep pets out of the way
- remove ashtrays and odour of smoke
- keep an up-to-date service record of all appliances that need care, e.g., furnace, hot water heater
- clean chimneys, ashpits, sump pits, gutters, perimeter drainage.

Here are some points to make the exterior more attractive to inspection first impressions. Again, if you are buying a home, look for the absence of these positive features to improve your negotiating price position:

- maintain your landscaping
- remove junk
- know where things are located and the age of items, e.g., main underground water and sewage waste line, natural gas line, water shut off valves, electrical circuit breaker box, perimeter drainage, sump pits. (How can you sell anything if you don't know where they are or when they were last serviced?)
- organize items you have outdoors to look neat and tidy
- repair necessary exterior items of home
- consider painting the house
- make the front door house numbers and mail box look attractive.

The preceding hints are simply basic guidelines to remind you how important it is to set the correct mood and environment for a person to want to buy your property. As mentioned earlier, the best approach is to try to see your property through the eyes of a prospective buyer. Don't make your decision to buy based mainly on advice given by people trying to sell. No house is perfect every house is repairable at a price and every house is a good house at the right price. Keep a level head while house hunting.

Condition of Houses
Built Pre- and Post-1950

THE METHOD AND materials used in house construction varies widely over time. In Canada the most drastic changes occurred in the 1950s, so inspecting a house built before or after 1950 will be quite different. This section highlights typical Canadian vintage homes built between 1900 and 1950 and what you can expect to find in these homes today. Houses built from 1950 to the present day will also be discussed to highlight other areas to focus on during the inspection process.

Houses Built between 1900 and 1950

It is fair to say that most, if not all, houses built between 1900 and 1950 have undergone some degree of remodelling. The fact that the natural lifespan of construction materials is limited means that through natural wear and tear, items will have been replaced using modern-day materials and methods. Most often kitchens, bathrooms, electrical wiring, heating and plumbing are areas most needing upgrading, if only for convenience and safety reasons. Unfortunately, though, a lot of do-it-yourself and quick-fix-it repairs have brought about houses that have been "remuddled" rather than remodelled! Other houses, being upgraded for a sale, have veneer finishes to give the appearance of being remodelled. One owner boasted that the plumbing had been upgraded to include all copper pipes. However, a closer look revealed that the visible copper piping under the sink didn't lead anywhere; the actual old lead pipes were still being used behind the cupboard wall veneer. Buyer beware!

The diagram on page 217 illustrates common problems found in houses built between 1900 and 1950. When inspecting houses of this age, be especially cautious about the major items such as concrete footings, foundations and load-bearing components. For your convenience, major trouble areas noted below are indicated by a double exclamation point (!!) as a critical warning sign. If serious problems exist in these areas, chances are you will not be able to recoup your investment dollars on the resale of the property. You will be constantly faced with costly repairs and your insurance rates undoubtedly will be high. In addition, the house will be a high safety risk, for you and your family.

1. (!!) Extensive chimney deterioration and rot around the top and inside. No chimney flue liner. Chimney leaning due to moisture getting into mortar and brick cracks. Expansion of the mortar due to freezing and reaction of sulphur dioxide with lime mortage as a result of seepage from the combustion of sulphur-containing fuels through unlined flues. The side of the chimney that carries wind-driven rain will behave differently from the dryer side. Rain hoods were not used because the chimney was constantly in operation from wood-stove use, therefore evaporating any moisture within the chimney.

2. (!!) Roofing material or tar used for flashing. Flashing material deteriorated.

3. (!!) Mortar between the brick soft and running out, creating openings. Often you will see the chimney has been extended by using inferior materials like rocks, cement and recycled concrete blocks. Some bricks can be removed from chimney with bare hands.

4. (!!) Sagging ridge. Roof at ridge not properly capped, allowing water to run along the inside of the roof rafters.

5. Roof area has sagged. Missing shingles. Extensive moss growth all along the north side.

6. Roof edge and fascia boards have rotted. All areas are well covered with paint.

7. Rafter tail ends rotting. Often there are as many as five different roofing materials on top of one another. Roof rafter ends are exposed. No soffits were provided and fascias are seen only at gable ends. No attic ventilation. Rain gutters made of wood. Downspouts drain to the surface of the soil.

8. Thin-paned, aluminum-framed windows have replaced wooden sash and frames. Often the sills have rotted out due to condensation and aluminum sweating. Often there is a mixture in quality of windows.

9. Stucco is hanging on side of walls, ready to fall off, if hit hard enough. Often stucco is badly weathered under eaves due to prevailing winds.

10. Old wood siding or stucco covered up by vinyl or aluminum siding.

11. No ridge board; rafters are toe-nailed together.

12. (!!) Rafters are splintered, broken, missing, spliced or irregularly spaced more than 24 inches apart. Wide boards nailed horizontally or diagonally are used as sheathing. Knots have fallen out of the wood or battens are seen to which wood shingles have been attached, on which at least four other different types of roofing have been added. Undersized rough-sawn 2"x 4" rafters and joists. Inadequate bracing or supports. Often any wood used has been recycled. Ceiling joists not secured to rafters at the top plate.

DIAGRAM 9: Common Problems Found in Homes Built between 1900 and 1950

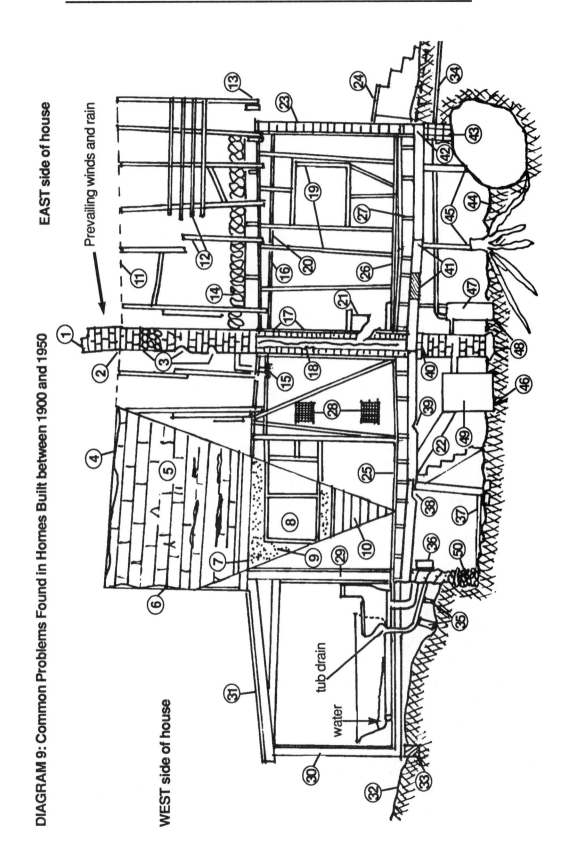

EAST side of house

Prevailing winds and rain

WEST side of house

tub drain

water

13. (!!) Little or no roof overhang or rake causing extensive wall weathering. Rot and blistering paint. Often exposed wood is covered using metal or vinyl.

14. Insulation has been added, along with a vapour barrier over old insulation that could consist of either seaweed, horsehair, sawdust, wood shavings, compacted newspaper, straw or other combustible materials; or areas with no previous insulation resulting in large voids. This allows convection currents to carry moisture to all wood surfaces. As well, in event of a fire, the fire and smoke will spread quickly, risking occupants' lives. Adding insulation makes the house "top heavy" when perimeter walls are not insulated and windows allow for air infiltration. Improper ventilation causes moisture problems.

15. Exhaust vent from kitchen and/or bathroom connected to chimney or leading only under insulation in attic.

16. (!!) High ceilings are common and were considered a symbol of wealth. False or furred-down ceilings leave room for fire to spread quickly throughout the structure. Decorative ceiling beams, plaster coves and ceiling medallions may have been removed or painted over many times. In the late 1950s asbestos-based spray-on ceiling finish was used. This material should not present a health hazard if painted.

17. (!!) Wood framing abutting chimney. Chimney framed or covered with combustible materials like wallpaper. Brick mortar crumbling and leaking carbon monoxide into living areas.

18. Old chimney breachings covered with flattened tobacco cans or openings filled with loose-fitting rocks.

19. (!!) Irregularly spaced rough-sawn 2"x 4"s often spaced more than 24 inches apart and balloon framed. Framing around doors and windows is of poor construction — e.g., without lintels over large openings. Of course, this is difficult to see behind finished walls but can be detected using an electronic stud-finder.

20. (!!) Often no attic access. If access is found, openings are small and covered with thick cobwebs. Often you will find information related to the house or personal information of previous owners buried under old insulation around the attic access.

21. Fireplaces were the primary source of heat along with a gravity furnace. That is why in older houses the chimney is centrally located. Some fireplaces have elaborate decorative elements featuring cast-iron, specialty millwork mantels and imported glazed ceramic tile. Fireplace has no damper or fresh air supply. Fireplace often has a large firebox. Brick and mortar inside the firebox is soft. Lime-based mortar was used and subsequent repairs have used stronger Portland cement based mortars, causing the brick to crack or shatter.

22. (!!) Stairs often very steep and narrow with low head clearance. Stair construction varies from timbers to recycled wood. Uneven risers and steps. No handrailing.

23. Often load-bearing brick was used on wood-framed floors or other under-designed bearing sources. Brick is soft and porous, and vulnerable to water damage from no roof overhangs, leaking gutters, poor flashings. Often the brick was painted to hide poor colour match or inferior quality, and to make the surfaces more water-resistant. The brick may have been directly exposed to sandblasting, which is not an acceptable practice.

24. (!!) Concrete or wood stairs have either settled out of place or rotted out. Stairs were seldom protected by a roof or overhang. This results in continuous weathering and deterioration.

25. On main floors, oak or hardwood strip flooring with a varnish finish was used along with occasional decorative borders. Strips varied from 5/16-inch thick by 1 1/2-inches wide. In drier climates the wood was subject to extensive cracking. Often softwood floor boards were used, usually in upper areas. They were difficult to clean and did not wear well. You will often come across these types of floors with many paint applications on them. Ceramic tiles were occasionally found in bathrooms. Battleship linoleum with asbestos composition could be found in kitchen and bath areas. Floor cloths, the forerunner of resilient flooring, can still be found in areas. Subflooring consisted of shiplap nailed horizontally or diagonally.

26. (!!) Plywood or wall panels have been shimmed and nailed over existing sagging flooring with carpet glued or firmly affixed over.

27. (!!) Floor joists rough-sawn 2"x 4"s, 2"x 6"s, 2"x 8"s, spaced irregularly with no cross-bracing resting on under-designed or recycled beams.

28. Pantry or cold-storage room had an upper and a lower screened vent. These openings are still evident, long after the disappearance of the pantry and cold-storage areas. Refrigerators were widely used in the mid-1940s. Before this time, ice was delivered to homes regularly during the summer months. Mice or other rodents and pests would find their way into unused openings and run along uninsulated wall cavities.

29. Wood lath and plastic walls. Gyproc lath and plastic used in the mid-1940s. Lead- and oil-based paints and decorative wallpaper can also be found under the faceplates of electrical outlets. Wall insulation was not always installed in this period. Over the years any insulation used may have settled to the lower half of the walls, leaving the top of the wall uninsulated. Wooden wainscotting and panelling has been removed. Kitchen walls were often finished with narrow tongue-and-groove panelling installed vertically.

30. Exterior cladding also consisted of asbestos shingles, asphalt shingles, wood clapboard and cedar shingles. Today most of these materials have been removed, whitewashed, painted over, replaced or covered up with vinyl or aluminum siding. Air barriers under the exterior cladding varied from building paper, kraft paper or aluminum-foil backing, to nothing at all. Under the cladding the corners of the house may have rotted due to

windwash and moisture. Structural lumber is very dry and hard, and difficult to work with.

31. (!!) Often porches or verandas have been converted into bathrooms or enlarged kitchens. There is really no solid footing under some of these structures. Slopes are significant enough that water won't find its way to the drain of the tub and you will slide from the toilet seat when you sit down. Bathrooms were constructed indoors when outhouses were no longer the norm.

32. (!!) Soil grades slope towards the house. Often original topsoil from the house excavation.

33. (!!) Wooden beams and floor joists resting on the dirt. No venting under the crawl space, giving the living quarters of the house an "old house smell."

34. After wells, lead or galvanized steel piping was used for hot and cold water supply lines. Cast iron was used for drainage piping, waste and vent for larger sizes and galvanized for small requirements. Often this plumbing is still in place in inaccessible wall cavities and connected to newer plumbing. The use of lead in piping and paints is a health concern.

35. (!!) Rusted cast-iron plumbing drains held in place with wooden blocks resting on soil and tied to rope or wires from the structure. Vent pipes may only stick outside of walls. Cement asbestos pipe is sometimes used for the main sewer lines and in-coming water line to the house. Toilets and tubs are often raised so they could be fitted to the city sewage line, whereas earlier they drained to a septic tank. Grey water from sinks runs into a cesspool or perimeter drainage system.

36. (!!) Knob and tube wiring was common. Once the wire and insulating porcelain elements are damaged the system-short circuits and/or becomes a fire hazard. Homes during this period had few electrical outlets and minimal electrical service. When this old wiring is spliced into higher amperage, service overloading becomes a real problem. Low amperage service of 30 amps was only used for lighting. Back then, few appliances required electricity. During the early 1950s underground lumex wire became available. Fuse boxes were replaced with circuit-breaker panels. Main electrical box not certified. During late 1950s more electrical appliances were available and electrical service was increased to 60 or 100 amps. Also, grounded lumex wire became available.

37. (!!) Wood flooring over dirt, often hiding cracked load-bearing footings.

38. Load-bearing beam roughly notched out with an axe. Often these beams were rough-cut solid timbers of irregular sizes.

39. (!!) Recycled load-bearing beams notched out, reducing their structural strength.

40. Chimney used as a structural load-bearing surface for beam.

41. Beam spliced together or inadequately overlapped at load-bearing columns. The wood used in these beams is very dry and hard. Pounding nails or cutting them can be difficult without proper tools.

42. (!!) Load-bearing beams and foundation wall resting on an unknown boulder. You never know what rock consistency this boulder is made of or its depth in the ground. How will this boulder hold up a major portion of this house during an earthquake? Will the house slide from its footing?

43. (!!) Hollow unfilled masonry blocks resting on boulders, salts and acids in the soil will cause these old and untreated blocks to deteriorate.

44. (!!) Dirt floor often muddy, damp and wet. Perimeter drainage is non-existent.

45. (!!) Load-bearing columns inadequately supported and with footings that range from the top of old rotted tree stumps to the edge of large boulders.

46. (!!) Both hot-water tank and furnace not resting on solid footings.

47. Hot-water tank replaced many times. Exhaust vent not properly connected.

48. (!!) Masonry chimney has no adequate footing. Corroded clean-out door. Over the years, ashes have not been emptied. Brick at the base and mortar joints are deteriorating. Chimney has no flue liner and is exhausting deadly fumes throughout the house through the cracked brick and missing mortar. A single chimney flue serves the furnace, hot-water tank, fireplace, kitchen and bath exhaust. This is a very dangerous situation from the point of view of fires and combustion gas poisoning to the occupants of this house. In some areas the flue could be blocked with creosote.

49. New furnace either oversized or undersized for this old house. Complete heating ducts or pipes have not been replaced, leaving the old gravity system of heat distribution in place. Can cause inefficient heating and comfort problems. Old asbestos boards above the furnace and around heating ducts and pipes still in place. During the period 1900—1950 several types of heating systems were used — fireplace, coal and wood stove, low-pressure steam, gravity warm air, gravity hot water and forced warm air.

50. (!!) Concrete found in the footings and foundations is of poor quality. This is associated with the use of river stones as aggregate, use of mineral-laden water in the mix, poor compaction, poor grading of aggregates and exposure of concrete footings and foundation walls to poor soil drainage, as well as sulphate rich soils. You will also find sandstone, rubblestone or old timbers used as load-bearing footings and walls. If soil drainage has not been good over the years, expect severe problems. During the 1950s expect to find very little or undersized reinforcing used in concrete.

Houses Built 1950 to Present

With the advent of modernization, the construction industry went through drastic changes regarding house design, room features as well as new materials and methods. Public attention was drawn to the health hazards caused by materials such as asbestos, urea formaldehyde foam insulation, lead pipes and lead-based paints, which brought about the manufacture of safer products. In today's houses more emphasis is put on comfort, energy-efficient construction, use of quiet, energy-efficient appliances and low operational costs.

While most changes have been for the better, some countereffects have been realized. Some houses are built so airtight that adequate ventilation is lacking. Other houses may be constructed so quickly, that shortcuts have been taken to save on materials and labour, resulting in a poorer quality of construction. Houses built during a hot real estate market, for example, often miss out on quality finishing touches and attention to detail. Early in the 1980s most provinces in Canada implemented a New Home Warranty program to protect new-home buyers against sloppy workmanship. Homes built by certified builders under the program, are guaranteed to be free of faulty materials for a certain period of time. A description of the New Home Warranty Program is provided in Appendix 7.

The following diagram and points illustrate some typical concerns of houses built more recently than 1950.

1. No curbing or flashings around skylight. Single pane, no solar control over pane. Very large skylight for area of room. Skylights located directly above moist or grease-laden air in the kitchen and/or bathroom.
2. Extensive moss growing on north side.
3. No roof overhang (all sides of house). Rot at roof edges.
4. No rain hood, no chimney liner, chimney rot inside masonry/chimney, chimney not high enough, inadequate flashing around chimney.
5. Masonry chimney on outside wall, resulting in heat loss.
6. Cathedral ceiling, no attic, no venting. Cathedral ceilings are not meant for Canadian climates.
7. Overheating and overcooling problem because of no roof overhangs, inadequate mechanical and natural ventilation, little or no wall and attic insulation.
8. Built-up roofing system. Be careful with certain roofs older than 20 years. Low-sloped roofs or flat roofs. Less than 3 in 12 roof slope can cause numerous water leakage problems.
9. Small windows on south side of house. Window rot on sill due to direct weathering and no roof overhang.
10. No rain gutters, resulting in soil erosion below and water splashed lower wall surfaces, resulting in rot.
11. No roof venting.
12. Extensive wall weathering and wall rot due to lack of roof overhang.
13. High ceilings resulting in hot air raising and cold air at the floor level.
14. Direct-line thermostats controlling all electrical baseboard heaters or electric radiant ceilings.
15. Undersized electric baseboard heaters using aluminum wiring.
16. No curb under door opening. Water from patio or non-draining balcony runs under threshold of door. Promotes air/heat leakage under door and rot of the door frame.

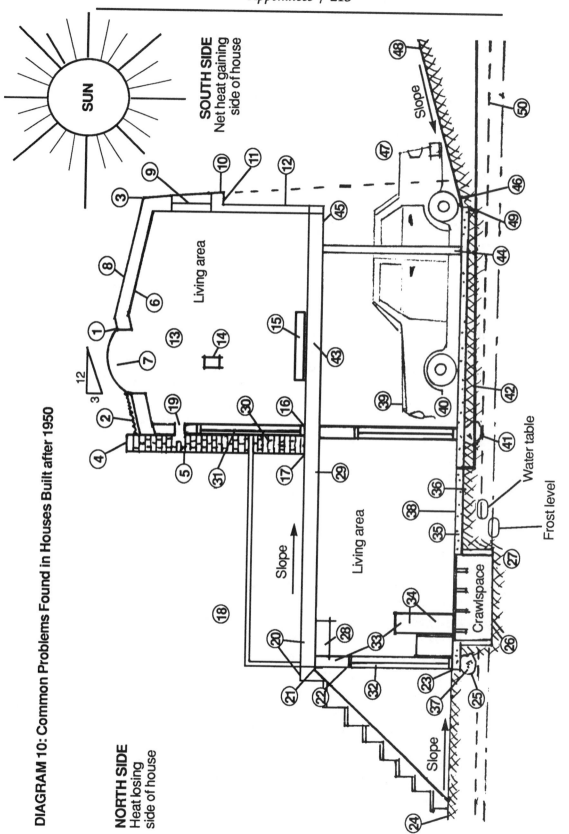

DIAGRAM 10: Common Problems Found in Houses Built after 1950

SUN

SOUTH SIDE
Net heat gaining
side of house

NORTH SIDE
Heat losing
side of house

Living area

Living area

Slope

Slope

Slope

Crawlspace

Water table

Frost level

17. Masonry chimney resting on wooden footing. No ash clean-out door on outside. Masonry veneer walls resting on wooden footings (wood rots and compresses). Exterior surfaces not moisture proof.
18. Extensive rotting of wooden handrail, making a safety problem. Handrailing open all round a danger to life.
19. Ventilation exhaust duct from kitchen laundry and/or bathroom venting into masonry chimney.
20. Balcony not completely protected by a roof, resulting in weathering and leaking areas below into the living quarters. Water running toward the walls of the house in winter, as snow melts on the north side of house last.
21. No balcony flashing, edge rot, no overhang, extensive weathering.
22. No drip cap, resulting in wood rot over frame.
23. No curb under door opening. Water from patio runs under door. Still rot. Door frame rot.
24. Patio sloping towards house. If concrete, no thickened edge, or slip resistant surfaces. If constructed of wood, no pressure-treated wood used, wood resting directly on soil, no ventilation under patio, pests gathered in rotting wood.
25. No adequate footing under load-bearing wall or column. No perimeter drainage or plugged perimeter drainage. Footings above the frost line. High water table.
26. Unvented crawl space. Crawl space below water table. If finished basement instead of crawl space, be careful of rot under finished floor and behind finished walls.
27. Crawl space load-bearing wall not resting on proper footings.
28. Air recovery ventilator inaccessible and not centrally located. Intake and exhaust openings side by side and close to the ground. No adequate mechanical or natural air ventilation in kitchen, bathroom, laundry room and bedrooms.
29. Not known if balcony leaks or if water is held back by insulation and vapour barrier. Difficult to add more insulation to ceiling area. No acoustical sound proofing from balcony above.
30. Improperly designed fireplace resulting in smoking, back drafting. If fireplace insert installed, it may not be approved by a certified testing agency or recognized by your insurance company.
31. Large windows or sliding glass doors on north side of house. Single-pane aluminum frames not insulated or thermally broken.
32. Large sliding glass doors on north side of house. Single pane aluminium frames not insulated or thermally broken. A security problem.
33. Urea formaldehyde foam insulation (UFFI) in walls and asbestos around furnace, heating pipes. Also no insulation in walls.
34. Hot-water heater and furnace or boiler not centrally located and inaccessible to get to come replacement time. Be careful with hot water tank

older than 12 years, forced air furnace older than 25 years, and boiler older than 30 years.

35. Radiant floor heating system embedded in concrete not professionally installed. If concrete slab breaks, so can the heating pipes. Also the heating system could be undersized or oversized. In many areas there are cold spots.

36. No rigid insulation under slab on grade concrete floor.

37. No rigid insulation around slab on grade concrete floor.

38. No floor drain.

39. Doors and windows that are easy to break-in because of semi enclosed non-light areas.

40. No curb under door. Water from sloped driveway runs straight into open carport.

41. Inadequate load-bearing footing. Footing above frost level.

42. Main water and/or sewage line and/or gas and/or main electrical lines running under concrete slab. Be careful with main water line older than 30 years. Inaccessible clean-out openings for sewage drains. Lead supply water lines. Low water pressure. Washroom toilets and drain pipes located in uninsulated areas above and beside eating areas.

43. Inadequate or no insulation in open carport ceiling above living area.

44. No footing under load bearing column, or undersized footing. Building site could possibly be an old land fill which is still settling.

45. Be careful also of cantilevered bay, bow or greenhouse windows or inadequate insulation in the floor joists.

46. No catch basin to take up water from sloped driveway.

47. Inadequate parking space.

48. Steep slope making winter access impossible. Soil and dirt erosion. Surfaces have large cracks. No moisture proofing.

49. No thickened edge of concrete slab.

50. High frost level, high water table, unstable soil. Problems with septic tank, septic field, well water supply or quality of water.

Average Life Expectancy of House Materials

I N CANADIAN CLIMATES the average life expectancy of some house items are as follows:

20 to 30 Years

- Furnace.
- Main underground water line, water pressure reducing value.
- Most types of roof not including quality slate, concrete and clay tile.
- Plumbing pipes, galvanized, copper. Some plastic piping. (Much depends upon the mineral content of the water.) Plumbing valves.
- Main waste drains under sinks. Underground clay sewage line.
- Masonry/chimney flue linings. Ashpit clean-out doors. Metal dampers. Masonry joints require repointing. Prefabricated metal chimneys and fireplaces.
- Gutters, downspouts, wire mesh used over attic vent openings and other types of vent screening.
- Perimeter drainage if made of clay or other porous material.
- Exterior doors and windows, depending on energy efficiency and original quality.
- Main electrical breaker switch. Also replacement of some circuit breakers.
- Roof flashing.
- Exterior siding not including brick, concrete or quality materials.

5 to 10 Years

- Air conditioner, heat pump parts and swimming pool components.
- Most types of resilient flooring and carpets in rooms and on stairs.

- Thermocouplers for natural gas furnace and hot-water tank.
- Hot-water heater.
- Most appliances — e.g., range, fridge, freezer, dishwasher, clothes washer, clothes dryer, water softener.
- Motors used in the most areas — e.g., furnace blower motor or pump, kitchen and bathroom fans, air-recovery ventilator unit, water pumps, built-in vacuum motor, garage door motor, sump and/or sewage pump.
- Wooden non-pressure treated decking, stairs, posts, columns, siding and other structural components not protected from the weather by a roof, paint, stain or other protective surface for door and window weather stripping.
- Electrical receptacles, switches in areas of heavy use, exterior metal light fixtures.
- Faucets and sinks in kitchen, bathroom, laundry, sink traps.
- Door and window locking hardware.
- Kitchen cupboards, bathroom vanities.
- House paint.

List of Tools and Materials Used During a House Inspection

TO CARRY OUT a satisfactory inspection you will need certain tools and materials. However, this does not necessarily mean that you need to purchase expensive tools. Instead, you can improvise by using many common household utensils and tools to achieve the same results. Below is a list of materials that will be useful when conducting a house inspection. You may wish to purchase some items that you presently do not own, as they will become handy for future annual maintenance inspections on the house that you decide to purchase.

Awl Tool with an insulated handle to prevent shock. Used to probe for wood rot, soft concrete and mortar.

Bandages For covering cuts made by refitting the furnace cover or similar work.

Binoculars For viewing distant items like chimney, roof, flashings, etc.

Blanket or Tarp (6'x6') To place under ladder when you are lifting the attic hatch, so that insulation and debris that may fall to the floor can be easily gathered.

Camera Photographic or video camera to take pictures of unknown conditions, like an unmarked electrical service box, for later review by a professional.

Carpenter's Level For checking horizontal surfaces for level and vertical surfaces for plumb. Helps to determine the amount of slope to a floor drain or slope of the roof in conjunction with a protractor.

Carpenter's Square To measure slope of roof.

Clear Plastic Bags Used for gathering samples of rot, infested tree leaves or insulation for further examination.

Coveralls Used to save your clothes from getting dirty and torn.

Crochet Hook or Wire Hook To pull out wall or ceiling insulation.

Crowbar Used for looking under exterior siding, finished basement floors, lifting sump lids and checking the edges of sidewalks for footing depth.

Curved Claw Hammer To pull away wall or ceiling panels, and lift up sump lids.

Drill This can be used to drill under cantilevered areas of the house or into walls under kitchen sinks that are located on perimeter walls to check for insulation.

truck *Electric Spotlight and High-beam Flashlight* Used with cord to light up crawl space, attic, and to see clearly into dark corners. If a battery is used, make sure that it will last the length of the inspection.

Electrical Tester To test electrical polarity and ground wires.

φ *Face Dust Mask* To prevent inhaling insulation dust in the attic and crawlspace.

Feather Glued to a Toothpick To check for air infiltration into the house around electrical outlets, glass fireplace doors, etc.

Garden Hose (100-foot) To see if the perimeter drainage system is functioning, or how gutters, patios and driveway are draining.

φ *Hard Hat* To prevent head injuries while in the attic or crawl space.

Knee Pads To protect the knees from injury when crawling about in crawl-space and attic.

φ *Knife* To determine the number of coats of paint on the surface areas of the house. Also useful, in place of an awl, to check for dry rot.

Magnet To see which metals are made of high or low quality alloys. A magnet will not adhere to items made of solid brass or to high quality stainless steel. Used to check for steel reinforcement in concrete or block foundation walls.

Magnetic Compass To find the orientation of the house; useful in the attic and crawlspace, or other enclosed spaces.

Magnetic or Electronic Stud Finder To determine the spacing of studs in the ceiling and wall framing.

Magnifying Glass To examine pest debris and extent of corrosion on metal surfaces.

Marbles (Large) To see if floor surfaces are level or to see if floor surfaces slope to a drain.

Metric Converter Calculator To assist with any metric conversions.

Mirror To have a closer look at hard-to-reach areas such as under sinks, under hot water heaters, inside the chimney and fireplace.

Moisture Meter To test the range of wood moisture content.

Notebook and Coloured Pens Preferably with lined or graph paper. Different coloured pens will assist in coding features on your sketches and notes. Graph paper makes it easy to draw straight lines and keep your sketches in proportion.

Pail To collect water from hot-water heater when sampling for cleanliness. Also used to pour water down basement floor drains or perimeter drains.

Penlight Helpful when looking into small holes and wall cavities without light reflecting back at you.

Pipe Wrench To check main plumbing drain for any blockage of debris.

Plumb Bob or Fishing Weight and String To check for insulation or any obstructions between the attic and the foundation. Useful in balloon framing.

hammer + nail – to test concrete

Pocket Whisk Broom and Wire Brush For brushing efflorescent concrete surfaces and to clean areas.

Pointed Six-Foot Wooden Pole To probe hard-to-reach areas like ends of fascia boards or rain gutters, and to test depth of perimeter drainage of sump openings.

Protractor To measure angles.

Putty in a Tube To repair and fill holes that were drilled to check for insulation.

Relative Humidity Indicator To check humidity of house. The substance changes colour in the high humidity levels. For use in attic, kitchen, bathrooms, crawl space, basement, etc.

Rubber Gloves To handle unpleasant matter, like pest debris or wet rot, or debris inside the fireplace.

Rubber Mallet To tap over surface areas (such as walls, floors, etc.).

Safety Glasses To prevent eye injury while in the attic or crawlspace, and when looking up inside the fireplace to check the chimney.

Safety Rubber-Soled Treaded Shoes To prevent electrical shock and stepping on rusty nails in the attic. Also can prevent falls on wet grass, slippery sidewalks and stairs.

Screwdriver Type with a multiple number of different heads issued to remove electrical panels and face plates.

Shovel To dig along suspect areas of footing or foundation walls.

Sling Psychrometer and Charts Used for determining indoor relative humidity. Tests can help pinpoint moisture problems.

Tape Used to hold thermostat in place.

Tape Measure A 100-foot tape measure is used to measure the property; a 25-foot tape measure is used to measure rooms, ceiling heights, etc.

Telephone Tester To see if the phone lines are properly polarized.

Test Kits Test kits are available for radon, air and water quality, lead-based paints, lead solder, urea formaldehyde foam insulation, asbestos, etc. It is recommended that a certified testing laboratory be consulted.

Thermometer To determine hot and cold water temperature, temperature in the attic and various rooms.

Toolbox To store most of the items in this list.

Towel Used to dry your hands after removing the soot and dirt when finished with the fireplace and furnace inspection.

Tri-square To check the squareness of doors and windows.

Water Pressure Gauge Used to test static water pressure at the faucet.

Wooden Six-Foot Ladder and Extension Ladder needed to inspect high areas such as eaves, ceilings and overhead lighting. Wood, vinyl or fiber-glass is used rather than aluminum, because it is a better insulator from electric shock and the wind will not blow over an unattended wooden ladder as easily as aluminum. As you walk from room to room, up stairs and along hallways with the ladder under your arm, it will give you a good idea of how easy it will be to move your furniture into the house.

▼

Master Checklist of Questions to Ask the Owner

MOST PROSPECTIVE PURCHASERS do not ask enough question or simply do not know what questions to ask when buying a house. The more information you are able to elicit from an owner, the better prepared you will be to make a careful, informed investment decision. You will find out how well the house and property have been cared for. Should you decide to buy, it will also assist you in maintaining the house and property, and to answer questions asked by prospective purchasers when you later sell the house.

The following is a summary of questions you should ask the present homeowner, regardless of the location or size of the house. Some questions will not pertain to the property or house you are inspecting. For convenience sake, you may wish to make a copy of this list and ask the owner to answer the questions to the best of his/her knowledge. However, personally asking the questions and maintaining good eye contact will give you a sense of the owner's confidence, honesty and integrity. Are your questions being answered thoroughly to your satisfaction? Many of the questions below have been coded with a "C" indicating the answer may have a CRITICAL bearing on your Offer to Purchase. You will want to review these answers carefully, and compare them with your physical inspection notes, before you finalize your purchase decision. The rest have been coded with an "I" to indicate the answer is merely INFORMATIONAL in nature for future care or maintenance.

Lot and Property

C   How many owners have lived in the house before you?
C   How long have you lived in this house? Why are you selling and where are you moving to?

I How long has the property been listed for sale? Has it ever been privately listed? Has it ever been independently inspected?

C Are there any covenants on the house or property? Has the title search been made?

C When was the property and house last assessed and appraised for taxation purposes? What was the annual taxation assessment?

C What form of zoning and bylaws exist for the neighbourhood?

I Are there any restrictions in this area such as watering, burning leaves, motor home or vehicle parking, pets, cutting down of trees, etc.?

I Is there unlimited or restricted parking on the street?

C Are the yard and streets well lit at night?

C What is the crime rate like in the neighbourhood? Has the house ever been burglarized since you've lived in it?

I Has the property or any buildings on it ever been hit by lightning? Is the house lightning protected?

I How far away is the fire hydrant or firehall?

C In which predominant direction does wind, rain and snow blow over the property and house? Does the wind blow in one direction more than in another at any time of the year?

C Has the property been tested for radon or methane gas leakage?

C Where is the property line and survey markers?

C Are there any property easements or rights of way?

I Who is responsible for maintenance, repair and upgrading of the perimeter fence around the property?

C How does water drain from the driveway and garage floor? Where does the water run to?

C How high does the groundwater table rise during various seasons of the year?

I When was an application of sealer last placed on the asphalt driveway?

I Has the concrete driveway ever been treated with a water repellant substance?

I How is household garbage disposed of?

I What services come to this house: milk and bread delivery, cable TV, newspaper delivery, mail, etc.?

Service Connections

C Where are underground service lines located? (e.g., water, sewage, storm, natural gas, electricity, oil, propane, etc.)

C How deep are they in the ground? Are they below the frost line?

I Has there ever been a power outage? Is there an auxiliary source of electricity?

C How old is the main underground water line leading up to the house? When was it last replaced? Is it copper or plastic pipe?

C Where is the main water shut off on the property and within the house? Where is the water meter located? Is there a water pressure reducing valve inside the house?

I If there is a culvert under the driveway, when was it last cleaned?

C When was the perimeter drainage system last cleaned or replaced? Who do you hire to clean or replace the perimeter drainage system?

C Are there separate storm and sewage lines on the property? Where does the water run to?

C Are there any unused oil tanks, septic tanks or cesspools buried on the property? How are they protected from caving in, or leaching their contents into the soil?

C Where is the septic tank and field located in relation to any wells?

C When was the septic tank, cesspool or dry well last cleaned?

C Is there a sump and sump pump on the property? When was it last cleaned?

I Are there any old mine shafts or water wells on the property? Was the well dug manually? What materials are used to line the walls of the well?

C Is the well deep or shallow? Has it ever gone dry during the year? When was the water last tested for bacteria? Have any pesticides been sprayed on the ground near the well?

Landscaping

I What types of plants and trees are in the yard and how are they cared for? Are plans available? If I purchased the house, would you draw a plan identifying the various trees and plants?

I Are there any tall trees on the property that require removal or topping?

C What type of pesticides do you use on your flowers, shrubs and trees?

I Has new topsoil been added to the garden or yard recently?

I How old is the lawn? Was the lawn started from sod or seed?

I When was the lawn last aerated?

I What type of fertilizer do you use on the lawn?

C Have you ever noticed any settling of certain areas of the lawn over the years?

C Do some areas of the lawn stay wet longer than others after rain? Do some areas stay greener than others?

C What is the geology of the area like?

C Does the yard receive equal amounts of sunlight throughout the day? How many hours of uninterfered daylight per day are there? Which areas of the property are mostly in shade?

Pools, Patios and Decks

C When was the swimming pool installed? Was a permit taken out at City Hall? Who installed the pool and furnace?

C How is the pool serviced? When was it last cleaned and when was the water heating furnace last serviced?

C How is the water in the pool treated? When was the water filter last cleaned or replaced?

I Are operations manuals available for the swimming pool, spa and sauna?

C Does the exterior balcony, landing, deck or patio have a floor drain?

C Was any pressure-treated wood used for the decks and patios?

House Exterior

C How old is the house? Does the house have any heritage features or record of a prominent citizen who lived in it or designed it?

C If it is a newer house, is it still covered by a New House Warranty program?

C Are original inspection certificates (e.g., building inspection, plumbing, heating, electrical, insulation and surveyors) for the house available?

I Who was the original contractor of the house? How many other houses have been built by this contractor? Is the contractor a member of a home builders association?

I Are construction plans and specifications available for the house?

C Has the house been raised or previously moved to the site?

C Before the house was built, what was the topography of the property like? Were there any underground streams, springs, marshes or old landfills? Was a soil test performed before the footings were poured?

C Does the house rest on any large boulders or pilings?

C Is the house built to specific performance standards for energy efficiency (e.g., Airtight Drywall Approach)?

C Are exterior faucets for garden hose connections or underground lawn sprinkler systems protected with an approved backflow preventer to prevent back siphonage?

C In an attached garage, are the walls finished with non-combustible materials? Are joints sealed to prevent carbon monoxide from entering the house?

C Has pressure treated wood been used in the house construction or yard outbuildings?

I What type of sheathing material is under the existing exterior wall surfaces?

C If aluminum or vinyl siding has been installed, what was the condition of the cladding before the new siding was added? Was wood rot removed? Do you have pictures of what the old walls looked like? Are there any manufacturers' guarantees left on the siding?

I When was the exterior of the house last cleaned or painted? What type of paint or stain was used? Where was it purchased?

C How old is the roof? How many layers of old roofing are under the present roof? What type of roofing material is it? Who installed it? Are there any guarantees or warranties left on the roof?

C   Are there soffit and gable vents?

I   When were the rain gutters last cleaned and checked for leaks?

C   When was the masonry chimney last cleaned? Who cleaned it? What was the condition of the liner? When were the bricks last repainted? Does the top of the chimney have a rain hood?

I   Where is the cleanout ash pit opening located for the masonry chimney and fireplace? Is it on the exterior or interior of the house?

C   Is the metal prefabricated chimney insulated and certified? Does it have a rain cap?

C   Is the fireplace insert or wood stove certified by a testing agency and approved by the insurance company?

C   How long have the cracks in the foundation and footings been present?

House Interior

I   How many occupants live in the house? Do any of them smoke?

C   Are there any earthquake resistant features to this house?

C   Did you ever have a fire inside the house or on the premises? Was there ever a fire safety inspection done on this house?

C   Are the interior rooms sprinklered or fire protected? How are the sprinklers serviced?

C   Does the house have a burglar alarm system? Who installed the system? Is it approved by a certified testing agency? Did your insurance company require a copy of the certificate?

I   Does the house have any safety features for children or the elderly?

I   Which windows are single glazed? Are there storm windows and insect screens?

C   Have you had any problems with condensation on walls and windows?

C   How well can the rooms be ventilated for fresh air? Do windows and doors permit cross ventilation?

C   Are some rooms colder than others? Do any rooms overheat in the summer months and stay cool during winter months?

C   Are the perimeter walls insulated? What kind of insulation was used?

C   Is there any asbestos used in the house, for instance, around heating ducts and pipes, or under ceiling and flooring tile? Is there any urea formaldehyde foam insulation in the walls?

C   Do all rooms get enough natural light during the day?

C   Which walls of the house are structurally load bearing?

C   Are there any wall and ceiling cracks? When did they first occur?

C   Are floors bouncy on the main and/or upper floors? Are they level?

I   Are there any squeaky floors or stairs?

I   How old is the floor covering in the house?

I   How often do you use the fireplace insert or stove? How often do you reload the fireplace, insert or stove with wood?

I   Do you have any special way of starting a fire? What type of firewood do you commonly burn?

C   Where is the attic access hatch or door located?

C   Is the attic insulated? What kind of insulation has been used?

C   How well is the attic vented? Does it often get very hot in the attic?

C   Has the attic ever been fumigated for rodents, ants, wasps, hornets?

C   Where is the basement floor drain located? Does it work?

C   Where is the access to the crawlspace? Has the crawlspace ever been cleaned?

C   Have there been any problems with moisture, condensation or water seepage along the floors or walls of the basement or crawlspace?

C   Has the basement or crawlspace ever flooded during the year or length of time you lived in the house?

C   Is a ground cover vapour retarder used over the soil in the crawlspace? Does the crawlspace have ventilation?

Electrical Wiring

I   Are all the circuit breakers marked for each room at the main electrical service panel? Is there a main breaker switch?

C   When you plug various appliances into electrical outlets in the kitchen, do any of the breakers overload or shut off at the main service panel?

I   Do the electrical outlets in the kitchen have split-type receptacles?

C   Which outlet is the deep freezer plugged into?

C   Are the electrical outlets in the kitchen, bathroom, garage, crawlspace and outdoor receptacles protected by certified electrical ground fault interrupters? Is all the electrical wiring grounded?

C   When was the electrical wiring last upgraded? Who was the electrical contractor?

C   Is there any aluminum wiring in the house? When were the connections last tightened? Are connections treated with an oxide inhibitor?

C   Is there any old knob and tube wiring?

C   How large is the electrical service and service panel? Is there a main breaker switch?

Heating, Plumbing and Ventilation

C   When was the plumbing last upgraded?

C   Where in the house is the water shut-off valve for the lawn faucets? Where are the other water shut-off valves throughout the house?

I   Are there any old galvanized or cast iron pipes within the walls? Was lead-free solder used on copper water pipes?

C Have there been any water leaks from pipes and drains? Where are the drain clean-out openings located? When were the plumbing drains last cleaned?

C Has there been any discolouration of the water during various times of the year? Has chlorine or fluoride been added to the main water supply?

I If not from a well, from what reservoir is the water supplied?

I If there is a basement or crawlspace sump, when was it last cleaned?

C Does the main waste line have a back water closing valve? When was this valve last checked?

C Where is the main fuel shut off valve located for the furnace or hot water heater (e.g., natural gas)?

C Do combustible appliances like furnace, hot water heater and fireplace have their own fresh air supply?

C How old is the hot water heater? Are there any guarantees and warranties left?

I How many gallons of water does it hold? Have you ever run out of hot water?

I When was the hot water heater last serviced? Who serviced it?

C Is the house's heating system approved and certified by the permits and licensing department of the municipality or city?

I How old is the furnace? How well does it heat the house without assistance from the wood stove or electric baseboard heaters?

C When was the furnace last serviced? Who serviced it? When were the forced air ducts last cleaned?

C If the house is heated with hot water, how is the water treated to prevent corrosion in the water lines?

I What type of thermostats are used to control the heating system and where are they located?

I Is the forced-air furnace, hot water boiler, hot water heater or space heater vented by means of a direct vent, induced-draft or natural vent?

I Do the mechanical ventilators in the kitchen and bathroom work? Where do they exhaust to?

I When were the air conditioner, air recovery ventilator, electronic air filter and humidifier last serviced? Specifically what parts were serviced? What company serviced them?

Overall Maintenance

C Has the house given you any problems? What do you find most irritating about the house, property and neighbourhood?

I What is the most recent item you have had to fix or repair in the house?

I What items have been renovated, repaired or replaced since you have owned the house? Who did the work? Where were the materials purchased? Are there any guarantees and warranties on the materials supplied such as doors, windows, cupboards, garborator, plumbing fixtures, etc.?

C Were building permits required for the renovation? Was the renovation inspected by the city building inspector? Is the documentation available?

I Did you make use of any government grants or assistance regarding oil conversion, home weatherization or renovation programs?

I What things have you done to improve the house to prepare for its sale?

I When were the interior walls and ceilings last painted? What type of paint was used?

I When were the carpets last cleaned?

I How are skylights and clerestory windows washed?

C Have you had any problems with pests in the house like cockroaches, carpenter ants, sow bugs, spiders, etc.? Has an exterminator ever been called?

C Do larger animals (like raccoons, deer, coyotes, bears, etc.) come around the house? What is used to control them?

C Is there anything in the house that will cause an allergy or health problem?

C What have been your overall operating costs for the house and yard?

C How expensive are your heat, hydro and water bills?

C Have heat loss/gain calculations been done on the house?

I What special features does the house have that will reduce insurance rates and property taxes?

I Are any items in the house under a service contract? (For instance, the heat pump, air conditioner, fuel for the furnace, swimming pool, gardens, lawns?)

I What fixtures and appliances are included in the sale of the house? How old are they? What condition are they in?

I Are the operations manuals available for the furnace, hot water heater, heat recovery ventilator, fireplace, air filter, garbage disposer, built-in vacuum, security system and other appliances and fixtures in the house? Are there manufacturer's guarantees or warranties left on any of these items?

Houses with Basement Suites

C Is the suite legal? (Obtain a letter from city hall to confirm.)

C Are there any liens against the property or the house that the tenant may have placed?

C How is the rent paid and when is it due? Is there any damage deposit? When was the last rent increase?

C Are there any restrictions placed on the tenant regarding children, pets, parking, smoking, music and parties?

C Are the interior partitions and ceiling fire rated?

C How are the acoustics? Can you hear sounds from above or below coming through the walls, ceilings, floors or heating ducts?

C How are utilities like cable TV, heating, water and electricity paid? Are there separate meters?

C Is the main water shut-off, hot water tank, furnace and main electrical service panel for the entire house in the rented suite? (This can cause problems for access.)

I Is there any problem with heating, hot water, water pressure or plumbing drainage?

I How long have the present tenants occupied the suite? When was the last time the condition of the suite was checked?

I Have the locks been changed after each tenant?

I What appliances or fixtures belong to the tenant?

I Is there a separate access to laundry and storage?

Suitability (To be answered by you)

C How much privacy is there in the yard — visual and acoustical?

C If you are affected by allergies or asthma, will the plants, shrubs, trees, humidity, etc. cause health problems?

C Is the property and house accessible to the aged and disabled?

C Is the area prone to hurricanes, tornadoes, earthquakes, polluted air, contimaned soil?

After discussing the above items with the owner, you will have a much clearer feeling about whether or not you wish to purchase the house. If you are interested in pursuing the purchase but have some concerns that were raised by the exploratory questionnaire, it is advisable to include a subject clause in the Offer to Purchase. The subject clause may stipulate the offer is "subject to satisfactory inspection of the house and property." The inspection may be done by you and/or a building inspector. If you feel you do not need a complete building inspection, then you could specify certain aspects such as "subject to inspection of the furnace, chimney, fireplace, stove, roof, structure and for pest and insect infestation." The purpose of inspecting these major items is that you will want to know their remaining life expectancy. Hopefully all of them won't need replacement at the same time, or soon after you take occupancy of the house. If the latter is the case, you may wish to negotiate an adjustment in the purchase price.

Also on the topic of subject clauses to include in an Offer to Purchase, is the condition that certain items are cleaned or serviced prior to closing date of the sale. Suggested items include: chimney cleaned, fireplace inserts certified and approved by the insurance company, gutters and perimeter drainage cleaned, hot water tank and furnace serviced, heating ducts cleaned, handrailings fixed, broken or cracked windows replaced, smoke detectors operational. Safety is your prime concern, although cost and convenience are also factors. After all, you wouldn't buy a dirty used car or one with an untuned engine.

The same principle applies to buying a house, unless of course, adjustments to the selling price have been made for servicing and cleaning.

When purchasing a brand new house, be certain to ask the builder for left-over supplies of finishing items such as touch-up paint and stain, spare floor and wall tiles, spare roof tiles or shingles, samples of other flooring used, etc. Once you move into a house, you will find areas that need touch-up for fixing and this will enable you to get an exact match with the original finishes.

▼

One-hour
House Examination

A THOROUGH INSPECTION REQUIRES a considerable amount of time and energy. Since you may be looking at a number of houses, you will want to invest a large amount of effort only on the ones you are seriously interested in buying. To find out if the house is worth inspecting in detail, therefore, the following one-hour examination will help you to eliminate those houses with major structural or mechanical flaws. The owner should be able to provide you with answers to the fact-finding questions and pointers noted below.

Exterior

A *Lot Location*
- How long has the property been listed for sale? Reason for selling?
- Has it been listed before by the same owner?
- Neighbourhood type, basic services, schools, bus, mail, police, fire hydrant or fire hall, church, garbage disposal, zoning.
- Duration of hottest and coldest temperatures of the year along with rain, snow, shade and darkness.
- Hours of sunlight and darkness throughout the year.
- Direction of prevailing winds during summer and winter.
- Lot size, shape, slope away from house, surface drainage.
- Topography, terrain, high or low elevation of lot in relation to others in the neighbourhood.
- Location of lot survey markers and bench mark.
- Location and age of items buried underground of lot — e.g., sewage, water and storm lines, cable, electrical and natural gas line, oil tank, well, cesspool, septic tank or other air and soil pollutants.
- Underground streams, geology of area.

DIAGRAM 11: One-hour House Inspection

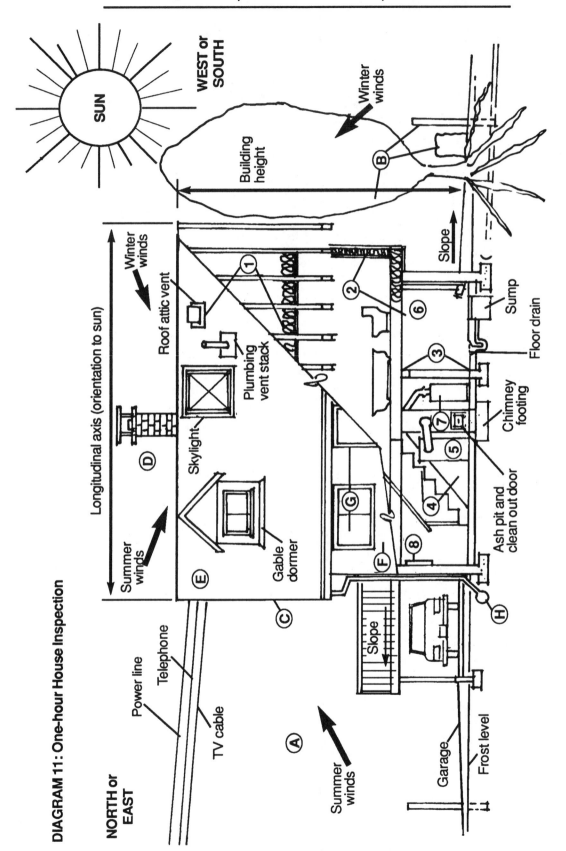

- Lot's visual and acoustical privacy.
- Lot easements or restrictions.

B *Landscaping*
- Identification of types of trees, shrubs and other vegetation.
- Age, height and how cared for.
- Types of pesticides and fertilizers used.
- Trees used for shade, windbreak, air filtration, acoustics or beauty.
- Pest problems.
- Concrete driveway last sealed.
- Condition of perimeter fence.
- Driveway and catch basins last cleaned.
- Adequate surface drainage?

C *House*
- Availability of house and survey plans.
- House built to energy-efficient performance standards?
- Quality construction materials used.
- Age, square footage, number of rooms and ease of maintaining house.
- Number of previous owners and size of families. (More owners and large families will show more wear of house components.)
- Orientation of house to natural elements.
- Number of previous renovations and/or rooms renovated.
- Number of house fires, conversions and uses — e.g., some houses may have been used for livestock or birds.
- Was house ever raised or moved?
- Total annual operating cost of house including taxes, insurance, repairs and replacement of components.
- Any component of house, yard, pool, ventilation, heating or air conditioning system under a service contract?
- How does the exterior of this house look in relation to all the others in the neighbourhood? Is it better?

D *Chimney*
- Type of construction, age, height, location on exterior or interior walls in relation to prevailing winds and the possibility of backdrafting.
- Chimney last cleaned.
- Number of flues side by side.
- Rain cap and/or hood.
- If masonry, condition and age of flue liner.
- Fireplace insert age and last inspected to meet fire insurance requirements.
- Chimney ashpit and clean-out door location.
- Chimney footing or foundation.

- Does fireplace have combustible fresh air duct?
- Exterior masonry chimney walls waterproofed?

E *Roof*
- Type, age, shape, slope, pitch, colour, orientation of roof ridge to the sun, blowing winds, rain and snow.
- Ridge straight with no sags over roof areas.
- Number and location of ridges, valleys, dormers, skylights.
- Overhang protecting all exterior wall surfaces and stairs.
- Roof last cleaned?
- Age and type of flashing — tar, aluminum or galvanized metal.
- Gutters last cleaned?
- Downspouts connected to perimeter drainage.
- Location of plumbing, vents, natural and mechanical air vents.
- Vent screens last cleaned?

F *Exterior Cladding*
- Type, age, colour.
- Last cleaned, stained, painted or otherwise finished?
- Surfaces exposed to weathering from wind, rain, sun, snow and uneven temperatures.
- Settlement cracks over wall surfaces?

G *Windows and Doors*
- Type, age, colour, last upgraded or replaced.
- Orientation of large windows, skylights and doors to natural elements in the north, south, east and west.
- Problems with fire escape, security or break-ins.
- Problems with condensation, overheating, cooling and natural ventilation.
- All doors and operable windows weatherstripped.
- Windows with thermally broken panes and frames.
- Number and thickness of panes.
- Exterior doors of solid construction with thermally broken frames.

H *Perimeter Drainage*
- Type, age and location of pipe.
- Last cleaned?
- Soil type, water table level, frost level.
- Good drainage around the house will prevent a wet basement, crawl space, slab, structural settlement, frost heaving problems, buildup of hydrostatic pressure on concrete floors and retaining walls. (Remember, during wet periods the water table will be close to the surface; during extended dry periods it can be many feet beneath.)
- Ask where water drains to from perimeter drainage.

Interior

1 *Attic*

- Attic access, location, size, number of access locations.
- Type of attic insulation and thickness.
- Natural, mechanical, soffit and gable ventilation.
- Type of roof framing trusses or rafters.
- Problems with truss uplift.
- Size, framing, spacing and bracing of rafters.
- Continuation of plumbing pipes and mechanical venting ducts through the roof.
- Frost or icing problems inside attic during winter and moisture problems during summer.
- Water leakage under valleys, around chimneys, skylights, mechanical and natural vents and other roof penetrations.

2 *Interior Living Quarters*

- Find out if all built-in features work — e.g., mechanical ventilators, intercom, computerized or remote controls, vacuum system, garboretor, vegetable sprayer, fire alarms or detectors, security system, ceiling fans, clock-controlled night lighting. Materials marked by a certification agency?
- Surfaces last painted, cleaned or otherwise finished.
- What is underneath the wall finish?
- Flooring type, age, last cleaned.
- Age and number of mechanical ventilators.
- Fresh air filters.
- Filters last cleaned?
- Motors lubricated or replaced.
- Chances of mechanical ventilators backdrafting living quarters.
- All perimeter walls insulated.
- Type of insulation used and thickness.
- Any urea formaldehyde foam insulation in walls or under bathtubs?
- Any unusual odours from cigarette smoke, cooking or moisture?
- Living quarters have visual and acoustical privacy.
- All appliances work that go with the sale of the house.
- Wall, ceiling or floor stains.
- Any illegal suites — how insured?

3 *Structural*

- What components are used to hold the entire building together?
- Type of structural framing and load-bearing materials used.
- Location of load-bearing columns, beams and walls.
- Type of foundation walls and footings.

- Where and how are they supported?
- Use of pressure-treated wood.
- Cantilevered walls, balconies or decks.
- Direction of water drainage from surfaces.
- Any balconies or decks over enclosed living quarters below?
- Areas of heat loss and water penetration.
- Any large boulders or dirt floors under the house, in the basement or crawl space?

4 *Stairs*
- Size, width, head clearance, handrailing, even risers and steps.
- If accessible, look underneath stair to determine type of wood used and quality of construction. This will give you a good idea how the structural components of the rest of the house are assembled with regard to quality of materials and workmanship.

5 *Mechanical Heating System*
- Type, age, location of unit — central or off to one side of floor plan.
- Combustible fresh-air duct.
- When were heating ducts, air filter and burner areas last cleaned?
- Motor last oiled?
- Electrical or hot-water baseboard convectors last cleaned?
- Water last treated in hot-water boiler?
- Expansion tank serviced?
- Furnace last serviced?
- Type, age, location and number of thermostats.
- Number of direct line or low-voltage thermostats in use.
- Use of any asbestos around heating ducts, pipes or around furnace.

6 *Plumbing*
- Age of all plumbing faucets and fixtures.
- Source of water supply, water purification, water pressure.
- Depth of well. Well close to septic tank?
- Well ever run dry during the year?
- Well pump last serviced?
- Types of supply lines, age, location of shut-off valves.
- Location of main shut-off valve on property and inside house.
- Location of backflow preventer, pressure reducing valve, air chamber, trap primer.
- Location of floor drain.
- Pipes insulated and protected from freezing.
- Pipes of drainage, waste and sewage.
- Age, location of secondary clean-outs, last cleaned.
- Location of main clean-out.

- Sewage pump last replaced and protected from freezing?
- Sewage backflow preventer, backwater closing valve, automatic air vents.
- Sump age, location, last cleaned.
- Grease trap.
- Water strainers last cleaned?
- Septic tank last cleaned?
- Clean-out opening location.
- Size of tank, number of gallons, type of tank construction.
- Any galvanized-steel or cast-iron piping still in use for drainage and water supply?
- Watering restrictions.

7 *Hot-water Tank*

- Type, age, number of gallons, location — central or off to one side of floor plan.
- Tank last drained or serviced?
- Tank components last replaced?
- Length of time to get hot water from furthest faucets.
- Combustible fresh air duct for natural gas hot water tank.
- Vacuum relief, temperature and pressure relief valve with extension pipe to floor drain or outside of house.
- Age of water softener, last serviced.

8 *Electrical*

- Location of main electrical breaker box and grounding wire.
- Type and size of wires amps/volts.
- Age of wiring, main breaker disconnect switch and circuit breakers.
- Circuit breakers all identified or marked.
- Problems with overloaded circuits.
- Electrical ground fault interrupters.
- Any aluminum or knob and tube wiring in use?
- How many power outages are there per year at this house?
- Type of breakers.
- Certification of electrical box.

Hiring a Residential Building Inspector

Y OU MAY DECIDE that you need the skills of a professional house inspector. A listing of inspectors can be found in your local Yellow Pages telephone directory under the heading Building Inspection Service. The best way to find an inspector is by word of mouth, since it usually comes with anecdotal comments about the quality and value of the service performed. However, beware of inspectors recommended by a real estate agent. Since the agent most often represents the seller of the house, inspectors they recommend may have a reputation for doing cursory inspections that will not "kill the deal." You need to hire an inspector who is unbiased and will represent you, the buyer.

Below are some pointers on how to evaluate the company and service to be provided.

Checking Out the Company

- How many years has the company been in the business of specifically inspecting houses? Is the company and inspector a member of a recognized credit association? Phone to see if there have been any unresolved complaints. Is the inspector bonded and does he carry liability insurance? You don't want to be held liable for missing items or damaged property.
- Does the company or inspector hold a membership in a professional organization? Is the company affiliated with any construction, real estate or other professional organization? Does the connection imply a conflict of interest? The inspection firm should be completely independent. A conflict may exist if the inspector stresses the need for repairs and is prepared to do them or recommends someone to do them.
- Which member of the company will be inspecting the house? What qualifications does the individual have to do a house inspection? Good inspec-

tors will have practical, technical and university training in the building sciences. You want to hire an individual who is a generalist. An engineer or architect, because of the amount of specialization in one area, may not always be your best choice. An ideal house inspector has been in the building industry most of his life and has acquired a working knowledge of all subjects related to residential construction. Can the inspector supply references? How large was the last house inspected? Where was it located and how long did it take to inspect? Will the inspector give you the name of the previous client as a reference? Do you feel at ease with the inspector? Are your questions answered fully?

Services to Be Provided

- How long will the inspection take? Good inspectors can take all day to inspect an average-size house. How many items are covered in the report? Good reports are written in point form narrative and should list hundreds of points to acquaint you with all possible troublespots. What tools does the inspector have for inspecting the insulation, the chimney, furnace, hot-water heater, electrical wiring and plumbing?
- Good inspectors will want you to come along for an oral report during the tour, and then provide a written report immediately after the inspection. The inspector should brief you beforehand on what will be inspected and how the inspection will be carried out. Has the inspector checked all the areas that were mentioned when you first arranged the appointment?
- Maintenance tips should also be included in the report. After you have purchased a house, ask if the inspector will make a follow-up visit to ensure nothing has been overlooked in the original inspection.
- What fees will be charged for the inspection? Rates will vary in different parts of the country and in rural and urban areas. You should expect to pay between $75 and $175 per hour for a qualified and experienced inspector. Some inspectors prefer to charge a flat fee for a one-hour, half-day or full-day inspection. Ask if there will be additional fees for inspecting outbuildings, swimming pools, yard and fireplace insert.

Checking Out the Inspector

Before you buy your next home, the following are points you should consider when hiring a home inspector.

- Credentials. How long has the inspector been in the business of inspecting homes or commercial dwellings?
- Professional training. Is the inspector trained as an architect, engineer, building technologist or certified builder from an accredited university, trade or technical college? Ask to see tickets and diplomas.

- Professional membership. Does the inspector hold a membership in a Canadian professional group?
- References. Be cautious of references or referrals from some realtors. This can lead to a conflict of interest.
- Business address. There should be an office you can visit. Cellular telephone numbers aren't enough.
- Business licence. Does the company have a current business licence?
- Length of inspection. A proper, comprehensive, professional home inspection performed by the best inspectors can take all day.
- Accompanying the inspector. You should tag along. You will learn a lot about what you are buying. You will also know how much time you are paying for.
- Cost. Be sure to get an estimate so you know exactly what the inspection covers and at what rate.
- Inspection format. Does the inspection include a comprehensive narrative or only a checklist?
- Items covered. Check for items not covered in the report and/or visual inspection. How many items are covered, for example radon, air quality, wood rot, mold and pest infiltration? Are there any hidden or additional costs?
- Client briefing. Does the inspector brief the client beforehand as to what will be inspected?
- Who is doing the inspection. Is the owner of the home inspection company doing the inspection or the employees of the company who may have little experience or who may not be accredited?
- Inspection report legitimate. Find out if the inspector will back his report in court, if necessary.
- Personality. Do you feel at ease with the inspector? What other things does the inspector do besides house inspections?

Why Hire a Home Inspector?

- Peace of mind. You know that the house you are buying is what you think you are buying.
- Make sure you end up with a cool-headed assessment. Know the condition of the property in advance.
- Protect the biggest investment of your life. You don't want to put your investment at risk and have to face heavy repair costs.
- Learn how your house works. Learn where things are and what requires maintenance before you buy.
- Strike yourself a better deal. You can have the inspection take place before you make an offer, or make an inspection a condition of your offer. Allow yourself time to arrange and complete a proper inspection.

Other Services a Company Can Offer

- Building specification, plan and design review.
- Consumer information and building product analysis.
- Energy conservation audits and reviews.
- Security and burglar protection analysis.
- Historical preservation research and restoration documentation.
- Building condition survey and technical audits/maintenance programs.
- Building problem anaysis and investigations.
- Enviromnmental assessments, and hazardous and toxic substance inspections and monitoring.
- Ventilation and indoor air quality studies.
- Fire protection and safety plans.

New Home Warranty Program

THE NEW HOME Warranty Program is operated by the Housing and Urban Development Association of Canada (HUDAC). Most provinces have a New Home Warranty Program, although there are differences between the provinces in terms of coverage under the program. In some provinces the program is mandatory by law, whereas in others it is an optional program that builders may or may not be involved in.

It is important to contact the New Home Warranty program in your province to get further information on the exact warranty coverage provided. The limitations and exclusions could cost you a lot of money later. NHWP coverage generally includes incomplete work allowance, warranty protection up to one year on specific items, basement protection for two years and major structural defect protection for five years. A list of contact addresses in various provinces is listed below.

The overall program applies to houses, condominiums, apartments, townhouses, and other forms of residential homes. Under the provisions of the Program, it is the builder's responsibility to repair, without charge, defects in materials and/or workmanship and structural problems, according to the terms of the New Home Warranty Certificate. In addition, any remainder of the warranty coverage applying to the previous owner is generally extended to subsequent buyers for a fixed period of time.

If a problem occurs, the homeowner notifies the builder; if the problem is not sufficiently addressed, the NHWP officials attempt to mediate the matter and rectify the problem within the limits of the coverage.

It is the builder who pays for the program, but sometimes the builder passes on the cost for each individual unit to the purchaser or otherwise adds it into the purchase price.

Here is a listing of the current NHWP contact addresses and phone numbers. Naturall, these are subject to change.

New Home Warranty Program of British Columbia & the Yukon
#760 - 1441 Creekside Drive, Vancouver, B.C. V6B 3R9
Phone:(604) 736-9231

New Home Warranty Program of Alberta
#201 - 208 - 57th Avenue S.W., Calgary, Alberta T2H 2K8
Phone:(403) 253-3636

New Home Warranty Program of Saskatchewan Inc.
3012 Louise Street, Saskatoon, Saskatchewan S7J 3L8
Phone:(306) 373-7833

New Home Warranty Program of Manitoba Inc.
#220 - 1120 Grant Avenue, Winnipeg, Manitoba R3M 2A6
Phone:(204) 477-1877

Ontario New Home Warranty Program
660 Eglinton Avenue East, Toronto, Ontario M4P 1P3
Phone:(416) 488-6000

La garantie des maisons neuves de l'APCHQ
5800, boul. Louis-H. Lafontaine, Ville d'Anjou, Quebec H1M 1S7
Phone:(514) 353-1120

Atlantic New Home Warranty Corporation
P.O. Box 411, Halifax, Nova Scotia B3J 2P8
Phone:(902) 425-7225

▼

Conversion Factors

T HE FOLLOWING TABLE provides conversion factors for some units used in this book to express measurement, as well as others that you will come across during your inspection. Of course, if you have a metric converter calculator, you will not need to use this manual method of conversion.

Acres	x	0.405	=	hectares
Celsius	x	1.8 + 32 degrees	=	Fahrenheit
Centimetres	x	0.39370079	=	inches
	x	0.01	=	metres
	x	10	=	millimetres
	x	0.0109361	=	yards
Chains (Gunter's)	x	66	=	feet
	x	20.1168	=	metres
Fahrenheit	–	32 degrees, ÷ 1.8	=	Celsius
Feet	x	30.48	=	centimetres
	x	12	=	inches
Gallons (Imp)	x	4.5459	=	litres
Gallons (US Liq)	x	3.785306	=	litres
Half Sections	x	129.504	=	hectares
Inches	x	2.54	=	centimetres
	x	0.0254	=	metres
	x	0.0277	=	yards

Kilometres	x	100,000	=	centimetres
	x	3280.839	=	feet
	x	1,000	=	metres
	x	1093.613	=	yards
Litres	x	0.219975	=	gallons (Imp)
	x	0.264179	=	gallons (US Liq)
Metres	x	100	=	centimetres
	x	3.2808399	=	feet
	x	39.370079	=	inches
	x	0.001	=	kilometres
	x	0.0006213711	=	miles (statute)
	x	1.09361	=	yards
Miles (statute)	x	5,280	=	feet
	x	1.60934	=	kilometres
	x	1,760	=	yards
Millimetres	x	0.1	=	centimetres
	x	0.00328083	=	feet
	x	0.03937007	=	inches
Pints (Imp)	x	0.56824	=	litres
Quarts (Imp)	x	1.13649	=	litres
Quarter Sections	x	64.752	=	hectares
Rods	x	0.25	=	chains (Gunter)
	x	16.5	=	feet
	x	5.0292	=	metres
RSI	x	5.678229	=	R-Value
R-Value	÷	0.1761093	=	RSI
Sections	x	640	=	acres
Square Miles	x	640	=	acres
	x	258.998	=	hectares
Tons (long)	x	1,016	=	kilograms
Tons (short)	x	907.185	=	kilograms
Yards	x	91.44	=	centimetres
	x	0.4545454	=	chains (Gunter)
	x	3	=	feet
	x	0.9144	=	metres
	x	0.181818	=	rods

▼
Selected Canadian
Real Estate/Business Books

Condominiums
Gray, Douglas A. *Buying, Owning & Selling a Condominium: A Guide for Canadians.* Toronto: McGraw-Hill Ryerson Limited, 1989.

Home Buying
Gray, Douglas A. *Home Buying Made Easy.* Toronto: McGraw-Hill Ryerson Limited, 1993 (forthcoming).

Mortgages
Gray, Douglas A. *Mortgages Made Easy: A Canadian Guide to Home Financing.* Toronto: McGraw-Hill Ryerson Limited, 1992.

Real Estate — Commercial Business
Gray, Douglas A. and Diana Gray. *The Complete Canadian Small Business Guide.* Toronto: McGraw-Hill Ryerson Limited, 1988.
———. *Home Inc.: The Canadian Home-Based Business Guide.* Toronto: McGraw-Hill Ryerson Limted, 1989.

Real Estate — Financing
Gray, Douglas A. and Brian F. Nattress. *Raising Money: The Canadian Guide to Successful Business Financing.* Toronto: McGraw-Hill Ryerson Limited, 1992.

Real Estate — General
Gray, Douglas A. *The Complete Canadian Real Estate Guide.* Toronto: McGraw-Hill Ryerson Limited, 1993 (forthcoming).

Real Estate — Investment
Gray, Douglas A. *Making Money in Real Estate: The Canadian Residential Investment Guide.* Toronto: McGraw-Hill Ryerson Limited, 1992.

Glossary

Air Barrier A continuous network of durable materias and joints to prevent air leakage.

Adfreezing When water in the foundation and the adjacent soil freeze together, bonding the structure to the heaving ground. As the ground heaves, the foundations of unheated spaces like garages also move.

Backfill The material used to refill an excavation around the outside of a footing and/or foundation wall, retaining wall or pipe trench.

Beam Also known as girder. A horizontal structural member that usually runs down the centre of the longest axis of a house. They support vertical loads and are made of timber, laminated wood, steel or reinforced concrete, or a combination of different materials.

Cant A wedge or triangular-shaped piece of wood generally installed in the deck of a flat roof around the perimeter or at the junction of the roof and an adjoining wall.

Certified Testing Agency An accredited organization that provides standards, certification, testing and inspection on the performance of a product under various conditions before it is available for public use. The tested product will bear the testing agency's certification mark. The mark indicates that representative samples have been tested and meet the requirements of accepted standards for desirable levels of safety and/or performance, and that the manufacturer is committed to an ongoing program of production review by the testing agency. The major certifying agencies and laboratories in Canada are Canadian Standards Association (CSA), Underwriter Laboratories of Canada (ULC), Canadian Gas Association (CGA) and Warnock Hersey Inc. (WHI).

Control Joint A straight line joint placed in concrete to form a plane of weakness to prevent random cracks from forming due to shrinkage or stress. If stress or movement is sufficient, the cracks will occur at the control joints and thus be inconspicuous. This can be a saw cut (a groove formed with a hand-finishing tool) or a pre-molded strip. On a concrete slab, control joints permit horizontal movement. The depth of the joints should be one-quarter of the slab's thickness.

Damp-proofing To make a surface proof against the penetration of dampness from adjacent ground or from driving rain. The purpose of damp-proofing is to prevent the capillary movement of moisture into the wall system and to the interior of the foundation. Used where water is not exerting pressure on the outside surface of walls.

Dehumidistat An electronic control and sensing device used to regulate mechanical ventilation according to relative humidity. When the relative humidity surpasses the preset limit, the dehumidistat activates the ventilation system to exhaust house air and bring in drier outdoor air.

Dewpoint The temperature at which a given air/water vapour mixtures is saturated with water vapour (i.e., 100% relative humidity). Consequently, if air is in contact with a surface below this temperature, condensation will form on the surface.

Dormer A small gable in a pitched roof, usually bearing a window or windows on its front vertical face.

Drip Continuous recess cut under a sill or protection to throw off water and prevent it from running down the face of the wall or any other vertical surface.

Dry Rot A wood-destroying fungus that particularly attacks soft wood. Most often found in damp or unventilated conditions, and is later able to spread to dry wood, owing to the development of special water-conducting organisms. The fungus breaks down the cellulose in the wood and the timber becomes brittle. Often referred to as wet rot, soft rot or wood rot. The fungus requires moisture to survive.

Duckboard Narrow slatted boards which are used to form a path over a wet floor, wet ground, etc.

Easement The right held by one person over another person's land for a specific use; rights of tenants are excluded.

Eaves The bottom of a pitched roof slope or edge of a flat roof, usually overhanging the wall.

Edge Grain Wood in which the annual growth rings are at 45 to 90 degrees to the width surface of the piece.

Efflorescence Crystalline deposit appearing on cement or brick surfaces due to the evaporation of water containing soluble salts. The salts left behind on the wall surface have a crystal-like appearance.

Electrolysis Production of chemical changes by passage of an electrical current through a non-metallic conductor.

End Grain The surface of timber exposed when it is cross-cut.

Envelope The exterior surface of a building including all external additions, e.g., bay windows, chimneys, etc.

Exhaust Breaching Chimney pipe used to lead the products of combustion safely from the furnace or hot water tank to the chimney.

Expansion Joint Also known as "Isolation Joints". Forms a separation between adjoining parts of a concrete structure to permit horizontal and vertical movement (such as those caused by thermal changes) to occur independently between abutting faces of the area. Expansion joints are commonly found between the floor slab and fixed parts of the house, such as walls or columns.

Fascia Board Any board set vertically on edge, covering the end of roof rafters at the eave line.

Fire Bricks Used in the firebox of fireplaces. A brick capable of withstanding high temperatures (1,600 degrees Celsius), made from clay with a high quartz content.

Fire Clay Mortar Specially prepared mortar used to hold fire bricks in place.

Flammable Capable of being easily ignited, burning intensely, or having a rapid rate of flame spread.

Flashing A strip of thin impervious material, often flexible metal (lead, aluminum, copper or zinc) but sometimes bitumen felt, thick plastic sheet or asbestos-based material. Used to weatherproof a joint between two materials in the external shell of a building.

Flat Grain Lumber sawn in such a way that the annual growth rings form an angle of less than 45 degrees with the wide surface of the piece.

Frost Line Also known as "frost level." The maximum depth at which water freezes within the soil below ground in winter. Will vary according to geographic location.

Furring Strips of wood applied to a wall or other surface as nailing support for the finish material, or to give the wall an appearance of greater thickness.

Gable An end wall of a building housing a triangular-shaped upper portion formed by a sloping roof on either side of a ridge.

Galvanic Action The term used when corrosion is caused by dissimilar metals touching each other and some moisture is present.

Grade The level of the ground surface around the foundation wall.

Grain The pattern created by the annual rings and the other growth patterns and fibre arrangements of wood.

Ground Water Water in the soil below the standing-water level. It is primarily caused by rainfall percolating into the soil.

Hard Water A term used to describe water with poor sudsing ability due to impurities in the water such as calcium and magnesium ions. Water softeners are used to remove impurities and provide easier sudsing.

Header (Framing) A wood member at right angles to a series of joist rafters at which the joists or rafters terminate. When used at openings in the floor or roof system, the header supports the joint or rafters and acts as a beam.

Heart Wood The dense and often dark-coloured wood that lies in the inner part of a trunk; the superior timber in a log, as compared to the sapwood, which was the living tissue of the tree when felled, and is softer and paler.

Humidistat An instrument for regulating or maintaining the degree of humidity.

I-Beam A steel or wooden beam with a cross-section resembling the letter "I".

Joist Hanger Any of a variety of strap-like metal hangers used to support the ends of wood.

Kerf Groove formed in wood by a saw cut.

Lintel A horizontal structural member that supports the load over an opening such as a window or door.

Load Bearing Building material or element subjected to or designed to carry loads in addition to its own dead load.

Newel Principal post at the foot of a staircase; general support of a winding flight of stairs.

Nosing The rounded and projected edge of a stair tread, window sill, etc.

Parapet Wall The part of an exterior, party or firewall extending above the roof line; a wall which serves as a guard at the edge of a balcony or roof.

Parging A coat of plaster or cement mortar applied to masonry or concrete walls, or to the inside of the smoke chamber of a fireplace. Parging of a masonry wall delays the transfer of moisture until the parging is saturated.

Pier A column of masonry or concrete used to support and distribute the structural load of the building over short lengths instead of a continuous foundation.

Pitch or Slope Slope or angle of a roof indicated in inches per foot in relation to a horizontal plane.

Pointing Final filling and finishing of mortar joints that have been raked out.

Purlin Timber supporting several rafters at one or more points, or the roof decking directly above it.

Radon An odourless and colourless radioactive gas formed by the natural decay of radium, which comes from uranium. It is present in rock, ground water and soil in varying concentrations in all regions of North America. Some medical reports claim it has been associated with adverse health effects and can cause lung cancer.

Radiant Heating A method of heating, usually consisting of coils or pipes or electric heating elements placed in the floor, wall or ceiling.

Rake A board or molding placed along the sloping sides of a frame gable to cover the ends of the sliding.

Relative Humidity The amount of moisture in the air compared to the maximum amount of moisture that air at the same temperature could retain. The ratio is expressed as a percentage.

Ridge Board In a pitched roof the horizontal board which forms the peak of the roof.

Saddle Two sloping surfaces meeting in a horizontal ridge, used between the back side of a chimney or other vertical surface and a sloping roof. Also called a cricket. Commonly used on wide chimneys and skylight curbs.

Sap Wood The outer, more recently grown wood of a tree. It occurs between the back and the heart wood, and is lighter in colour than the heartwood, more prone to rot but easier to treat with preservatives.

Sheathing The first layer of exterior wall or roof covering nailed to the framing of the house.

Shiplap Lumber that is edge-dressed to make a close-rabbeted or lapped joint.

Sill Plate A structural member anchored to the top of a foundation wall, upon which the floor joists rest. Also called "Foundation Sills." Holes are drilled through the sill plate and anchor bolts passed through them to secure it to the foundation.

Soffit The underside of the roof overhang. Generally any undersurface other than a ceiling.

Spall To split off from the surface, as in deterioration of brick, stone or concrete.

Subfloor Boards of sheet material laid on joists under a finish floor.

Sub-Grade The natural ground, graded and compacted, on which the floor is built. Sub-grades are improved through soil stabilization, compaction and drainage.

Top Plate In building the horizontal member, nailed to the top of the partition or wall studs.

Valley The intersection between the sloping pitched roof surfaces belonging to two abutting roofs, usually meeting at right angles.

Vapour Barrier Also known as "Vapour Retarder." Any material of low vapour permeability used to restrict and slow both air movement and water-vapour diffusion located on the warm side of surfaces because it keeps the warm moist air in the house from coming in contact with temperatures below the dew point.

Wall Plates In wood-frame construction the horizontal members attached to the ends of studs. Also called top or bottom plates, depending on their location.

Water Proofing To make a surface resistant to water penetration. Used where there is a definite water problem.

Water Table The surface of underground, gravity-controlled water; the level below which the ground is saturated with water.

Weep Holes Small holes provided in the sill section of a sash to allow water or condensation to escape, and that might otherwise accumulate in a window sill; drainage opening in retaining wall; openings placed in mortar joints of brick or block facing material at the level of flashing to permit the escape of moisture.

Bibliography

Books, Periodicals, Journals, Magazines

Builderburg Partners, Ltd. *The Journal of Light Construction*. New England Edition, Washington, D.C.

Currie, J.C. and Robertson, J.S. *House Building Regulations Simplified—An Illustrated Commentary on Housing Regulations in Canada*. Victoria, B.C.: Text Research Inc., 1988.

Hunter, Linda Mason. *The Healthy Home*. New York: Pocket Books, a division of Simon & Schuster Inc., 1990.

Labine, Clem and Flaherty, Carolyn (editors). *The Original Old-House Journal Compendium, Volume 1*. Woodstock, New York: The Overlook Press, 1983.

McAlester, Lee and Virginia. *A Field Guide to American Houses*. New York: Alfred A. Knopf, 1988.

National Research Council of Canada. *Canadian Building Digests*. Ottawa: Division of Building Research.

Poore, Patricia and Labine, Clem (editors). *The Old-House Journal New Compendium*. Garden City, New York: Dolphin Books, Doubleday and Company, Inc., 1983.

Rodale Press Inc. *Practical Homeowner*. Emmaus, PA, 18078.

Rousseau, David, W.J. Rea, M.D., and Jean Enwright. *Your Home, Your Health and Well-Being*. Vancouver: Hartley & Marks Publishers, 1988.

Southam Communications Ltd. *Select Homes*. Don Mills, Ontario.

Taunton Press Inc. *Fine Home Building*. Newtown, CT, 06470.

Organizations and Government Agencies

Booklets, pamphlets and newsletters published by the following organizations and government agencies, as well as individuals employed by these organizations, were consulted for this book. In addition, reference was made to numerous North American residential building, plumbing, electrical and fire codes.

Alberta Department of Energy, Energy Conservation Branch

Alberta Municipal Affairs, Innovative Housing Grants Program

American Concrete Institute

American Institute of Architects

American Society of Heating, Refrigerating and Air-Conditioning Engineers

American Society for Testing and Materials

Association of Consulting Engineers of Canada

British Columbia Hydro, Energy Conservation Division

Canadian Construction Association

Canadian Gas Association

Canadian Home Builders Association

Canadian Masonry Contractors Association

Canadian Mortgage and Housing Corporation

Canadian Standards Association

Canadian Wood Council

Construction Specifications Canada

Consumers Association of Canada

Energy, Mines and Resources Canada

Engineering Institute of Canada

Masonry Institute of British Columbia

National Fire Protection Association

National Research Council of Canada

Office of the Fire Commissioner, Ministry of the Attorney General

Province of British Columbia

Ontario Ministry of Energy

Portland Cement Association

Real Estate Board of Greater Vancouver

Royal Architectural Institute of Canada

Underwriters' Laboratories of Canada

Washington Energy Extension Service, Seattle, Washington

Workers Compensation Board of British Columbia